ROMMEL'S
DESERT COMMANDERS

ROMMEL'S
DESERT COMMANDERS

*The Men Who Served
the Desert Fox,
North Africa, 1941–1942*

Samuel W. Mitcham, Jr.

PRAEGER SECURITY INTERNATIONAL
Westport, Connecticut • London

Library of Congress Cataloging-in-Publication Data

Mitcham, Samuel W.
  Rommel's desert commanders : the men who served the Desert Fox,
North Africa, 1941–1942 / Samuel W. Mitcham, Jr.
    p. cm.
  Includes bibliographical references and index.
  ISBN 0-275-99436-8 (alk. paper)
  1. Germany. Heer. Panzerarmeekorps Afrika. 2. Germany. Heer—
Officers—Biography. 3. World War, 1939–1945—Campaigns—Africa,
North. 4. World War, 1939–1945—Regimental histories—Germany.
I. Title.
  D757.55.A4M568 2007
  940.54′13430922—dc22   2006038662

British Library Cataloguing in Publication Data is available.

Library of Congress Catalog Card Number: 2006038662
ISBN-10: 0-275-99436-8
ISBN-13: 978-0-275-99436-5

First published in 2007

Praeger Security International, 88 Post Road West, Westport, CT 06881
An imprint of Greenwood Publishing Group, Inc.
www.praeger.com

Printed in the United States of America

The paper used in this book complies with the
Permanent Paper Standard issued by the National
Information Standards Organization (Z39.48–1984).

10 9 8 7 6 5 4 3 2 1

CONTENTS

Photo essay follows page 68.

LIST OF FIGURES

List of Figures

PREFACE

Perhaps the most famous soldier to fight in World War II was Field Marshal Erwin Rommel, who achieved immortality as "the Desert Fox." He is also one of the most admired.

In 1941 and 1942, in Libya and Egypt, Rommel battled and usually defeated enemies who were vastly superior to him in the numerical sense. He kept Mussolini's Fascist Empire afloat and tied down huge numbers of Allied formations, which otherwise could have been used most dangerously elsewhere. By stabilizing Hitler's southern flank and keeping pressure off of his western flank, he enabled the Nazi dictator to turn his attention to the East. In doing so, he made the D-Day invasion and the Allied return to Europe impossible until 1943 at the earliest; in practice, it was mid-1944 before they landed. When they did land, they had to face the Desert Fox and all of the cunning of a first-rate military genius.

A great deal of attention has been paid to Field Marshal Erwin Rommel and justifiably so. What most military historians and the general public have failed to notice is that he enjoyed a cast of supporting characters who were also first rate. To my knowledge, no historian has ever systematically dealt with the talented cast of characters who supported the Desert Fox in 1941 and 1942. No one has ever attempted to tell their stories. The purpose of this book is to remedy this deficiency.

I wish to thank my good friend, the late Theodor-Friedrich von Stauffenberg, who first called my attention to the relatively large number of future generals who served in the 7th Panzer Division, which Rommel led in France in 1940. Stauffenberg identified seven of them in the late 1980s, but it turns out that there were even more. (Friedrich was an expert on the German panzer officers and was the first cousin of the colonel who came so close to assassinating Hitler in 1944.) This revelation led to my writing *Rommel's Lieutenants: The Men Who Served the Desert Fox, France, 1940.* In many ways, this book is a sequel. The Desert Fox had a large number of top-notch subordinates in France and Belgium in 1940; he had even more—and even better— subordinates in 1941 and 1942. Even this list is incomplete, because the men of the Luftwaffe are omitted. These included flak commanders who used their guns—especially their 88s—in a most devastating manner. They were certainly instrumental in winning more than one of Rommel's victories and must be given credit for saving the Afrika Korps (and thus the panzer army) during the Battle of the Gazala Line. The air force pilots and paratroopers also played significant roles in the North African battles. Length, however, can be to an author what the friction of space can be to a military commander, and it is simply impractical to cover everything and everybody. A book on the Luftwaffe in North Africa—especially the flak units and their commanders—would be an excellent addition to the literature of World War II. I hope someone writes it someday.

I also wish to thank my long-suffering wife, Donna, who has had to put up with a lot over the years in the interest of my research, and who turned out to be an extraordinarily competent proofreader. Professor Melinda Matthews, the head of the Interlibrary Loan Department at the University of Louisiana at Monroe, is also deserving of special praise for putting up with my insatiable requests for books and documents. (If Melinda can't locate it, it probably doesn't exist.)

I alone assume responsibility for any deficiencies or mistakes in this book.

CHAPTER I

THE SOURCES OF ROMMEL'S OFFICERS

Rommel's officers came from three overlapping sources: the Imperial Army (the Kaiser's army), the *Reichsheer* or "Treaty Army" (as the German Army from 1919 to 1935 was called), and the *Heer*, which was Hitler's army. The term *Wehrmacht* is also sometimes used to refer to Hitler's army, but that term literally means "armed forces" and would thus include the navy and *Luftwaffe* (air force).

Rommel and his officers inherited a legacy that dates back to the days of Prussia and the rise of what became the House of Hohenzollern in the early fifteenth century. The modern Prussian Army was built anew after 1806 under the "reformers," led by General Johann von Scharnhorst, who shifted the emphasis of Prussian military thought and doctrine from a volunteer army obsessed with iron discipline and rigid drill to a conscripted army, stressing technological expertise, operational planning, flexibility, and a highly trained and dedicated professional officers' corps. Among other things, Scharnhorst and his young assistants, who included Karl von Clausewitz, founded the Prussian General Staff and the War Academy (*Kriegsakademie*). They also laid the foundations for a tradition of military excellence that endured until 1945. Indeed, if there is one common characteristic that links the Imperial Army, the Reichsheer, and the Heer, it is institutionalized military excellence.[1]

If the Prussian General Staff was considered a model for others to follow, German diplomacy after Wilhelm II ascended to the throne in 1890 was not. He sacked the legendary "Iron Chancellor" Otto von Bismarck and maneuvered the Reich into a strategic corner by August 1914, when it was faced with a two-front war without a single strong ally, against all the other great powers of Europe and later

Figure 1.1
Europe, 1920–1938

the United States as well. After four years of war, in which its army performed well and sometimes brilliantly, Germany was finally forced to sue for peace. Its representatives signed the armistice on November 11, 1918.

During World War I, the corporate tactical and operational excellence of the Imperial Army was proven on the battlefield. French General Charles de Gaulle, for example, wrote, "The superiority of good troops was abundantly clear. How else is one to explain the prolonged success of the German armies against so many opponents? For 1,700,000 deaths ... the Germans, better trained than anyone else, killed 3,200,000 enemies; for 750,000 prisoners which they lost, they took 1,900,000."[2] De Gaulle, of course, was no admirer of Germany or the Germans.

The military clauses of the Treaty of Versailles attempted to reduce the German armed forces to the status of an armed police and coast guard force, by limiting the German Army to 100,000 men, of which only 4,000 could be officers.[3] So that it could never again wage offensive warfare against its neighbors, it was forbidden to have tanks, aircraft, poison gas, or field pieces larger than 105 mm. To ensure that no significant reserves were created, privates and noncommissioned officers (NCOs) had to enlist for 12 years, while officers were required to commit themselves to 25 years' service. The General Staff, the War Academy, and the cadet academies were banned; a yearly personnel turnover of more than 5 percent was prohibited; and even its ammunition supply was limited, to prevent stockpiling for a major war. All of its activities were subject to inspections by the International Control Commission.

To defend the Weimar Republic (as the German nation from 1919 to 1933 was called), the *Reichstag* (parliament) created the *Reichswehr* (Reich Defense Force), which consisted of the *Reichsheer* (Army) and *Reichsmarine* (Navy). The army played such a predominant role (it must be remembered that Germany was traditionally a land power) that many came to consider the Reichswehr and Reichsheer identical. The tiny navy amounted to little until after the rise of Adolf Hitler. Under the terms of the Treaty of Versailles, Germany was not allowed to have an air force.

In 1919 and 1920, the German Army was frequently called the *Uebergangsheer* or transitional army. During these years, it transitioned from the large wartime Imperial Army into the peacetime Reichsheer. It also fought "the war after the war" against Communists and other rebellious forces that sought to overthrow the republic, as well as Poles on the eastern border, who hoped to expand Poland at the expense of Germany. Because the army did not always want to become directly involved in these activities, the actual fighting was left to the *Freikorps*—a loose collection of right-wing paramilitary groups, consisting of volunteers and often led by former generals. Many of Rommel's future officers served in the Freikorps, and Rommel himself fought in this struggle, which lasted until 1923. Ironically, the last rebellion occurred in November 1923, when Adolf Hitler and the Nazi Party attempted to overthrow the government of Bavaria in the "Beer Hall Putsch." Among those who helped put it down was Ritter Wilhelm von Thoma, the future commander of the Afrika Korps.

The true functional heart of the German Army was the *Wehrkreise* (military districts). Each Wehrkreis was a corps-level territorial command that was responsible for recruitment, mobilization, supply, administration, logistical support, and all territorial and military-political (or military-civilian) matters within its area. Later, when the German Army took the field, the Wehrkreise assumed responsibility for training as well. Initially there were seven military districts, all designated by Roman numerals (I through VII). By 1939, there were 16 (see Figure 1.6). By 1940, there were 18 Wehrkreise, numbered I

Figure 1.2
General Regions of the Third Reich

through XIII, XVII, XVIII, and XX, as well as Wehrkreis Bohemia and Moravia (in what had been Czechoslovakia), and Wehrkreis *General Gouvernement* in what had once been Poland. In addition to directing the military activities in his territories, each Wehrkreis commander before 1935 was also the commander of an infantry division, which bore the same number as the Wehrkreis, although the two commands were technically separate. Germany also had three small cavalry divisions, which did not have territorial responsibilities.

The most important officer on the divisional staff was the Ia, the chief of operations, who was, in effect, divisional chief of staff (although this term was only used at the corps level and higher). When the division went to the field, the staff usually divided into three separate operational groups: the *Fuehrungsabteilung*, the *Quartermeister*, and the *Adjutantur*. The *Fuehrungsabteilung* (or operational detachment) was the most important. Directed by the Ia, it formed with division's tactical nerve center and was known as the division's command post (CP). It also included the intelligence staff, which, under the Ic (chief intelligence officer), was subordinate to the Ia.

The supply headquarters (*Quartermeister*) was headed by the Ib (chief supply officer, or divisional quartermaster). Physically separated from the CP, it included the IVa (chief administrative officer), IVb (chief medical officer), and V (motor transport officer), each of whom directed his own section. Most of these officers were not members of the General Staff; as a general rule, only I-type officers (the Ia, Ib, and so on) were War Academy graduates.

The personnel group (or *Adjutantur*) was the third staff grouping. Generally some distance to the rear, it was directed by the IIa (chief personnel officer or adjutant). He supervised the IIb (second personnel officer, who was in charge of enlisted personnel matters), the III (chief judge advocate), and the chaplains (IVd), as well as various other units necessary to keep a staff headquarters and divisional rear-area functioning normally. These included security detachments, construction engineer units, labor battalions, and field replacement units.

In 1920, before the 100,000-man army could be established, tens of thousands of officers and hundreds of thousands of other ranks had to be involuntarily discharged from the service. Some generals wanted to retain primarily frontline soldiers, but Colonel General Hans von Seeckt, the chief of the Army Command, wanted to keep as many General Staff officers as possible.[4] Seeckt would be the undisputed dictator of the German armed forces for the next six critical years (1920–26). He had a unique opportunity to build an army in accordance with his own ideas, and he took full advantage of it. By the time he was finished, the Reichsheer was heavily stocked with aristocrats and General Staff officers—as well as highly talented and veteran officers and men.

Seeckt would not tolerate prima donnas in his army. "The form changes, the spirit remains," he said when he set up the *Truppenamt* (Troop Office, as the clandestine General Staff was called). "It is the spirit of silent, selfless devotion to duty in the service of the Army. General Staff officers have no names."[5] For him, it was intolerable for officers to meddle in politics (although he periodically did so himself). "Great achievements, small display; more reality than appearance" became a motto of the General Staff officer.[6]

After the initial selections for the Reichsheer, the decision on which officers to choose for the regimental- and company-level appointments usually fell to the colonel involved. As one might expect, this man almost invariably selected candidates whom he believed to have outstanding leadership potential, largely because it was in his own best

Figure 1.3
Major Cities of the Third Reich

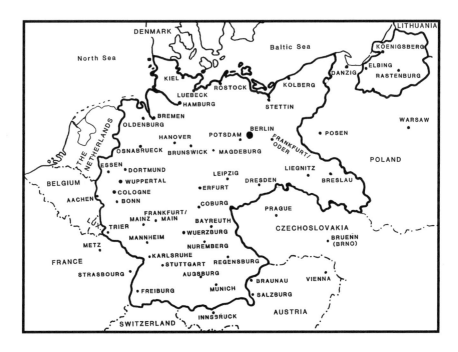

interests to do so. Many exceptionally talented privates and NCOs entered the service through this door and eventually earned their commissions in this way.

Once an officer was selected for the Reichsheer, his rate of promotion was very slow, as is still typical in a small army. Erwin Rommel, for example, entered the Reichsheer as a captain in 1919, having been promoted the year before. He was not promoted again until 1932, when he had 14 years' time in grade. Kurt Student, a future colonel general, army group commander, and "father" of the German parachute branch, was a captain from 1917 until 1929. Bernhard Ramcke, a second lieutenant in 1918, was not promoted to first lieutenant until 1921 and did not become a captain until 1927. He spent 16 years as a company grade officer. Ramcke was a lieutenant general when he led the 2nd Parachute Division against the Americans at Brest in 1944. Most other junior officers were promoted with equal slowness. In fact, several future World War II generals served full 12-year enlistments without ever receiving their commissions. Examples of these include Ludwig Heilmann, the future commander of the 5th Parachute

Division; Willi Bittrich, who became a general of *Waffen-SS* (armed SS) and achieved fame as the commander of the II SS Panzer Corps in the Battle of Arnhem; and Sergeant Helmuth Becker, a future major general of SS and commander of the 3rd SS Panzer Division "Totenkopf" on the Eastern Front.

The postwar intake of potential officers was very small; therefore, the standards they had to meet were very high. Preference went to those under 21 years of age with a higher education. They normally served 15 months in their regiments as enlisted men and, if still considered suitable, took their *Fahnenjunker* examination. Before World War I, officer candidates coming straight out of schools or universities entered the ranks as *Fahnenjunkern* (officer-cadets). They ate in the officers' mess (but were not allowed to speak unless spoken to) and could sleep in private accommodations after six weeks' service. Then they went on to a war school (*Kriegschule*). These procedures were similar during the Reichswehr era, but the standards were much higher. If the Reichsheer candidate passed his Fahnenjunker exam, he was promoted to *Faehnrich* (senior officer-cadet or officer candidate) and sent to the corporals course at the Infantry School at Dresden, regardless of his branch. Then he took the officers examination. If the candidate passed, he was promoted to *Oberfaehnrich* (roughly equivalent to ensign or senior candidate) and joined the officers' mess of his regiment. After a certain period of time, he was accepted or rejected for the rank of second lieutenant by a vote of the officers of his regiment. This was usually just a formality; if the colonel wanted an Oberfaehnrich commissioned, it would be highly unusual for the officers to reject him. In any case, the entire process took between four and five years from the date of his enlistment.

Under Seeckt's supervision, the army became a state within a state, but it was a highly professional body of dedicated men, all trained to assume command of the unit above their own. It was an army capable of extremely rapid expansion, should an emergency arise; that, indeed, was the cornerstone of its existence, what its members longed for. The German Army practiced mobile operations with dummy tanks and used balloons to simulate airplanes. Its sergeants were trained to be platoon leaders, its lieutenants were fully qualified as company commanders, and its captains were perfectly capable of commanding battalions. Its field maneuvers and training problems were the best in the world, and its men almost turned the staff study and war game into an art form, they became so good at them.[7]

"The officer instruction program of the Reichswehr was one of the most strenuous officer training systems ever devised," historian James Corum wrote later.[8] Typically, training for a potential new officer began with 18 months in a line regiment, during which time he served

Figure 1.4
The Eastern Front

as a recruit, private, and junior NCO. This was followed by two years at an officer training school. At the Infantry School at Dresden, the first year included 24 hours per week in academic classes and 13 hours of practical training. The academic instruction included an emphasis on tactics, as well as classes on weaponry, military engineering, geography, motor vehicles, and aerial warfare, among other subjects. Practical training included athletics, horseback riding, infantry exercises, combat engineering, and a variety of live-fire exercises, including artillery, mortars, and machine guns. During the second year, about half of the instruction was on general army subjects, while half was branch specific (i.e., specific to the infantry, artillery, or cavalry). Common subjects included military history, army administration, weapons training, and close air support for ground forces.[9] These vigorous courses of instruction had a very high failure rate (unfortunately exact figures are lacking), but they also produced the best junior officers in the world by the late 1920s.

Even in this highly skilled collection of soldiers, the General Staff officers stood out. (Seeckt clandestinely reintroduced General Staff training almost as soon as the Allies outlawed it.) By 1920, for example, all officers who reached 10 years of service were required to take the Wehrkreis exam, which measured their professional ability. It lasted several days. An officer had to write three papers on applied tactics, one on theoretical tactics, one on military engineering, another on map reading, and another on weapons and/or equipment. There were also general knowledge questions dealing with history, military history, civics, economic geography, mathematics, physics, and chemistry. The exam was not a rehash of the officer candidate exams but went well beyond them. It included complicated problems in logistics, resupply, motorized warfare, artillery and mortar fire support plans, and so on. The test, which was changed every year, was a major event in an officer's career and was graded by General Staff officers in Berlin. If an officer failed the test, he was required to take it again the next year. A second failure could result in the loss of one's commission.[10]

Only those in the top 10 to 15 percent were considered for General Staff training. (Erwin Rommel was among those who did not score high enough for General Staff selection.) Of those selected, only about a third passed the rigorous course and became General Staff officers. Their training, of course, could not be conducted at the Kriegsakademie, which had been closed in March 1920 under the terms of the Treaty of Versailles. Under Seeckt and his successors it was carried on in the Wehrkreise and by special courses held by the Truppenamt. Other than that, however, little had changed. The course was just as rigorous as it had ever been.

Figure 1.5
The Western Front

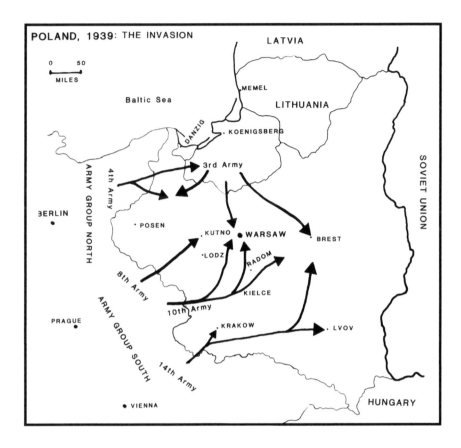

The third source of Rommel's officers were those who entered the service in 1935 or after—that is, those who were commissioned during the Hitler era. For the most part, these men were the company commanders and junior staff officers of the Afrika Korps and Panzer Army Afrika. They were the products of the officer training schools (*Kriegsschulen*). Rommel himself was part of this system. He taught at the War School at Potsdam (1935–38) and was the commandant of the War School at Wiener-Neustadt (1938–39).[11]

The officer training schools taught officer candidates a much narrower range of lower-level tactical skills (battalion level and below) for the various arms, as opposed to the War Academy, which taught higher-level tactics and operational and strategic skills. The emphasis was on infantry training, which every would-be officer had to undergo.

Figure 1.6
The Wehrkreise, 1939

Basic training in the Wehrmacht in 1936 was somewhat similar to American basic training. Artillery, Panzer, and the soldiers of other noninfantry branches underwent six weeks of training (as opposed to 12 months for infantry troops). They learned infantry tactics, how to handle and clean rifles, how to parade, how to read a tactical map, how to throw hand grenades, and how to operate machine guns. During this phase, the day usually ended at 10 P.M., when the recruits fell into bed, nearly exhausted. Then they began their three months basic branch training. Once their basic training was completed, exceptional soldiers were sent to officer training schools, if they wished to earn a commission.

In the late 1930s, there were four grades of officer candidates: *Fahnenjunker-Gefreiter* (equivalent to corporal), *Fahnenjunker-Unteroffizier* (equivalent to sergeant), *Fahnrich* (officer candidate), and *Oberfahnrich* (senior officer candidate or "almost an officer"). Candidates could be promoted to Fahnenjunker-Unteroffizier before beginning their intensive officer training at a Kriegschule. Rommel's own school at Potsdam was typical. The barracks at Potsdam were divided into

11

suites, with four candidates per suite. All four men in each suite were from different branches of the service. Each suite was divided into a large study room with four desks and a bedroom with four beds, four lockers, and four washing facilities. There were approximately 1,000 students in the school at any one time, and there were four such schools in Germany. The Potsdam school was divided into two groups, and each group had 16 platoons of 32 men each.

One measure of the quality of the school and the quality of the training the young men received is the caliber of the officers responsible for their training. The school commandant at Potsdam was Colonel Wilhelm Wetzel, who went on to command the 255th Infantry Division, V Corps, and LXVI Corps in World War II. He ended the war as a general of infantry, commanding Wehrkreis X. One of the two group commanders was Lieutenant Colonel Erwin Rommel, the future "Desert Fox." His book, *Infantry in the Attack*, was then being used as a textbook in the course. The other group commander was Lieutenant Colonel Johannes Friessner, who rose to the rank of colonel general during World War II and commanded the 102nd Infantry Division, XXIII Corps, Army Detachment Narva, Army Group North, and Army Group South Ukraine (later South). The platoon leaders and tactical officers also distinguished themselves during the war.

One of the unofficial instructors was also noteworthy. She was Lucie Rommel, the wife of the future field marshal, who assisted her husband on "evenings out," when the future officers were taught the social graces. Lucie, who had been a dance student in Danzig when she met her future husband in 1912, helped teach the young cadets proper social behavior and how to dance. By all accounts, the young men looked forward to and thoroughly enjoyed their evenings out.

At Potsdam, all of the candidates were treated as infantry, and the mission of the school was to teach them all how to lead an infantry platoon, company, and battalion in combat. (They were, however, not subjected to the verbal abuse the NCOs heaped on them in basic training.) They studied topography, map reading, engineering, the construction and demolition of bridges, basic artillery, drill, parade, physical education, Luftwaffe coordination, and how to ride a horse. They spent six hours each day in the classroom and three in the field, and they had a major exam every week. The most important subject was tactics, which counted more than all of the other subjects combined. In their tactical problems, there was no single "school solution"; the candidates had to formulate, defend, and execute their own plans, and their success was based on how well they did it. They all had the chance to "play" battalion commander, as well as to serve as company commander and in various staff positions. They also spent a great deal of time studying military history (mostly the Prussian battles of the seventeenth and eighteenth centuries), and often took trips (now called "staff rides") to the actual battlefields. One trip to East Prussia lasted two weeks. They also studied the tactics of Alexander, Caesar, Napoleon (Rommel's favorite), and Frederick the Great, and the battles of ancient Greece and Rome. They learned how to handle barbed wire, antitank mines, dynamite (for demolitions), and various types of machine guns. They also participated in sports, including swimming, highdiving, boxing, fencing, horseback riding, running, tennis, pistol shooting, cross-country running, and other activities. In addition, the school owned some small sailing boats, and everyone learned how to sail.

"Our lives were quite pleasant at Kriegsschule Potsdam," Fahnenjunker Siegfried Knappe recalled.[12] Their training was excellent, interesting, and challenging. Their mess hall was a like a cafeteria; the food was simple but good, and usually consisted of meat, potatoes, vegetables, and bread. The hall was used only for the noon meal. Each room was issued a two-pound loaf of *kommissbrot* (army bread) every other day, and they were issued butter, jam, and coffee every morning. Dinner was dispensed from the mess hall and eaten in the suite. It consisted of liverwurst or cheese, butter, and bread.

In addition to their military training, they received training in the social graces as well. They often had formal dances, to which the daughters of older officers and the local gentry were invited. They were held in large ballrooms, with live orchestras, and dance classes were provided for those who needed them.

Just before graduation, all of the candidates were asked if they would like to join the Luftwaffe. If not enough candidates volunteered, a number were drafted into the air force. The other Fahnenjunkern then returned to their units as an *Oberfahnrichen*, to complete their specialty training. No officer-candidate could be assigned to a base where he had served as an enlisted man.

When an officer-candidate returned to his unit, his superiors could be sure that he had received the best military training available anywhere in the world. Most of the new officer-designates also had faith in their country and in the peaceful goals and ideals of their Fuehrer. They had no idea that they would be required to use what they had learned in the very near future.

CHAPTER II

THE FIRST CYRENAICAN CAMPAIGN

The first divisional commander of the Afrika Korps was Johannes Streich. He and Erwin Rommel had one thing in common: they could not stand each other.

An East Prussian, Streich was born in Augustenburg in the Sonderburg District on April 16, 1891. After matriculation, he joined the 2nd Railroad Regiment at Berlin-Schoeneberg as a Fahnenjunker in 1911. He completed his officer training and was commissioned *Leutnant* (second lieutenant) in 1913. During World War I, he served in Belgium, France, the Russian Front, Serbia, and Romania. He emerged from the conflict as a first lieutenant and a company commander, with both grades of the Iron Cross.

Selected for the Reichswehr, Streich was one of the first to see the potential of the tank and was an early convert to the concept of motorized warfare. As early as 1921, he commanded a motor transport company stationed at Hanover, and in 1923 he assumed command of a company in the 2nd Motor Transport Battalion at Stettin. He was promoted to captain that same year.

Streich became a technical instructor in the Motor Transport Training Branch in 1928, and in 1930 he was named technical advisor in the Army Ordnance Office, where he played a significant role in developing the Panzer Mark I through IV. He was promoted to major in 1933, shortly after Hitler came to power. Promotions to lieutenant colonel (1935) and colonel (1938) followed. Meanwhile, on October 1, 1935, he assumed command of the 15th Panzer Regiment at Sagan.

Although he got along well with Franz Halder and the other senior generals in Berlin, Johannes Striech did not do a particularly good job at Sagan. He was "at best a difficult person to work for," Friedrich von Stauffenberg wrote later.[1] Neither of his battalion commanders—Major

Rudolf Sieckenius and Major Paul Goerbig—could get along with him. "As a result," Stauffenberg recorded, "15th Panzer Regiment lacked much in espirit de corps, though, for that matter, none of the 8th Panzer Brigade was particularly noteworthy."[2] This climate of dissension existed for more than a year. Although the details are not known, an open explosion of tempers occurred in January 1939. General Heinrich von Vietinghoff, the divisional commander and future commander of the 10th Army and Army Group C in Italy, had to intervene, and his solution was to transfer both battalion commanders to other posts. Both later became generals in World War II.[3]

Streich's regiment was part of the 5th Panzer Division, which took part in the occupation of the Sudetenland and played an "inconspicuous" role in the Polish campaign of 1939, according to Allied intelligence documents.[4] It took part in the conquest of Belgium, the encirclement and destruction of the main French armies in the Lille Pocket, the liquidation of the Dunkirk Pocket, the drive to the Seine, and the capture of Rouen. Before the campaign was over, Streich's regiment had pushed almost to the Spanish border and had taken 20,000 prisoners. This total was not unusual for a panzer unit in France, however, and the performance of the 5th Panzer Division in general had not been outstanding. Even before the campaign was over, the even-tempered and objective General of Infantry Hermann Hoth, the commander of the XV Motorized Corps, became so dissatisfied with its performance that he relieved the division's commander—Lieutenant General Max von Hartlieb—of his command.[5]

In France, Streich also had a heated argument with the commander of the adjacent sector, Major General Erwin Rommel, the leader of the 7th Panzer Division, over some bridging equipment. The evidence concerning the dispute is fragmentary but seems to indicate that Rommel acted in a high-handed and undiplomatic manner, because the equipment in question did belong to the 5th Panzer Division. On the other hand, Rommel was trying to retain the momentum of a pursuit, and Streich was moving very slowly. Neither was known for his selfless cooperation. Whoever was right, the incident resulted in hard feelings on both sides. This mutual dislike would only intensify in the year ahead.

In early 1941, Streich received three promotions. In January, he was named commander of the 5th Panzer Brigade. On February 1, he received an accelerated promotion to major general, and six days later he was named commander of the recently activated 5th Light Division. (The original division commander during the formation phase was Major General Baron Hans von Funck, who later commanded a panzer corps on the Western Front.) Meanwhile, the 5th Panzer Regiment was transferred from France to Wuensdorf, the home of the Panzer School, and it

Figure 2.1
The Mediterranean Theater of Operations

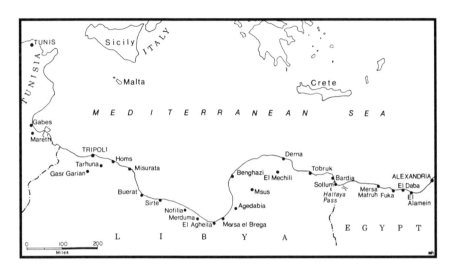

was incorporated into the 5th Light on February 18, the day it was formally activated. The 5th Light also included the 104th Motorized Infantry
Regiment, the 155th Panzer Artillery Regiment, the 3rd Reconnaissance
Battalion, the 39th Antitank Battalion, the 200th Panzer Engineer Battalion, and the 200th Panzer Signal Battalion. Streich's joy at his promotions, however, was tempered later that month when the 5th Light was
alerted for movement. It was being sent to Libya, where it would be one
of the two divisions in another new command. This one was the Afrika
Korps, which was to be commanded by Lieutenant General Erwin
Rommel. Figure 2.1 shows the Mediterranean Theater of Operations.

The 5th Light arrived in Tripoli in February and March 1941. (The
other division in the Afrika Korps—the 15th Panzer—would not arrive
until late April and early May.) Streich himself came ashore on February
25, but the 5th Panzer Regiment did not complete its disembarkation
until March 11. Rommel threw it into the attack on March 31, when he
began his First Cyrenaican Campaign. The Germans broke through the
main British position at Mersa el Brega late that afternoon, capturing 30
British trucks and 50 Bren carriers in the process. Rommel set off in immediate pursuit. Agedabia fell on April 2, and the spearheads of the
5th Light Division turned into the desert, heading for the main Allied
supply depot at Msus. The French garrison saw tanks approaching,
assumed they were German, and blew up the depot, including the vital
fuel tanks. The tanks belonged to the 5th and 6th Royal Tank Regiments of the British 3rd Armoured Brigade, which intended to refuel at

17

Msus. They now lacked the petrol to reach Mechili, where the British 2nd Armoured Division was attempting to concentrate. By transferring the fuel from their worst tanks to propel their best, the 3rd Armoured was able to reach Mechili the following night, but it was down to a strength of 10 tanks and was effectively eliminated as a major combat force.

On April 8, the Afrika Korps completed the destruction of the 2nd Armoured Division. Major General Michael D. Gambier-Parry, the commander of the 2nd Armoured, and Brigadier Vaughan, the commander of the Indian 3rd Motor Brigade, were captured, along with 3,000 of their men. Four of the 3rd Armoured Brigade's tanks managed to escape in the direction of Tobruk, but German pursuit forces destroyed all of them before they could get there.

Although Johannes Streich played a major role in the destruction of the British 2nd Armoured, the Desert Fox was dissatisfied with his overall performance. Rommel believed that Streich's headquarters was too luxurious and that the general himself lacked boldness and imagination. This opinion was confirmed in Rommel's mind on April 3, when Streich demanded that the offensive be halted on the grounds that his vehicles needed maintenance. Rommel harshly denied this request and ordered Lieutenant Colonel Baron Irnfried von Wechmar, the commander of the 3rd Reconnaissance Battalion, to capture Benghazi, the capital and only major city of Cyrenaica. Wechmar was only too eager to comply. The city fell the next day. "I could not allow this [Streich's maintenance problems] to affect the issue," Rommel commented later. "One cannot permit unique opportunities to slip by for the sake of trifles."[6]

Streich and his principle subordinate, Lieutenant Colonel Dr. Herbert Olbricht, the commander of the 5th Panzer Regiment, both opposed Rommel's plan to capture Benghazi. They were also too slow for Rommel. The 5th Panzer did not reach the smoldering ruins of Msus until almost nightfall on April 5, and the next day—when Rommel expected it to attack Mechili—it was 85 miles to the west and was strung out over 30 miles of desert. To make matters worse, Olbricht got lost and further delayed the advance. Rommel, meanwhile, had pushed to within 15 miles of Mechili, but he had only a single battalion with him. He fumed in impotent rage while his reconnaissance troops looked for Streich and Olbricht. They finally located them—more than 70 miles from where they were supposed to be. Rommel jumped into a small Storch reconnaissance aircraft and flew to Streicht's command post, where an angry confrontation occurred. (The fact that Rommel's airplane was hit by British fire during the flight did nothing to improve his mood.) The Desert Fox demanded that Streich attack Mechili the next day. This Streich refused to do on the grounds that

Figure 2.2
Rommel's First Cyrenaican Campaign

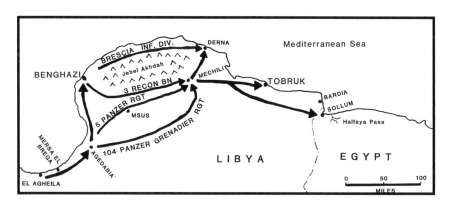

his division was scattered over 100 miles of desert and many of vehicles had broken down or had overheated engines. Rommel lost control of his temper and called Streich a coward. This was too much for Johannes Streich, who took off his Knights' Cross and roared: "Withdraw that remark, or I'll throw this at your feet!" Rommel muttered a halfhearted apology, but the meeting ended with hard feelings all around.[7] Fortunately for the Germans, the British did not take advantage of the delay to extricate the 2nd Armoured, and Rommel was able to destroy it at Mechili two days later. Figure 2.2 shows Rommel's First Cyrenaican campaign.

After the Battle of Mechili, Rommel continued the pursuit to Tobruk, which he attacked on April 12, despite the objections of Streich and Olbricht. It failed. Another attack during the night of April 13–14 also failed, and the 5th Panzer Regiment retreated without orders, leading to the virtual destruction of the 8th Machine Gun Battalion. Rommel gave Streich and Olbricht another fierce dressing down and accused them of leaving the infantry in the lurch. Streich tried to make excuses, but Rommel would have none of it. He ordered another attack for the night of April 16–17 and told Streich and Olbricht: "I expect this attack to be made with the utmost resolution under your personal leadership!"[8] This was clearly a "come back victorious or don't come back at all" order. It was clear that Rommel was giving Streich one last chance.

At least one neutral observer present felt Rommel was bullying Streich and his chief of operations, Major Wolf Ruediger Hauser. Heinz Schmidt, Rommel's own aide, recorded: "I like the friendly and considerate Streich, whom I regard as an extremely brave man, and Hauser, too, and feel sorry that they are being treated so remorselessly."[9]

Remorseless Rommel was. For the attack of April 16–17, Rommel reinforced Streich with the Italian Ariete Armored Division and the 62nd Infantry Regiment of the Trento Motorized Division. The Italians scored a major initial success by capturing Hill 187 (Ras el Madauer), thus threatening the integrity of the entire Allied defense, but then the Australians who formed the Tobruk garrison launched a sharp counterattack, which routed the Italians, many of whom surrendered. The German elements did not panic, but neither did they score any significant victories. Rommel nevertheless allowed Olbricht and Streich to direct another series of attacks in late April and early May. When these also failed, Rommel relieved them of their commands. Streich was temporarily succeeded by Major General Heinrich Kirchheim on May 16. Olbricht was temporarily replaced by Major Ernst Bolbrinker, who was soon succeeded by Lieutenant Colonel Friedrich "Fritz" Stephan, an "up and coming" young panzer officer.[10] At the same time, Rommel set about "cleaning house" in the Afrika Korps. He had been given a group of commanders and General Staff officers not of his choosing and several of them were not loyal to him; their loyalties lay with Field Marshal Walter von Brauchitsch, the commander-in-chief of the army, and Colonel General Franz Halder, the chief of the General Staff.[11] Rommel replaced them all, including Streich; Olbricht; Colonel Klaus von dem Borne, the chief of staff of the Afrika Korps; Major Ehlers, the Ia (chief of operations) of the Afrika Korps; Hans-Henning von Holtzendorff, the commander of the 104th Rifle Regiment; and several others. There were howls of anguish from Berlin, of course, but at this point in the war, Rommel was in high favor with Adolf Hitler and Halder was not, so the protests came to nothing.

Normally, when an officer is relieved of his command, his career is effectively over. Streicht's career, however, was not ruined. Franz Halder saw to that. He was given command of a battle group on the Eastern Front. When Lieutenant General Sigfrid Henrici, the commander of the 16th Motorized Infantry Division, fell ill in October, Streich was given temporary command of the division during the last German drive on Moscow. During these desperate battles, Streich was again slow and earned the censure of Colonel General Heinz Guderian, the commander of the 2nd Panzer Army. When Henrici returned in November, Streich was sent back to Berlin. This second failure was viewed as much more serious than his failure in North Africa, and he was unemployed for seven months.

Johannes Streich's career was effectively ruined after November 1941, although he managed to return to active duty as inspector of Mobile Troops in Halder's OKH (on June 1, 1942). He even managed to secure a belated promotion to lieutenant general on October 1, 1943, but he never held another important command. He was named commander of Recruiting Area Breslau in June 1943, a posting that can only be viewed as another demotion. When the Russians encircled the city in February 1945, Streich managed to escape and was named commander of Recruiting Area Berlin in early April 1945. He also managed to vacate the capital of the Reich just before the Soviets surrounded it. He surrendered to the Anglo-Americans at the end of the war. After the Allies released him in 1948, Johannes Streich settled in Hamburg, where he died on August 20, 1977.

Like their commander, Streich's two principle regimental commanders did not have particularly distinguished careers after they left North Africa.

A Silesian, Herbert Olbricht was born in Breslau on September 11, 1895, and entered the service as a Fahnenjunker in the 16th Foot Artillery Regiment when World War I broke out in August 1914. He was commissioned second lieutenant the following year. He survived the Great War, was selected for the Reichsheer, and earned a doctorate in engineering in 1929. Assigned to the staff of the High Command of the Armed Forces (OKW) in 1938, he missed the Polish and French campaigns. On November 13, 1940, however, he succeeded Streich as commander of the 5th Panzer Regiment. His tour of duty in North Africa was not a successful one (as we have seen), but he was nevertheless given command of the 35th Panzer Regiment of the 4th Panzer Division on July 2, 1941. Although the Russian campaign had only begun on June 22, the 35th Panzer had already suffered severe casualties in the Battle of Minsk. Olbricht led his regiment at Gomel, Bryansk, Vyazma, and other bitterly contested battles on the road to Moscow. He fought in the winter battles of 1941–42 and at least partially redeemed his reputation. He was then transferred to the south, where the 13th Panzer Division had suffered heavy casualties during the winter battles around Rostov and the Mius. Here, Olbricht was given command of the 4th Panzer Regiment, his third regimental command of the war. The 4th Panzer took part in the Caucasus campaign of 1942 and spearheaded 1st Panzer Army's drive on the Soviet oilfields. In early September, after successfully crossing the Terek River at Ischerskaja (within 15 miles of the critical oil city of Grozny), the 4th Panzer was subjected to repeated and heavy Soviet counterattacks. The forward battle group alone destroyed 33 Soviet T-34 and KV-1 heavy tanks in two days. German casualties were also heavy. Among them was Colonel Dr. Herbert Olbricht, who was killed in action on September 10, 1942. When OKH learned of his death, he was posthumously promoted to major general, effective September 1.

Hans-Henning von Holtzendorff was the second of Streich's regimental commanders to be sent back to Germany "on his camel" by Erwin Rommel.

21

Born in Neuenahr on August 2, 1892, he entered the service as a Fahnenjunker in the 2nd Guards Regiment of Foot in September 1910. He was commissioned second lieutenant in early 1912 and fought in the First World War but was not selected for the Reichsheer. Discharged as a captain in 1920, he returned to the army during Hitler's secret military expansion of 1934 as a major. He was promoted to lieutenant colonel in 1937. Recognizing the potential of the panzer branch, he managed to be assigned to the staff of the Panzer Troops School in 1938 and was named commander of the Berlin/Potsdam 561st Antitank (later Tank Destroyer) Battalion when World War II broke out. He led this army-level General Headquarters (GHQ) unit with considerable success in Poland (1939) and France (1940).[12]

Holtzendorff was promoted to colonel in September 1940 and was named commander of the 104th Motorized Infantry (or Rifle) Regiment on December 11, 1940. It was incorporated into the 5th Light Division in February 1941 and was sent to North Africa in March. In the eyes of Erwin Rommel, Holtzendorff performed better in Libya than did Streich or Olbricht, but that was apparently not enough to satisfy the Desert Fox. Holtzendorff was replaced as commander of the 104th on July 10, 1941, and returned to Germany.

After several weeks of unemployment, Hans-Henning von Holtzendorff was given another motorized regiment in September 1941. This was the 40th Rifle, which was part of the 17th Panzer Division on the Eastern Front. This unit fought very well and destroyed dozens of Soviet units during the battles of 1941–42. It also suffered very heavy casualties. During the retreat from Moscow, for example, it lost all of its armored cars and most of its trucks. Holtzendorff himself was transferred back to Germany in late 1941 (he gave up his command on December 18, 1941), apparently by his own arrangement. This three-month regimental command on the Eastern Front was very brief for someone who was not wounded. In January 1942, he became director of training at the Panzer Troops School but held no further active commands. On March 1, 1943, however, he was promoted to major general and was named commander of the Motor Pool Troops School in July. He remained in this post until "final victory" and, while in captivity, wrote a rather frank report for the United States Army entitled "Reasons for Rommel's Successes in Africa, 1941–1942." It is a surprisingly even-handed document, in which Holtzendorff praised Rommel's "skillful leadership" and "iron nerves." He had particularly high praise for Rommel's ability to get the maximum effort from the Italian units "within the limits of their capacity." "To be sure," the former regimental commander noted, "he did make extreme demands on troops and material, and his subordinate commanders frequently groaned at his stubbornness and his personal interference."[13] Nevertheless, Holtzendorff rated Rommel high on his scale of generals and felt that the one commander in world history who most resembled him was Hannibal.

General Holtzendorff was released from prison in 1948 and settled in Hanover. He died on September 28, 1982, at the age of 90.

About the only senior officer with the 5th Light Division whose career was not damaged in North Africa was Wolf Ruediger Hauser, the young Ia (chief of operations).

Hauser was born in Strassburg, Alsace (now in France), on July 22, 1906. Too young to fight in World War I, he joined the Reichsheer as a Fahnenjunker in 1923. Four and a half years later he was commissioned second lieutenant in the 18th Cavalry Regiment. Selected for General Staff training early in his career, he was a captain and adjutant to the chief of operations of the General Staff (OKH) in 1938. After the completion of the Polish campaign, the capable Hauser was named chief of operations of the 68th Infantry Division and fought in France. He was promoted to major on October 1, 1940, and, early in 1941 became Ia of the 5th Light Division.[14]

Unlike the case with almost every other officer in authority with the 5th Light, Erwin Rommel liked Wolf Hauser. Even when Rommel was in a fine rage, in the middle of chewing out Streich and Olbricht for their lack of resolution and ordering them to attack Tobruk at once, Hauser got away with interrupting. He informed Rommel that they were expecting another 12 mobile guns and recommended that they postpone the attack until they arrived. Rommel paused and then agreed.

The extremely efficient Hauser remained divisional chief of operations under Streich's successor, General von Ravenstein. In September 1941, however, he was promoted to chief of operations of the 1st Panzer Group on the southern sector of the Eastern Front. After a leave in Germany, he assumed his new post on November 21, 1941. Initially, his commander was Colonel General Ewald von Kleist. A year later, Kleist was succeeded by another cavalry-officer-turned-panzer-leader, Eberhard von Mackensen. As Ia of the 1st Panzer, Hauser participated in the Rostov campaign, the retreat to the Mius in the winter of 1941–42, the drive to the Don, the initial phases of the Stalingrad campaign, the drive to the Caucasus, and the retreats and counterattacks of 1943, including Manstein's brilliant recapture of Kiev. Hauser, meanwhile, was promoted to lieutenant colonel on April 1, 1942, and to full colonel effective New Year's Day, 1943. By now, he had a solid reputation as a capable and highly effective General Staff officer.

In November 1943, Colonel General von Mackensen was transferred to northern Italy to assume command of the newly formed 14th Army. Mackensen took Hauser with him as chief of staff.

In February 1944, the Anglo-Americans landed at Anzio. Hauser did his usual highly competent job of rushing reinforcements to the threatened sector and keeping them well supplied, despite Allied air superiority. Mackensen, meanwhile, launched several ill-planned counterattacks on the U.S. VI Corps and was eventually relieved of his command by Field Marshal Albert Kesselring, the commander-in-chief of OB Southwest. Kesselring, however, attached no blame to Hauser. Although German army and army group commanders often carried their chief of staff with them when they were given new posts (as Mackensen had done in 1943), Hauser was nevertheless retained by all of the subsequent 14th Army commanders, including General of Panzer Troops Joachim Lemelsen, General of Panzer Troops Fridolin von Senger und Etterlin, General of Artillery Heinz Ziegler, General of Panzer Troops Traugott Herr, and General of Infantry Kurt von Tippelskirch. Hauser, meanwhile, fought in all of the major battles (and retreats) in Italy from Anzio to the Po. He was promoted to major general on September 1, 1944. He had just turned 38 years old.

In mid-February 1945, Wolf Hauser left Italy for the last time. He had been named chief of staff of the 1st Army, which was now defending the Black Forest and southern Germany from the Franco-American invasion. Initially, his commander was General of Infantry Hans von Obstfelder, but he was replaced by General of Infantry Hermann Foertsch on February 28. Foertsch, however, retained the brilliant young Hauser, who remained at his post until Germany surrendered on May 8, 1945.

An example of the old General Staff axiom "General Staff officers have no faces," Hauser is virtually unknown today but is nevertheless an excellent example of the kind of unseen officer without whom Rommel and the other major German commanders of World War II could not have won their victories. After spending more than two years in various POW camps, Hauser was released and settled in Bad Cannstatt, where he died on August 9, 1965.

Captain Dipl. Ing. Dr. Ernst Eberhard Bolbrinker was one of the heroes of the 1st Cyrenaican campaign.

He was born in Graz, Austria, on October 23, 1898, and joined the German Imperial Army as a private on June 1, 1916. He fought in World War I as a member of the 144th Infantry Regiment, where he earned the Iron Cross, 1st and 2nd Classes, as well as a promotion to second lieutenant in the fall of 1917.

Bolbrinker left the service in 1920 and decided to complete his education, which had been interrupted by the war. He received an advanced engineering degree (the *Dipl. Ing.*) and later a doctorate of engineering with a specialization in motor vehicles. In August 1936, he was recalled to active duty as a first lieutenant of reserves. He was soon transferred to the motorized branch (for obvious reasons), promoted to captain in 1937, and given command of a company in the 1st Panzer Regiment the following year. He fought in Poland and was promoted rapidly. After Warsaw fell, he was transferred to the staff of Lieutenant General Erich Hoepner's XVI Motorized (later Panzer) Corps. Six months later, on April 1, 1940, he was promoted to major, assigned to the 5th Panzer Regiment of the 3rd Panzer Division, and soon given command of the I Battalion. He fought in the Netherlands, Belgium, and France, where he was involved in the Battle of the Somme.[15] That winter, the 3rd Panzer Division (which had two panzer regiments) returned to Germany, where it was greatly reduced in size. Bolbrinker, along with the rest of the 5th Panzer Regiment, was transferred to the 5th Light Division, which was activated on February 18, 1941. It was already on its way to Libya.[16]

The regiment began disembarking at Tripoli on March 11 and was immediately rushed to the front. Bolbrinker was soon involved in the capture of Mersa el Brega. Shortly thereafter, he spearheaded the attack on Mechili. With four panzers, he followed a British column into the fortress and stormed it. He lost three of his four tanks but knocked out all of the British antitank guns and sealed the doom of the fort. Two thousand British soldiers were forced to surrender, along with two generals. For his bold action, the major was decorated with the Knight's Cross. A few days after, during the drive on Tobruk, he was wounded in action and was left with a nasty facial scar, which he bore for the rest of his life.

Bolbrinker fought in the drive to Tobruk and in Operations Brevity, Battleaxe, and Crusader. In the summer of 1941, he briefly served as acting commander of the 5th Panzer Regiment. In August, Dr. Bolbrinker was recalled to Germany and assigned to the staff of the Panzer School. On January 20, 1942, he was transferred to the Special Tropical Staff, and on April 1 he was promoted to lieutenant colonel.

Dr. Bolbrinker was transferred to the staff of Guderian's Panzer Inspectorate as a department chief on May 10, 1943. He worked for General Guderian and his successor, General of Panzer Troops Baron Leo Geyr von Schweppenburg, until the end of the war. He was promoted to colonel on May 1, 1943, and to major general on July 1, 1944.[17]

After the war, Ernst Bolbrinker was placed in an Allied POW camp, where he wrote a study of the 5th Panzer Regiment's actions on April 13 and 14, 1941, for the Historical Section of the U.S. Army, Europe.[18] After he was released from prison, he settled in Bielefeld, where he died on July 2, 1962.[19]

Heinrich Kirchheim was born in Gross-Salze in the Kreis Calbe/Saale on April 6, 1882. He entered the service as a Fahnenjunker in the 15th (2nd Westphalian) Infantry Regiment on May 1, 1899. He received his commission in 1900 and spent the next 10 years as a second lieutenant. In October 1904, he was sent to German South-West Africa (now Namibia), where a rebellion of the native Nama/Hottentot tribe had begun in January. Lieutenant General Lothar von Trotha, the military commander of the colony, put it down with extreme brutality using concentration camps, forced labor, deportations, and mass executions. The revolt ended in early 1907. Kirchheim, however, remained in the region until early 1914. In the process, he came to be known as an expert on tropical and desert warfare.

Kirchheim was assigned to the 4th Jaeger Battalion and became a company commander when World War I broke out. He was promoted to captain on September 15, 1914, and was seriously wounded nine days later. After he recovered, he returned to his battalion where he remained until August 1916, when he was named commander of the Hanoverian 10th Jaeger Battalion. He led it until the end of the war. In October 1918, a month before the end of the conflict, he was decorated with the *Pour le Merite*, a medal roughly equal to the Congressional Medal of Honor when awarded to someone of such junior rank.

After the armistice, Captain Kirchheim fought in "the war after the war," in which he led the Hanoverian "Volunteer Jaeger Battalion Kirchheim" against Communists and other leftists. Later, he was attached to the Prussian War Ministry (which later became the German Defense Ministry).

Kirchheim was selected for retention in the Reichsheer and became a company commander in the 17th Infantry Regiment in January 1921. He remained in this post until April 1, 1923, when he was promoted to major. He was then transferred to Frankfurt/Oder, where he spent the next three years on the staff of the 1st Cavalry Division. From 1926 to early 1930, Kirchheim commanded an infantry battalion. He was promoted to lieutenant colonel in 1928. His last assignment in the Weimar era was as commandant of Glatz. He became a colonel in 1931 and retired on March 31, 1932.[20]

Colonel Kirchheim was recalled to active duty in late 1934 as commander of the training battalion of the Arnsberg Infantry Regiment. Six weeks later, on November 15, 1934, he was named commandant of Military Zone Cologne (*Wehrbezirkskommandos Koeln*), which was then part of the demilitarized Rhineland, a post he held until after the German Army reoccupied the region. From 1938 to 1939, he headed a military zone in Vienna.[21]

Heinrich Kirchheim was promoted to major general on August 27, 1939, four days before the start of the war. On October 1, 1939, he was named commander of the 276th Infantry Regiment, which was then forming in Brieg, Frankenstein, Freiwaldau, and Goerlitz. This unit was later assigned to the 94th Infantry Division and was destroyed in

Stalingrad.[22] The regiment was a step below Kirchheim's rank, and he only commanded it for two months. On December 1, 1939, he was given command of the 169th Infantry Division, which was then forming at Frankfurt/Main. It was soon placed in positions near Offenbach on the Western Front. The division was in OKH reserve during the German drive to Dunkirk but played a part in the mopping up operations when the Wehrmacht finished off the Third Republic.

After France surrendered, Kirchheim and his division remained on occupation duty in Lothringen (Lorraine) until February 1941. The OKH, which considered him an expert of tropical (desert) warfare, then sent him to North Africa in charge of Special Staff Libya. Here, he ran across Erwin Rommel for the first time. Rommel basically dissolved Kirchheim's staff and named the excess German general of the Italian 27th "Brescia" Infantry Division.

Kirchheim and his men played a role in the capture of Benghazi, but Rommel was dissatisfied with their speed. Rommel also used Brescia to attack the Australian garrison at Tobruk. Here, the Desert Fox was dissatisfied with the division's courage and with Kirchheim's leadership—even though the older general was wounded in action and remained in command. Rommel was, however, more satisfied with Kirchheim than Streich. On April 30, he placed Kirchheim in charge of a battle group consisting of the 5th Panzer Regiment, the 2nd and 8th Machine Gun Battalions, two engineer companies, and antitank, artillery, and other elements of the 5th Light Division—i.e., he took most of Streich's men and placed them under Kirchheim. Unfortunately for Kirchheim, this assault also failed, at a cost of 1,400 German and Italian casualties. The battle lasted until May 5.

Although Kirchheim temporarily replaced Streich as commander of the 5th Light Division in the second half of May 1941, he held the post only until the permanent commander, General von Ravenstein, arrived on May 31. Rommel decorated Major General Kirchheim with the Knight's Cross and sent him back to Europe "on his camel."

Being sacked by Rommel did not count against Kirchheim when Franz Halder was chief of the General Staff. Halder named him commander of Special Staff Tropical (*Sonderstabes Tropen*; later Special Staff C) on June 15, 1941, and had him promoted to lieutenant general on July 1, 1942. Kirchheim, however, was merely an advisor to OKH and no longer had any influence on events in North Africa.

In the fall of 1944, Kirchheim had a chance to get a measure of revenge on Rommel when he was appointed to the "Court of Honor," which investigated German soldiers suspected of participating in the anti-Nazi coup of July 20, 1944. Among those brought before the court was Rommel's chief of staff in Normandy, Lieutenant General Dr. Hans Speidel. The Nazi civilian courts could not try soldiers unless they were expelled from the army. Although Speidel was guilty, Kirchheim passed up the opportunity to take secondhand revenge on the Desert Fox. He voted with the court in discharging Speidel from the service instead of expelling him. The distinction saved Speidel's life. As a discharged soldier, he could not be hauled before Judge Roland Freisler's People's Court, which undoubtedly would have hanged him. Speidel spent the rest of the war in prison, but he did not die until 1984.[23]

In October 1944, while he continued to sit on the Court of Honor, Kirchheim was named Inspector of Replacement Units in Berlin. He held this post until April 1, 1945, when he was placed in Fuehrer Reserve. He promptly left the capital of the Reich and headed west, where he surrendered to the Anglo-Americans on April 12. Kirchheim was discharged from the POW camps in October 1947. He retired to Luedenscheid and died on December 14, 1973.

CHAPTER III
THE SIEGE OF TOBRUK

The second of Rommel's divisional commanders to reach North Africa was Major General Heinrich von Prittwitz und Gaffron. He had proven himself to be an excellent panzer commander in Poland, France, and Belgium, and no doubt would have excelled in the Western Desert as well. Unfortunately, he did not live that long.

The descendant of an ancient and distinguished Prussian military family, Prittwitz was born in Sitzmannsdorf on September 4, 1889. He entered the service as a Fahnenjunker in April 1908 and was commissioned second lieutenant in the 3rd *Ulan* (Lancer) Regiment the following year. Later, he became a member of the General Staff. He fought in World War I, joined the Reichsheer in 1920, and was an early convert into the panzer branch. A major when Hitler took power in 1933 (and thus senior to Rommel), he was promoted to lieutenant colonel in 1934 and, on April 1, 1935, assumed command of the newly activated 2nd Panzer Regiment at Eisenach.[1] A promotion to colonel came the following year.

Prittwitz's regiment was part of the 1st Panzer Division—the first armored division in the history of the world. By the late 1930s, the colonel was apparently considered a solid tank commander but not a brilliant one. He took part in the occupation of Austria (March 1938) and the Sudetenland (September–October 1938) and performed well enough to make his next promotion. He took command of the 2nd Panzer Brigade of the 2nd Panzer Division at Vienna on November 10, 1938.

In 1939, the 2nd Panzer Brigade consisted of the 3rd and 4th Panzer Regiments, which were equipped with inferior Panzer Mark I and II tanks. (The much better Panzer Mark III was just coming into series production.) Prittwitz led it with distinction in central Poland, where it suffered severe casualties in heavy fighting. He was rewarded with a promotion to major general, effective October 1, 1939, as soon as the campaign ended.[2] It turned out to be his last—at least while he was alive.

The 2nd Panzer Division was quickly transferred to the West in the fall of 1939 and became part of General of Panzer Troops Heinz Guderian's XIX Motorized Corps during the French campaign. Prittwitz, therefore, had a chance to perform under the eyes of the "Father of the Blitzkrieg," who was also the former commander of the 2nd Panzer Division. Prittwitz's brigade excelled during the decisive Battle of Sedan (May 15–17, 1940), when Guderian broke through the French line. It then took part in the pursuit of the dissolving Anglo-French forces across the Aisne and in the drive to the sea, which ended in the isolation of the British Expeditionery Force (BEF), the 1st and 7th French Armies, and the Belgium Army in the Dunkirk Pocket. After the BEF was evacuated and the pocket was cleared, Prittwitz's brigade participated in the mopping up operations to the south and surrounded thousands of French Maginot Line soldiers in the Belfort Gap region.

After the French campaign, the 2nd Panzer Division was transferred back to the Reich and in September was sent to Poland. Meanwhile, because of his outstanding performance in France, Prittwitz had been earmarked for greater things. Hitler had decided to increase the number of panzer divisions from 10 to 20 by dividing the existing divisions in half. Prittwitz assumed command of the 14th Panzer Division at Dresden on October 1, 1940.

The 14th Panzer Division was formed from the old 4th Infantry Division, which included the 52nd, 103rd, and 108th Infantry Regiments. To form the 14th Panzer, it gave up the 52nd Infantry Regiment and received the 36th Panzer Regiment from the 4th Panzer Division. It also received the newly formed Staff, 14th Rifle Brigade, and the 64th Motorcycle (formerly 7th Machine Gun) Battalion, but gave up the III Battalion of both the 103rd and 108th Infantry Regiments, which were meanwhile motorized. Prittwitz oversaw the formation and unit training of the 14th Panzer Division and no doubt enjoyed the cultural delights of the beautiful Saxon capital, but when his unit arrived in Hungary that spring, Prittwitz was not with them. He had been named commander of the 15th Panzer Division effective March 23, 1941, exchanging commands with Major General Friedrich Kuehn. Prittwitz's new division was in or en route to Italy and was preparing for transport to Libya.

Why Prittwitz and Kuehn exchanged commands is not known, but it was highly unusual—especially when one considers the timing. The 14th Panzer would be in action in the Balkans campaign on April 6, and the 15th Panzer would also be in combat by the second week in April. To give both units new commanders was quite strange, especially at this stage of the war. In addition, Kuehn was no expert on the

Balkans, and Prittwitz certainly had no special qualifications for a desert command. Only two explanations are possible: 1) Rommel did not want Kuehn, or 2) Kuehn did not want to serve under Rommel. The second explanation is far more likely. Colonel General Franz Halder, the chief of the General Staff, was certainly no friend of Rommel's but he did respect Kuehn, who was an expert on motorization. (Later, in 1942, he appointed Kuehn chief of army motorization.[3]) At this time, Halder was referring to Rommel as "this soldier gone stark mad." He had already clearly demonstrated that he was not above filling Rommel's command with "spies" (i.e., officers who were loyal to OKH and who were disloyal to Rommel). Clearly, Halder would not have ordered Kuehn and Prittwitz to exchange commands had the idea originated with the Desert Fox; obviously, the request must have come from Kuehn—or perhaps it was Halder's own idea.

When the vanguards of the 15th Panzer Division arrived in North Africa, the other division of the DAK—the 5th Light—was chasing the British across the desert in the direction of Tobruk. Landing with his forward troops, General von Prittwitz promptly joined the pursuit with his vanguard. Rommel ordered him to prevent as many Allied troops from escaping as possible and to prepare to capture Tobruk. On April 10, 1941, his first day in action in North Africa, General Heinrich von Prittwitz und Gaffron was killed by a blast from an Australian antitank gun while probing the defenses of Tobruk. He was buried in the German Military Cemetary at Derna. Germany had lost an "up and coming" panzer leader.

Heinrich von Prittwitz von Gaffron was posthumously promoted to lieutenant general, effective April 1, 1941. He was succeeded by Colonel Hans-Karl von Esebeck, the commander of the 15th Panzer Brigade.

Esebeck was born in Frederick the Great's garrison town of Potsdam on July 10, 1892. The descendant of an old Prussian military family, he was educated in various cadet schools and entered the Imperial Army as a Fahnenjunker in the elite 3rd Guards Ulam Regiment on September 25, 1911. He was promoted to *Faehnrich* (senior officer-cadet, sometimes translated as ensign) on June 19, 1912, graduated from the War School at Anklam in early 1913, and was commissioned second lieutenant on February 18, 1913.

Esebeck spent most of his pre-World War II career in the cavalry. During the first three years of World War I, he served with his regiment, primarily on the Eastern Front, and was promoted to first lieutenant in 1916. Later he worked on the staff of the VI Corps (1917–18), as adjutant of the 3rd Guards Cavalry Brigade (1918) and as a member of the Military Commission to St. Petersburg (1918). After the armistice, he remained in the East, leading the Volunteer Squadron of the 3rd Guards Ulam in the struggle against the Soviets in the Baltic States. He returned to Germany as adjutant of the 115th Cavalry Regiment in late 1919 and was selected for the Reichswehr. In 1920, after the 115th Cavalry was dissolved, young Esebeck joined the 4th Cavalry Regiment at Allenstein, East Prussia. Except for a four-month tour of duty with the Staff, 1st Cavalry Division, he remained with his regiment for eleven years (1920–31). Promoted to *Rittmeister* (captain of cavalry) in March 1931, he became senior station officer for the small detachment at Perleberg late that year and was still there when Hitler took power in early 1933.

Esebeck was a simple, decent soldier with no other ambition than to serve his country. He had little interest in politics, at least until the 1940s. In 1934, he joined the staff of the Infantry School at Dresden, where Erwin Rommel was a fellow instructor. The following year, however, Esebeck became an instructor at the War School at Hanover. When this assignment was completed, he returned to East Prussia, where he was named commander of the 1st (Prussian) Cavalry Regiment at Insterburg. He assumed command on October 6, 1936. He had already been promoted to major (1933) and lieutenant colonel (January 1, 1936). He was promoted to colonel on June 1, 1938.[4]

To date, Esebeck's career had been that of a regular (i.e., active army) cavalry officer, with little or no diversification. He saw that the wave of the future, however, did not lie with the horse. After successfully commanding the 1st Cavalry, he left his beloved mounted branch and, on April 1, 1939, became the first commander of the 6th *Schuetzen* (Rifle) Brigade of the 1st Light Division.

The Rhinelander-Westphalian 6th Schuetzen (which can also be translated as Motorized) was based at Iserlohn and included the 4th Rifle Regiment (three battalions) and the 6th Motorcycle Battalion. Esebeck led it in the Polish campaign; then it returned to its home station, along with the rest of the 1st Light Division, which was quickly converted into the 6th Panzer Division. When the reorganization was completed, the division deployed on the lower Rhine and, in May 1940, took part in the invasion of Belgium. It fought its way through the frontier defenses, forced its way across the Meuse, and played a prominent role in the drive to the English Channel, during which it drove forward 217 miles in nine days. It was involved in heavy fighting in Flanders and played a role in the destruction of the 1st and 7th French Armies. It was then shifted south, where it advanced from the Aisne River to the Swiss border. He was awarded the Knight's Cross on July 4, 1940.

After the end of the French campaign, Esebeck's brigade returned to its base, where it was reorganized again, losing the 3rd Rifle Regiment but picking up the 114th Rifle Regiment (two battalions). It was then sent on to East Prussia, where it prepared for the invasion of the Soviet Union. Esebeck, however, gave up command in late February 1941, and traded the snows of Prussia for the sands of Africa. He assumed command of the 15th Rifle Brigade on March 13, 1941.

Esebeck's lateral transfer was undoubtedly arranged by Lieutenant General Erwin Rommel with the cooperation of his personal friend, Colonel Rudolf Schmundt, the chief army adjutant to the Fuehrer and the Supreme Commander of the Wehrmacht. At the time, Esebeck's brigade was in Italy and Sicily, en route to Benghazi. Before Hans-Karl von Esebeck could even reach the front, however, word arrived that his divisional commander, Heinrich von Prittwitz und Gaffron, had been killed in action near Tobruk. Rommel appointed Esebeck acting commander of the 15th Panzer Division effective April 13, 1941. Two days later, the longtime Prussian cavalryman received a special promotion to major general. His, however, was not destined to be a long appointment.

Rommel hoped to capture Tobruk before the Australian and British garrison could properly organize their defenses, so Esebeck and his men were in the attack almost as soon as they arrived. Despite several attempts, the 15th Panzer Division was unable to break the Allied defenses. On May 13, after exactly one month in command, General von Esebeck was seriously wounded by a shell splinter near the Tobruk perimeter. After his condition stabilized he was sent back to Europe, where he spent more than two months in the hospital, followed by another month on wounded leave. He did not return to active duty until August 1941.

Both Esebeck and Rommel wanted him to return to North Africa, but it was not to be. Rommel's hated enemy, Colonel General Franz Halder, the chief of the General Staff, refused to allow it. Esebeck was sent to the Eastern Front instead.

On August 24, 1941, General von Esebeck assumed command of the 11th Panzer Division, replacing Lieutenant General Ludwig Cruewell, who had recently departed for Libya to assume command of the Afrika Korps. He led it in the battles of Zhitomir, Uman, Kiev, and Moscow, among others. Esebeck also took part in the early stages of the Soviet Winter Offensive of 1941–42. On December 28, 1941, he was either wounded or fell ill; in any case, he left the Russian Front and did not return to active duty until February 17, 1942, when he assumed command of his old division, the 2nd Panzer, which was then fighting in the Rzhev salient. The Russians tried several times to crush this position (to no avail), and Esebeck was involved in heavy fighting for most of the year.

On November 22, 1942, Baron von Esebeck was named commander of the XXXXVI Panzer Corps on the central sector of the Eastern Front.

This led to his promotion to lieutenant general effective December 1, 1942. He led the corps until June 30, 1943, when he was placed in charge of Korps von Esebeck, an ad hoc three-division battle group under Army Group Center.

After Korps von Esebeck was dissolved, General Esebeck was sent west. From November 30, 1943, to early 1944, he was acting commander of the LVIII Reserve Panzer Corps, which was on occupation duty in the Toulouse area of southern France. He was promoted to general of panzer troops on February 1.

Esebeck was replaced as leader of the LVIII Panzer when its permanent commander, General of Panzer Troops Walter Krueger, arrived in February 1944. (Sources differ as to the exact date.) In any case, Esebeck was a supernumeracy officer with OB West until April 1, 1944, when he was placed in Fuehrer Reserve. (Apparently, there was no position open for an officer of his rank.) He remained in limbo until June 7, 1944, when he was named commander of Wehrkreis XVII in Vienna.

Baron von Esebeck had knowledge of and was sympathetic to the anti-Hitler conspiracy. On July 20, 1944, he cooperated with the conspirators. The following day he was arrested. He spent the rest of the war in concentration camps. It is not clear why he was not hanged, like most of the others.

Liberated at the end of the war, he had been impoverished by the conflict. He lived the rest of his life in relative poverty and died in Dortmund on January 5, 1955.

CHAPTER IV

CRUSADER

Johann Theodor von Ravenstein was chosen to replace Johann Streich as commander of the 5th Light Division. A cultured aristocrat with an anti-Nazi political background, he was not expected to get along with Rommel, who was an outspoken (and somewhat tactless) commoner and who was considered pro-Nazi in 1941. Surprisingly, they made a very effective team.

"Hans" von Ravenstein was born in the small garrison town of Strehlen, Silesia, about 20 miles south of Breslau, on January 1, 1889. His father, Fritz, was an officer in the Silesian Brown Hussars, but there was distinguished military stock on both sides of his family. His paternal great-grandfather had been one of Bluecher's adjutants, was a liaison officer to the Duke of Wellington during the Battle of Waterloo, and had been personally decorated by Kaiser Friedrich Wilhelm III. His mother, Baroness Margarete Maltzan of Mecklenburg, was a descendant of Baron Carl Friedrich Wilhelm von Korckwitz, who lost his arm serving as General von Seydlitz's adjutant during the Seven Years' War.

Despite their distinguished backgrounds, the Ravenstein home was not a happy one. Shortly after Hans was born, his father was thrown from a horse and suffered a brain injury. He then gave away the family estates piece by piece to his friends and treated Hans and his older sister, Margarete, with cruelty. This soon became too much for the now-impoverished baroness, who divorced her husband in about 1893 and set about supporting her family as best she could. Her ex-husband died in a private hospital in 1905 at the age of 42.

The family poverty and Fritz's tragic demise had no lasting impact on Hans, who grew into a fine and cultured young man. From the age of seven, his ambition in life was to be an Evangelical Lutheran pastor, and he wanted to attend a university and study theology. Unfortunately, there was no money to send him.

There were many financially challenged Prussian Junker families in the 1870–1945 period. Some were poor because they were bad businessmen and poor managers of their estates; others were impoverished as a result of the many selfless sacrifices they made for their country, their people, and their king. The Prussian Army offered the sons of both groups a free education to ensure a talented supply of future officers and to repay past loyalty.

At the age of 10, Hans von Ravenstein entered the Wahlstatt Cadet School. It was a harsh shock for the sensitive youth, because it had all of the vices and none of the virtues of the Prussian military system.[1] Here, bullying was mistaken for discipline, and the senior cadets were petty and mean to the younger cadets. Hans, however, was fortunate enough to have Senior Cadet Friedrich Wilhelm von Loeper—another future panzer general—as his protector. (The von Loeper and von Ravenstein families had been friends for decades.)[2] Although unpleasant enough, Ravenstein's time at Wahlstatt was not as bad as it might have been.

In 1903, at the age of 14, Ravenstein was admitted to the Cadet Academy at Gross-Lichterfelde—Germany's West Point—which was located in a district of southern Berlin. Here, the situation was much different. Although the military training and physical exercises were intense, the atmosphere was civilized, the staff was awesome, and individual cadets were treated with a degree of respect. In addition to military science, in which the academy excelled, Lichterfelde's courses included history, mathematics, sciences, modern languages, and Latin. Teaching standards were high, and Ravenstein received an education at least equal to that of a superior *Realgymnasium* (semi-classical high school), and he very much enjoyed his time at Lichterfelde.

During his last two years, Cadet von Ravenstein (along with other most-promising senior cadets) was called upon to serve as a page for the Kaiser and his guests during special occasions at the *Neues Palais* (New Palace) in Potsdam, and young Hans became friendly with Wilhelm II and Kaiserin Viktoria Auguste, the mother of six sons and a daughter. Throughout his life, Ravenstein retained his affection for the Royal family.

Hans von Ravenstein graduated from Gross-Lichterfelde in 1909 and was commissioned second lieutenant in the (7th) *Koenigsgrenadier* (King's Grenadier) Regiment on June 24, with seniority dating from March 23. Before joining his unit, Ravenstein did a tour of duty as Ordnance Officer (i.e., Orderly Officer) to the Kaiser. Shortly after joining his regiment at Liegnitz, he was invited to a party at the estate of Count and Countess von Oriola. Here, he met Countess Elisabeth von Oriola, a pretty, petite, 18-year-old ash blonde. He fell in love immediately.

The Oriolas were Portuguese. Elisabeth's great-grandfather had represented Portugal and Spain in the Congress of Vienna (1815). He traveled through Germany, bought an estate in Silesia, and became a naturalized German citizen in 1822. Elisabeth's parents opposed her possible match with Hans. He was of the wrong religion (they were Catholic), and he had no money. Hans nevertheless continued to woe Elisabeth and gradually wore her parents down.

In 1912, Lieutenant von Ravenstein was transferred to the 155th Infantry Regiment, which would be "his" regiment until the end of his life. Initially, he was a battalion adjutant. In August 1914, the German Army crossed the border in Belgium, and, on August 22, Ravenstein received his baptism of fire at Longwy. Ironically, less than a mile away, Lieutenant Erwin Rommel of the 124th Infantry Regiment also came under fire for the first time. (The two lieutenants would not meet for 26 years, when Ravenstein arrived in North Africa.) Ravenstein later remembered the battles around Longwy as some of the worse days of his life, because they involved frequent bayonet fighting. The following month, Hans took part in the initial attacks on Verdun. Here, in the trenches of World War I, he developed a reputation for boldness. He frequently led patrols, raids, and sorties into no-man's land, often bringing back prisoners. He successively advanced from battalion adjutant to company commander to General Staff Officer to battalion commander at the age of 29. He was promoted to first lieutenant in 1915 and to captain in 1918. He was also wounded several times. During a leave in the autumn of 1917, he proposed to Elisabeth von Oriola. Her parents had by now adjusted to the idea that their daughter was going to marry a penniless Protestant and supported her decision. Hans and Elisabeth were married during his next leave in February 1918. They honeymooned in the mountains of Silesia.

Ravenstein, meanwhile, had continued his professional advancement, had attended an abbreviated General Staff course (probably at Sedan), and was admitted to the General Staff. He was, however, unhappy with performing safe, rear-area staff duties when other men were dying, so he arranged to return to the front with his old regiment, the 155th Infantry.

"Yes, he ran away—ran away to the front!" his wife recalled. Naturally, she was very upset that he would risk death so soon after their marriage. She went to see her mother-in-law, to whom she poured out her heart. "You must accept him as he is," the baroness told her. "It is in his nature to do such things."[3] Elisabeth accepted her advice, although it is doubtful if it made her feel much better.

Meanwhile, at the front, Hans von Ravenstein ran wild. When the commander of the I Battalion was wounded during the Battle of the Marne (1918), command passed to Ravenstein. He broke through the French trench line, seized a bridge over the Aisne River near Chemin des Dames with only six men on May 27, and held it against repeated French counterattacks. On May 30, Ravenstein was leading an advanced patrol toward Chatillon when he spotted a French Negro Battalion led by white officers. He quickly set up an ambush and waited until the enemy was within 100 feet to open fire. The enemy battalion was taken completely by surprise and was routed—by 16 men. He pushed on toward the Marne, capturing more than 1,500 men, more than 30 guns, and 30 machine guns.[4] On June 9, the divisional commander decorated von Ravenstein with the *Pour le Merite*, the equivalent of the Congressional Medal of Honor when presented to a junior officer.[5] Shortly thereafter, Ravenstein was promoted to captain for bravery in the face of the enemy.[6]

In the last weeks of the war, Ravenstein commanded a battalion of the Imperial Guard at the Kaiser's headquarters at Spa. He was there when the Kaiser and Crown Prince abdicated on November 9, and the old order collapsed. For Ravenstein, however, the fighting was not over. He was sent to the East, where he helped the Freikorps defend Silesia against Polish attacks. Elisabeth joined him and cooked for the battalion staff, often quite near the firing line. After the Poles were checked, however, Ravenstein decided not to join Seeckt's 100,000-man army. He was discharged with an honorary promotion to major on March 31, 1920.

Meanwhile, Ravenstein prepared for civilian life. With no income and little savings, he entered a college at Essen and took a course in administration, from which he graduated in 1921. He then took a job with the Rhine-Westphalian Company, a huge electrical corporation. It paid him well and life was better. He and Elisabeth moved to Duisburg in the mid-1920s.

In Duisburg, Ravenstein became a close personal friend of Dr. Karl Jarres, the *Oberbuergermeister* (lord mayor) of the city and an influential politician who had been minister of the interior and vice chancellor under Chancellors Gustav Stresemann and Wilhelm Marx.[7] Jarres was nominated for the presidency of the Reich by both the People's and Nationalist parties after Friedrich Ebert died in February 1925. Dr. Jarres finished first in the first primary but then withdrew in favor of former Field Marshal Paul von Hindenburg, who was considered more likely to defeat the Social Democrats, the Catholic Center Party, the Communists, and the Nazis. Hindenburg was, of course, elected despite his advanced age of 78.

In 1926, Dr. Jarres offered Ravenstein a post in the Duisburg government as director of the tramway system. Despite his lack of training in civil transportation, Ravenstein did a brilliant job, so Jarres made him his personal assistant and promoted him to director of public relations. Ravenstein had this post until Hitler forced him and Jarres out of office in 1933.[8]

Domestically, the Ravensteins were very happy, except for their lack of children. Hans even underwent an operation to remedy this situation, but they were not lucky. Hans's sister Margarete, however, had a daughter, Christa, in December 1922. Her husband died of tuberculosis in 1925 and Margarete had to work, which made her less and less able to take care of her daughter. As a result, Christa spent more and more time at her aunt and uncle's. She soon regarded Hans and Elisabeth as sort of co-parents and called Hans father. He eventually adopted her.

Ravenstein, meanwhile, was not able to find a job. A known anti-Nazi, he was not in any danger of being thrown into a concentration camp in 1933–34 (as would likely have been the case a few years later), but employers were already afraid to hire prominent anti-Nazis. One profession, however, went on as before: the army was not yet under Hitler's thumb and would not be until 1938. It was also expanding and was in need of experienced and capable officers at every rank. It welcomed Major von Ravenstein back with opened arms. He returned to duty on May 1, 1934, as commander of the II Battalion, 60th Infantry Regiment (II/60th Infantry) at Luedenscheid in Wehrkreis VI. He was promoted to lieutenant colonel on October 1, 1936, was named commander of the Rhinelander-Westphalian 4th Rifle Regiment at Iserlohn in November 1938, and was promoted to colonel on August 1, 1939. The 4th Rifle was part of the 1st Light Division.

Ravenstein enjoyed his time in the prewar Wehrmacht, but he agonized over the direction Germany was heading. Far before most Germans, he recognized that Hitler was evil and was a criminal. He was still a strong Christian (as he would be until the day he died) and longed for a return to the days when Germany was Prussian, Christian, and conservative. But there was nothing he could do. The 4th Rifle, meanwhile, took part in the occupation of the Sudetenland (September–October 1938) and Czechoslovakia (April 1939). On September 1, 1939, the German Wehrmacht crossed the border into Poland. World War II had begun.

The 1st Light Division took part in the conquest of southern Poland but was then transferred back to Westphalia, where it was reorganized as the 6th Panzer Division. It was equipped mainly with Panzer Mark 35(t) Czech tanks, which were inferior to the Panzer Mark III and most of the British and French tanks. Ravenstein's regiment performed nevertheless exceedingly well in the Western campaign of 1940. The invasion began on May 10, 1940. Reinforced by several panzers, Battle Group Ravenstein crossed the Meuse near Montherme, broke through the main French line after destroying several bunkers, crossed the Serre, and finally captured Montcornet. On May 17, Ravenstein seized the vital bridge at Ovigny intact and began crossing the Oise. That afternoon, however, he ran into greatly superior French Char B tanks near LeCatelet and had to fight a two-and-a-half-hour battle. After overcoming heavy resistance, Ravenstein's men barrelled into Le Catelet, where they overran the Headquarters of the French 9th Army. Fifty French officers were captured, including the chief of staff. Only the army commander, General Giraud, escaped, because he was at his advanced command post. For this achievement, Ravenstein was awarded the Knight's Cross.[9] The 6th Panzer continued to advance and took part in the crushing of the Dunkirk Pocket and the mopping up operations south of the "Panzer Corridor." Afterwards, Ravenstein returned to Silesia, where he took part in the preparatory phases of Operation Felix—Hitler's plan to seize Gibraltar. The Spanish dictator Franco refused to cooperate, however, so the attack was cancelled. Meanwhile, on July 15, 1940, Ravenstein was given command of the 16th Rifle Brigade of the 16th Panzer Division. In November 1940, the colonel and his brigade were sent to the Balkans, where they remained until May 1941.

Initially, Ravenstein was part of the German Military Mission to Romania. In this capacity, he had his only conference with Hitler, who seemed impressed with the aristocratic holder of the Pour le Merite. Later, he took part in the campaign in Greece, which began on April 6, 1941. Finally, he was sent to Bulgaria as a German liaison officer to King Boris. Ravenstein liked the "Little Fox," as Boris was called, but his time in Sofia was short. On May 20, 1941, he was promoted to major general and was named commander of the 5th Light Division in Libya. He promptly flew to Berlin for a required medical examination, picked up his gear, and arrived in North Africa on May 31.

The 5th Light was deployed around Gambut, between Tobruk and the Egyptian-Libyan frontier, to rest and train while Major General Neumann-Silkow's 15th Panzer Division screened the frontier. Part of Rommel's army reserve, the 5th was ordered to be prepared to redeploy to the frontier if the British attacked, which is what Rommel expected.

The British offensive, which was codenamed Operation Battleaxe, began on June 15, and Rommel ordered the 5th Light to head south to cover the Axis right (desert) flank (Figure 4.1). Ravenstein, however, was 50 miles from the frontier and did not reach the combat zone until nightfall. The next day, he fought a running battle with the tanks of the British 7th Armoured Division north of Sidi Omar, in which both sides suffered severe losses. Unlike the British, however, he kept significant elements of his panzer regiment in reserve. That night, Rommel reinforced Ravenstein with the surviving tanks of the 8th Panzer Regiment (about 30 operational panzers) and ordered him to strike the extreme British left flank with everything he had. This was an exceedingly bold and dangerous move on Rommel's part, because it placed all of his German armor in the desert. All Rommel had left to defend

Figure 4.1
Operation Battleaxe

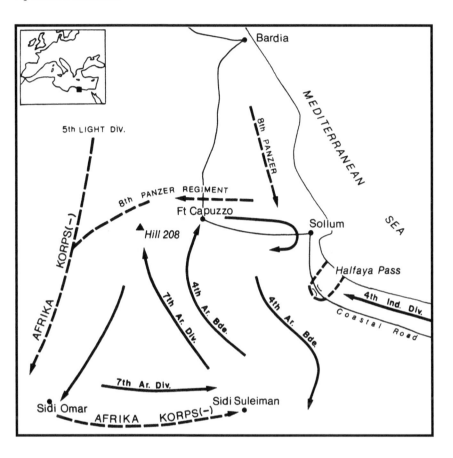

his center were a few immobile German detachments and the Italian Ariete Armored Division. A major Allied attack would lead to a major breakthrough, cutting off the entire Afrika Korps to the south, and the British had the forces on hand to do the job, including the 22nd Guards and 4th Armoured Brigades and elements of the 4th Indian Division. It was all a question of speed and Rommel, as usual, struck first. At dawn, the fast-moving Ravenstein caught the 7th Armoured Brigade (of the 7th Armoured Division) in an exposed position, smashed it, and drove into the Allied rear, heading for the besieged German garrison at Halfaya Pass. Now the British were faced with encirclement. Soon the 7th Armoured and 4th Indian Divisions, as well as the rest of the British Western Desert Force, were in full retreat. Many trucks were abandoned because of lack of fuel; damaged tanks, vehicles, and guns were also left behind.

The 7th Armoured Brigade had only 21 tanks remaining when it reached Egypt. In all, the British lost 100 tanks on June 17. Ravenstein lost 25—some of which were later repaired. And Nazi Germany had won its first major defensive battle in its history.

After "Battleaxe," the 5th Light was redesignated 21st Panzer Division but without any increase in its strength. It still included the 5th Panzer and 104th Panzer Grenadier Regiments, each with two battalions; the 155th Panzer Artillery Regiment (three battalions); and the 3rd Panzer Reconnaissance, 39th Tank Destroyer, 200th Panzer Engineer, and 200th Panzer Signal Battalions.

From June 17 until November 17, 1941—when the British launched Operation "Crusader," their next major offensive—a lull descended on the North African Front. Both sides desperately tried to build up the supplies for the next attack. Rommel wanted to overwhelm the Tobruk garrison before the British could strike; the British 8th Army wanted to relieve Tobruk before Rommel could attack. In this race, Rommel was handicapped by the Royal Navy and Air Forces at Malta, which were astride his supply lines. In July, 17 percent of his supplies were sunk before they could reach Libya. In August, this figure rose to 35 percent; it was 38 percent in September, and a whopping 63 percent in October. As a result, it was impossible for the Desert Fox to accumulate sufficient fuel and ammunition for his offensive. He was barely able to feed his men.

During the lull, Captain Heinz Werner Schmidt—Rommel's aide—visited the headquarters of the 21st Panzer Division, which Ravenstein had relocated under some palm trees west of Bardia, almost on the beach. Ravenstein loved beauty and tried to make his headquarters as comfortable and luxurious as possible, in marked contrast to the Spartan Rommel, who was completely indifferent to the creature comforts. "Here there were delicacies, including fresh eggs and cold beer, of which we never dreamed," Schmidt recalled. He was received cordially and invited to have an egg, which he consumed with concentrated enthusiasm. "Tastes good, eh, Schmidt?" General von Ravenstein asked with a twinkle in his eye. He pushed his own untouched egg over to the young officer. Schmidt tried to protest, but Ravenstein would hear none of it, so Schmidt ate the general's egg as well.[10]

Schmidt had been an officer-cadet in Ravenstein's battalion at Iserlohn in 1937, so the two renewed their acquaintanceship. Ravenstein invited Schmidt to accompany him on his evening walk. As Ravenstein strolled about the desert and commented on its beauty and serenity, Schmidt considered the differences between the two generals: "Von Ravenstein, the lover of beauty, the gentle, the humane, the considerate, for whom life contained poetry; and Rommel, supremely practical, hard, indifferent to the personal problems of others, concerned with personalities only in so far as they affected his military aims, for whom life was plain prose."[11]

Both Rommel and Ravenstein took two weeks' leave in Rome in October, and both were joined by their wives. They all stayed at the Hotel Eden. The couples ate together but spent most of the rest of their time separately. Rommel was too preoccupied with the military situation to enjoy himself, while Ravenstein was depressed by the Nazi regime and Hitler's amateurish handling of the war. When his airplane took off for North Africa, Elisabeth had no way of knowing that she would not see him again for six years.

Operation "Crusader" began on the night of November 17–18, 1941. It was an exceptionally complex battle—too complex to be described in depth here. Ravenstein, however, performed brilliantly. Shortly before his death, Rommel commented to his son that Ravenstein was one of his most brilliant generals. By 2 A.M. on November 26, the 21st Panzer Division was down to a strength of only 22 operational tanks. That evening, as the British tried to batter their way into Tobruk, Ravenstein led a successful counterattack, but his car sustained a direct hit, his driver was seriously wounded, and his orderly was killed. The battle continued at the same pace on November 27 and 28.

On the morning of November 29, Ravenstein set out with his new driver and orderly to attend a meeting at the headquarters of the 15th Panzer Division. Suddenly, he ran into an ambush, set by a New Zealand lieutenant. His tires were punctured, his radiator was shot up, and bullets and pieces of metal flew throughout the passenger compartment. The driver was hit in the shoulder. Ravenstein jumped out of the car and threw himself to the ground but was soon confronted by three New Zealand infantrymen. There was nothing to do but surrender. Hans von Ravenstein thus earned the dubious distinction of becoming the first German general to be captured in the Second World War.

The New Zealanders treated Ravenstein correctly. That night, they made contact with the Tobruk garrison and sent Ravenstein into the fortress. On December 5, with the battle still in progress, Ravenstein and 400 mostly British wounded were put aboard the transport ship, *Chakdina*, which set sail for Alexandria. That night, it was attacked by an Italian Savoia torpedo bomber and sank in three and a half minutes. Barefooted, Ravenstein jumped more than 20 feet into a lifeboat. Minutes later, however, the ship sank and the lifeboat was swamped by survivors. It was a dark and stormy night, and the waves were higher than houses. Ravenstein was about to drown when a plank with a handle for him to grip suddenly appeared before him—as if sent by God. This saved the general's life. A young Englishman, who was weak and was probably one of the wounded, joined him and held on to the plank. Ravenstein implored him to hang on and repeated the Lord's Prayer to him again and again in broken English. The private was too weak, however, and he let go and drowned. Tired, naked, and cold, Ravenstein was rescued by a British corvette two hours later. Less than half of the passengers and crew of the *Chakdina* survived.

Ravenstein finally arrived in Alexandria on December 8 and faded from the stage of history. He was imprisoned in Egypt, Durban, South Africa, Ontario, Canada, and in the German Generals' Camp at Bridgend, United Kingdom. He was promoted to lieutenant general on October 1, 1943, despite the fact that he was a prisoner of war. Ravenstein was medically repatriated to Germany on November 25, 1947 (he had developed heart trouble while in prison) and immediately returned to Iserlohn. Elisabeth later commented that it was as if he had been gone three days, not six years. "It was wonderful!" she declared.[12]

Because of the personal instructions of Field Marshal Montgomery, the Ravenstein home was never requisitioned by the Allies. After working for the Duesseldorf Corporation for a year, Ravenstein was offered his old job with the city administration in Duisburg. He worked there until his retirement in 1954. Christa, meanwhile, earned her Ph.D. in history and German literature. After Karl Jarres died in 1951, his daughter, Lore Kruse-Jarres, invited the Ravenstein family to occupy what had been Dr. Jarres's apartment in her home. She wanted him to act as a father figure for her three children, which he did with great success. Meanwhile, King Farouk of Egypt offered Ravenstein command of the Egyptian Army, no doubt hoping Rommel's former deputy would lead it against the Israelis. He declined.

In retirement, Hans von Ravenstein devoted himself to his many interests and hobbies. He was active in the Lutheran church, in the German Rotary movement, in the Duisburg Zoo, and in various veterans' and horticultural organizations. On March 26, 1962, he kissed his wife good-bye for the last time. That evening, in the middle of a very positive speech to his parish, he suddenly dropped dead of a heart attack.

Ludwig Cruewell was one of the best panzer commanders, not only in the Afrika Korps but in the entire German Army. This is why Erwin Rommel made him his deputy army commander.

Cruewell was born in Dortmund on March 20, 1892, and was just a few months younger than the Desert Fox.[13] He entered the service as a Fahnenjunker in the 9th Dragoon Regiment on March 6, 1911, and attended the War School at Hersfeld from October 1911 until the end of June 1912. He was commissioned second lieutenant in the 9th Dragoons on August 18, 1912. He served with his regiment for most of

World War I, fighting on both the Eastern and Western Fronts. He was a patrol leader in France, fought in the Battles of Kudno and Lodz in Poland, was promoted to first lieutenant in January 1916, and became regimental adjutant in September. The following year, he was selected for General Staff training, and thus was given a wide variety of assignments to broaden his experience and expertise. He was attached to the 1st Orderly Officer of the 233rd Infantry Division in Flanders (late 1917–January 1918), the 233rd Artillery Command (January 9, 1918), and the staff of the 233rd Infantry Division (March 17). He served briefly as adjutant of the 19th Landwehr Infantry Brigade (May 3–June 2) and then did a tour on the General Staff of the 52nd Special Purposes Corps, where he underwent a three-month course of formal General Staff classroom instruction. He was assigned to the General Staff of the 33rd Infantry Division on September 14, 1918, and remained with this unit until after the armistice, fighting in the 2nd Battle of the Marne and at Verdun in the process.[14]

Lieutenant Cruewell returned to Germany and in January 1919 rejoined his old regiment, the 9th Dragoons. In April he was recalled to Berlin and attached to the Great General Staff, where he apparently underwent further training. He was named defense ministry liaison officer to the 1st Cavalry Division in late 1920.

From 1919 on, Cruewell's career was fairly typical of a Prussian general-in-training. He served in the Defense Ministry (1921), on the staff of the 9th Cavalry Regiment under the commandant of Berlin (1921–22) where he almost certainly fought Communist insurgents, back to the defense ministry (1922), to the staff of Group 1 in Berlin (1922–23), to the defense ministry again (1923–25), and to the staff of the 2nd Cavalry Division in Breslau (1925–28). While he was in Berlin, he finished his General Staff training. After a brief course at the Cavalry School at Hanover, he was a squadron commander in the 12th Cavalry Regiment from 1928 to 1931. He served on the staff of the 3rd Cavalry and 6th Infantry Divisions from 1931 to 1934 and was chief of operations of Wehrkreis VI and VI Corps in Muenster, Westphalia (1934–36). Meanwhile, he was promoted to *Rittmeister* (captain of cavalry) (1922), major (1931), lieutenant colonel (1934), and colonel (1936).

Cruewell was a special purposes officer to the commander-in-chief of the army from April to October 1936. In this position, he was able to influence his own next assignment, and by now Cruewell had seen and recognized the potential of the tank. He became commander of Antitank Troop V in Stuttgart on October 6, 1936. This headquarters (HQ) controlled all antitank units (motorized and towed) in Wehrkreis V (Wurttemberg, southwestern Germany). He took over the 6th Panzer Regiment of the 3rd Panzer Division in Neuruppin near Berlin on February 1, 1938, and led it for the next 13 months. Then, he returned to Berlin as the chief of the 6th Branch at OKH. In this post he was chief supply and administrative officer for the German Army—a very important post indeed for a mere colonel.

Meanwhile, over a period of years, Ludwig Cruewell lost all of his hair and became bald, except for a little on the sides, which he kept cut very short.

Cruewell became chief quartermaster of the 16th Army under the harsh pro-Nazi Colonel General Ernst Busch on October 23, 1939, and was promoted to major general on December 1, 1939. He directed the quartermaster staff of the 16th during the campaign in Belgium and France in 1940 and was a tremendous help to General Busch, who was not competent to command an army. After Paris fell, Cruewell was attached to the Lieutenant General Joachim Lemelsen's 5th Panzer Division for a month to study how to command a panzer division. Then, after a brief leave, he assumed command of the 11th Panzer Division at Maneuver Area Neuhammer on August 1, 1940, the day it was activated. The home base of the new division was Sagan, Silesia (Wehrkreis VIII).

The 11th Panzer was created by expanding the 11th Rifle Brigade and adding to it the 15th Panzer Regiment (from the 5th Panzer Division), as well as the 61st Motorcycle Battalion, 231st Reconnaissance Battalion, and the 61st Antitank Battalion from the 231st Infantry Division; the 341st Signal Battalion from the 311th Infantry Division; the 209th Engineer Battalion from the 209th Infantry Division, and the 119th Artillery Regiment from the 4th and 231st Infantry Divisions and General Headquarter (GHQ) units. The new division was much smaller than previous German panzer divisions and only had four rifle battalions (instead of six), two panzer battalions (instead of three or four), and three artillery battalions (instead of four).[15]

Initially, the 11th Panzer was sent to Poland in December 1940, but a month later it was transferred to Romania. As part of the 1st Panzer Group, it played a major role in the German invasion of the Balkans and the conquest of Serbia and Greece. Cruewell's division took both Belgrade and Salonika. For his part in this victory, Ludwig Cruewell was decorated with the Knight's Cross.

The 11th Panzer was briefly sent to Austria to refit in May and June 1941 but hurriedly rejoined the 1st Panzer Group that summer, because the invasion of the Soviet Union had begun. The division fought in the early victories at Zhitomir, Uman, and Kiev under Cruewell, but he was replaced by Colonel Guenther Angern on August 15, 1941.[16] He had been ordered to North Africa, where he assumed command of the Afrika Korps on September 15.[17] He was promoted to lieutenant general and awarded the Oak Leaves to his Knight's Cross on September 1.

The straight-laced Cruewell was known throughout the Panzerwaffe as a highly competent, steady, and dependable General Staff officer, but his promotion to the command of the Afrika Korps was unusual because it was exceptionally rapid. Despite his promotion, he was still a grade below normal corps commanders' rank, and he was the most junior corps commander in the Wehrmacht at that time. Why, then, was he named commander of the Afrika Korps? There is no evidence that Rommel asked for him (although they briefly met in France), but he was well known and highly respected in OKH. It seems extremely likely that Field Marshal Walter von Brauchitsch, the commander-in-chief of the Army, and General Halder, the chief of the General Staff, picked him as a potential balance to what Halder perceived as Rommel's rashness. If so, they must have been extremely pleased with their pick, for events worked out exactly as they planned.

Cruewell's Afrika Korps consisted of the usual GHQ units, the 15th and 21st Panzer Divisions, plus a few attached Italian units. Rommel planned for the reinforced 21st Panzer Division under General von Ravenstein to screen his desert front, while the 15th Panzer Division spearheaded the attack on Tobruk. This never happened, however, because the British struck first.

Of the Crusader battles (called the "Winter Battles" by the Germans), Brigadier Desmond Young later wrote:

It was a real soldier's battle, a "proper dog-fight," like those great aerial mix-ups which we used to watch over the lines in 1918. It was fought at such speed, with such swiftly-changing fortunes, under such a cloud of smoke from bursting shells and burning tanks, such columns of dust ... in such confusion ... that no one knew what was happening a mile away. Even today it is hard to follow....[18]

Rommel was planning to launch his all-out offensive against Tobruk on November 23, 1941. The British 8th Army, however, preempted him by starting their own offensive on November 17–18. Rommel, who was preoccupied with his plans to capture Tobruk, at first refused to believe that the British offensive had begun. (He could be bullheaded and, on this occasion, let his tenacity affect his good judgment.) General von Ravenstein, the commander of the 21st Panzer, was closer to the front, and he had reports from Lieutenant Colonel von Wechmar that the 3rd Reconnaissance Battalion was being attacked by 200 tanks. He reported to Cruewell who, in turn, went to Rommel's headquarters on November 18. The Desert Fox, however, refused to believe that his Tobruk attack (which he had been preparing for months) had been spoiled. Declaring that the British advance was a mere reconnaissance-in-force, he became rather irritated at Cruewell and sent him away with the warning that he must not lose his nerve. The next day, however, the British 8th Army continued to push back the 21st Panzer and

Figure 4.2
Operation Crusader, November 17–18, 1941

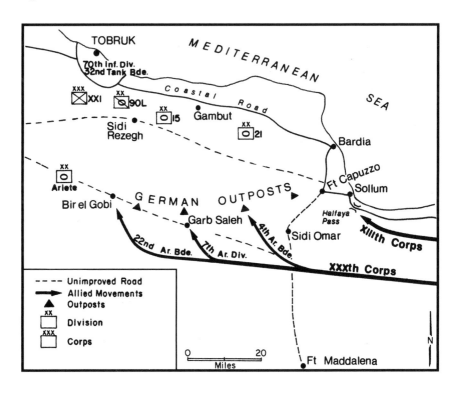

even (unsuccessfully) attacked the Italian Ariete Armored Division at Bir el Gobi (Figure 4.2).

That morning, November 19, Ludwig Cruewell turned up at Rommel's headquarters, determined to make his army commander see sense. He abandoned his more diplomatic approach of the day before and, in uncompromising terms, informed Rommel that he had been wrong the day before—that the British move was a major offensive, not a reconnaissance-in-force. The tough Rhinelander's arguments received a boost from an unexpected source: the enemy's news media. The British Broadcasting Corporation's Cairo station aired a story that the 8th Army—with 75,000 men—had launched a general offensive aimed at nothing less than destroying the German-Italian forces in North Africa.[19] This report, coupled with Cruewell's arguments, convinced Rommel, who reluctantly released Major General Walter Neumann-Silkow's 15th Panzer Division from the Tobruk offensive and allowed Cruewell to assemble it south of Gambut, where it could aid the embattled Ravenstein. This move was tantamount to canceling the Tobruk attack altogether.

Operation Crusader showed Ludwig Cruewell at his most brilliant, constantly leading from the front, constantly fighting separated Allied formations with inadequate resources (especially fuel), and turning back attempt after attempt to relieve the Tobruk garrison in increasingly desperate situations. His best day was November 23, which the Germans celebrated as *Totensonntag* (literally the Day of the Dead), when the Fatherland honored its fallen heroes of World War I. It was the fourth and final day of the Battle of Sidi Rezegh, which pitted the armored British XXX Corps against the Afrika Korps. Cruewell and his chief of staff, Fritz Bayerlein, left Afrika Korps Headquarters at Gasr el Arid at 5:30 that morning. The British 7th Armoured Division had pushed to within three miles of the Tobruk perimeter and was hedgehogged at Sidi Rezegh, preparing to link up with the garrison, which was attacking the Italian Pavia Division from the north. Rommel and Cruewell were determined to personally lead the attack against the 7th Armoured Division and to smash it before it could make contact with the garrison.

Cruewell had only been gone a half an hour before the 2nd New Zealand Division burst into Gasr el Arid and captured the headquarters of the Afrika Korps, including its chief of operations and most of his staff. Rommel was just approaching the place, attempting to reach Cruewell, when the New Zealanders struck. They spotted Rommel and chased him across the desert, but he was able to reach the 361st Infantry Regiment of the 90th Light Division, which was guarding the eastern approaches to Sidi Rezegh at Point 175. The New Zealanders quickly all but surrounded this isolated regiment, but it was a very tough unit and included many Germans who had served in the French Foreign Legion. The New Zealanders tried to crush and destroy the 361st all day long but were unable to do so. Rommel, however, was pinned down until after nightfall and was thus, for all practical purposes, eliminated as the German commander on Totensonntag. Command of Panzer Army Afrika devolved onto Ludwig Cruewell. This was an excellent choice for the Germans, even if it was accidental and made under duress.

At Sidi Rezegh, the British 7th Armoured Division controlled the 5th South African Brigade, the 22nd Armoured Brigade, and the 7th Support Group, which was equipped with artillery and antitank guns. With what was left of the Afrika Korps, Cruewell swung behind the South African brigade and attacked from the south. The British did not expect an attack from this direction, and the panzers burst into the South African camp before anyone realized what was happening. The 15th Panzer Division quickly overran the brigade's transport columns, while the 21st Panzer crushed the remnants of the 7th Support Group. The British and South Africans fought tenaciously, and the Battle of

Totensonntag was one of murderous intensity, with dust, smoke, and flames everywhere.

Without their transports, the South Africans went to ground behind their artillery batteries. Cruewell's men were forced to destroy the South Africans gun by gun, which is exactly what they did, despite the attempts of the British 22nd Armoured Brigade to intervene.

Cruewell directed the battle from a captured Mammoth, a large British-armored command and communications vehicle that had been captured at Mechili some months before. At one point during the battle, Cruewell's Mammoth pushed too far forward and was surrounded by British tanks. The British, however, were not aware of the prize that was within their reach. One British soldier became curious as to who was in the Mammoth, however, so he got out of his tank and knocked on the hatch of Cruewell's vehicle with a crowbar. Imagine his surprise when the general himself opened the hatch, and the soldier found himself staring face to face with the commander of the Afrika Korps! At that exact moment, a German 20-mm anti-aircraft gun opened up on the British soldier, who immediately ran to the cover of his own tank and disappeared. Cruewell's vehicle sped away in the confusion. Apparently, the British tanks were out of ammunition because no one fired on the Mammoth. There were no casualties in the incident.

To the north, the Tobruk garrison (the British 70th Infantry Division and the 32nd Army Tank Brigade) attacked the Pavia Division with infantry and 50 tanks, in hopes of forcing Cruewell to transfer troops from Sidi Rezegh to the siege perimeter. Pavia—a "marching" infantry unit that did not have a single tank—again demonstrated its unpredictability by rising to the occasion and defeating the attack without the aid of a single German soldier. The siege line held. Meanwhile, Cruewell organized a massive strike. At 3 P.M., he advanced with 150 panzers. The fighting was bitter, but the 5th South African Brigade was overwhelmed and destroyed. It lost 3,394 of its 5,700 men (mostly captured), and the 22nd Armoured Brigade lost a third of its remaining tanks before it escaped to the east. General Gott, the commander of the 7th Armoured Division, also escaped with the remnants of the other elements of his command. More than 300 British tanks lay burning or burned out over the 30-square-mile battlefield; another 150 had been heavily damaged. Cruewell had lost 60 tanks on Totensonntag.

Fortunately for the British, Rommel was carried away by Cruewell's success and ordered a premature pursuit to the Egyptian frontier, which is now known as "the dash to the wire." This gave 8th Army (and especially XXX Corps) time to recover and try once again to relieve Tobruk (Figure 4.3). Rommel and Cruewell defeated this attempt but could not defeat the next one. The Siege of Tobruk was lifted on December 5, 1941, after 242 days. Panzer Group Afrika abandoned eastern Libya, including

Figure 4.3
Operation Crusader, November 19–20, 1941

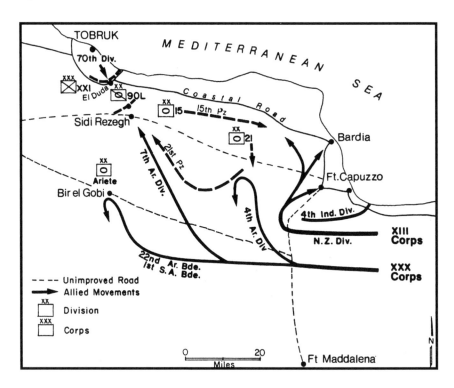

the important port of Benghazi, and fell back to the very strong position of Mersa el Brega, south and west of the Libyan "bulge."

Ludwig Cruewell's abilities as a corps commander had been proven during the Winter Battles to the satisfaction of the entire world. He was promoted to general of panzer troops on December 17, 1941, with an effective date of rank of December 1, 1941, after less than four months as a lieutenant general.

Cruewell's next battle was Rommel's 2nd Cyrenaican campaign, which began on January 21, 1942. After their victory in Crusader, the British did not bring their entire army to the front lines, but merely screened it with the 1st Armoured Division and the 201st Guards (Motorized) Brigade, while the 4th Indian Brigade lay nearby at Benghazi. They assumed that the Desert Fox would not be strong enough to launch a major offensive for months—if ever. Because of this complacency, Rommel succeeded in surprising the 8th Army, which regarded Panzer Group Afrika (now Panzer Army Afrika) as a spent force they would destroy and finish off completely as soon as they built up their supplies. During the first three days of the offensive, Ludwig Cruewell engaged the British 1st Armoured Division in a running battle, during which he destroyed 100 of their 150 tanks, 33 pieces of field artillery, and several armored cars, and captured thousands of men. He also captured the divisional staff, as well as 30 Valentine tanks, which he took when he overran a rear-area supply depot. He immediately incorporated them into the Afrika Korps.[20]

On January 25, the 15th Panzer Division burst into the critical British supply depot of Msus and took it almost intact. After the first five days of the offensive, the British had lost 299 tanks and armored vehicles, 147 guns, and 935 prisoners, mostly to the Afrika Korps. Rommel reported his own losses as three officers, 11 enlisted men, and three tanks.

Benghazi fell to the 90th Light Division on January 29, along with another 1,000 Allied prisoners. The German pursuit ended at the Gazala Line on February 6. Both sides then began to dig in and build up their supplies for the next offensive. Meanwhile, rewards came from Berlin. For his absolutely brilliant campaign, Rommel was promoted to colonel general. Cruewell was promoted to deputy commander of Panzer Army Afrika, indicating that the High Command had earmarked him for an army command of his own one day. General of Panzer Troops Walter Nehring succeeded Cruewell in command of the Afrika Korps. Rommel, meanwhile, went to Europe from March 9 to 19, and General Cruewell served as acting commander of Panzer Army Afrika in his absence.

On March 20, 1942, General Cruewell's 50th birthday, he visited his former headquarters at Umm er Rzem. Some enlisted bakers had managed to cook up some cream and chocolate tarts for the popular general, and Rommel and Walter Nehring produced a huge birthday cake from somewhere. Real French champagne was brought out of hiding, officers and men mixed together to toast the guest of honor, and the desert echoed with the sounds of happy celebration. It was a good thing that none of them could see into Ludwig Cruewell's future. It would have ruined the party.

A few days later, Cruewell received crushing personal news. His wife, who was only 34 years old, died suddenly of scarlet fever. He rushed home and made arrangements for the care of their four children. He then returned to North Africa just before Rommel's next offensive began.

For his offensive against the Gazala Line, Rommel divided his army into two components: a strike force under his personal command and a pinning force under General Cruewell. Rommel's force included the Afrika Korps, half of the 90th Light Division, and the Italian XX

Motorized Corps. Cruewell commanded the ad hoc Group Cruewell, which included the Italian XXI and X Infantry Corps plus two regimental battle groups from the 90th Light Division under Staff, 15th Rifle Brigade. His task was to launch diversionary attacks against the British front-line forces on the Gazala Line, to tie down the 1st South African and British 50th Infantry Divisions, and to force the 8th Army to commit as many of its reserves as possible against Group Cruewell; meanwhile, Rommel was to turn the line south of Bir Hacheim and emerge in the British rear. This time, however, things did not go as planned for the Rommel-Cruewell team.

Rommel outflanked the Gazala Line during the night of May 26–27, but was immediately subjected to a series of uncoordinated but nevertheless dangerous counterattacks from the British mobile reserves, which were much stronger than Panzer Army intelligence had estimated. By nightfall on May 27, Rommel's strike force was isolated and far behind British lines. Rommel decided to relieve the pressure on the Afrika Korps by having the Italian Sabratha Infantry Division of Group Cruewell break through the British minefields from the northwest and establish a supply corridor to the strike force. On May 28, Ludwig Cruewell visited Major General Krause, the commander of the Panzer Army Artillery, at his headquarters, where they planned the fire support for the Italian attack. Then, Cruewell flew on to the front line, but the flares that were supposed to be shot off to mark the front were not fired. Cruewell suddenly found himself over British lines at an altitude of only 500 feet. His airplane was quickly riddled by enemy machine gun fire, and the engine was knocked out. Even more horrifying, one burst hit the pilot, who slumped over the controls, dead.

Cruewell was in a Storch light reconnaissance aircraft, in which the passenger sat directly behind the pilot. There was no way the general could reach the controls. Helpless, Ludwig Cruewell could only await death. Then, a small miracle occurred. As if guided by the hand of God, the airplane landed itself. General Cruewell was removed—unhurt—by members of the British 150th Infantry Brigade. After the war, Cruewell learned that the officer who was supposed to fire the flares had been called to the telephone moments before the Storch reached Axis lines.

The British treated the depressed Cruewell with great respect and immediately fried him a huge steak. They then sent him to the rear. A few days later, Rommel overran the 150th Brigade and captured the men who had captured his deputy. By then, however, Cruewell was in Egypt, where he conducted himself with typical Afrika Korps spirit. When he was shown the famous Shepheard's Hotel in Cairo, he took one look at the luxurious accommodations and declared: "It will make a grand headquarters for Rommel!" Adolf Hitler was so pleased with the remark that he had Cruewell's words broadcast around the world.[21]

With that, Ludwig Cruewell faded from the stage of history. He spent the next five years in prison camps. He returned to Germany in April 1947 and was released, but the world he had known had vanished forever. After 36 years of service, he retired to the Essen suburb of Stadtwald, not far from his hometown of Dortmund. He died in Essen on September 25, 1958.

Ravenstein was succeeded as commander of the 21st Panzer Division by Karl Boettcher, Panzer Group Afrika's artillery commander.

Boettcher was born in Thorn, West Prussia, on October 25, 1889. He was educated at various cadet schools and entered the service as a Faehnrich (senior officer-cadet) in the 5th Foot Artillery Regiment on March 13, 1909. He was sent to the War School at Hersfeld the following month and, after graduating in December, was commissioned second lieutenant on January 27, 1910. For reasons not made clear by the records, he did not return to active duty for almost four years, except for a three-week temporary duty assignment to the Rifle Manufacturing Plant at Danzig in April 1912. For the last three months of 1913, he attended a training course at the Military Technical Academy but did not return to full-time active duty until the spring of 1914, when he attended an aerial observer course near his hometown of Thorn. He became a battery commander in the 5th Reserve Foot Artillery Battalion when World War I broke out in August 1914. He was part of the initial invasion of France and fought at Namur. Then, he and his unit were sent to the Eastern Front, where they fought in southern Poland.

In December 1914, Boettcher was assigned to the 46th Air Group (*Flieger-Abteilung 46*) as an artillery observer and was promoted to first lieutenant in February 1915. Four months later he was seriously wounded and did not return to active duty until June 1916. Even then he was not immediately sent back to the front but was assigned to the replacement battalion of the 5th Artillery. Once it was decided that he had fully recovered, he returned to the front as a battery commander in the 5th Foot Artillery Regiment and fought on the Somme (France) in Galacia, Lorraine, Ypres, and Alsace. He did well enough in this post to receive an accelerated promotion to captain (on August 18, 1917) and was given an instructorship at the prestigious Jueterbog Artillery School near Berlin in November 1917. He was given command of his own artillery battalion (the 149th) on September 29, 1918. After the war, young Boettcher was selected for the Reichsheer and did a tour on the staff of one of the battalions of the 7th Artillery Regiment in Bavaria (1919–20).

Karl Boettcher spent the next nine years in the isolated province of East Prussia, where an invasion by Poland seemed a very real possibility throughout the 1920s. He served as adjutant to the commander of Troop Maneuver Area Kummersdorf (1920), commander of the headquarters company in the same maneuver area (1920–21), and troop commander in the 1st Mobile Battalion (1921–25), where he gained valuable experience in mobile operations. He then became battery commander in the 1st Artillery Regiment at Koenigsberg (1925–27) and was assigned to the staff of the I Battalion/1st Artillery Regiment (I/1st Artillery) (1927–29). Boettcher finally left East Prussia in October 1929 and was assigned to the training staff at Jueterbog, where he remained until 1935. Promotions were slow in the Reichsheer (typical of a small army), and he was not promoted to major until November 1, 1930. Adolf Hitler came to power on January 30, 1933, and promotions would be much more rapid after that. Boettcher became a lieutenant colonel (May 1, 1934), colonel (April 1, 1936), major general (March 1, 1940), and lieutenant general (March 1, 1942).[22]

After five years at Jueterbog, Boettcher assumed command of I/59th Artillery Regiment at Berlin-Spandau on October 15, 1935. This battalion was an independent GHQ heavy artillery unit (i.e., there was no Staff, 59th Artillery Regiment) and was directly subordinate to Wehrkreis III. (Later, during World War II, it would be divided between the 23rd Infantry and 26th Panzer Divisions.) After another year in Brandenburg, Boettcher finally returned home to East Prussia and assumed command of the 1st Artillery Regiment on October 6, 1936. He remained in this post until the spring of 1939, when he became artillery officer to the fortress commander at Oppeln and later artillery officer on the staff of the commandant of Kattowitz. He was assigned to the staff of Frontier Guard Sector Command 3 in August 1939, just five days before the invasion of Poland began. After the Polish Army was defeated, he returned to the Berlin area, where the military expansion was continuing. On September 30, 1939, Karl Boettcher was named commanding officer of the 104th Artillery Command (Arko 104), a new unit that was then forming at the War School at Potsdam. This command would later achieve great fame in North Africa as Rommel's panzer army artillery and would be upgraded to Higher Artillery Command Afrika (Harko Afrika) on September 23, 1942, but this is getting ahead of our story.

Typical of the Arkos, the 104th consisted of special GHQ artillery battalions (including mortar and heavy artillery units and sometimes rocket units), as well as reinforcing artillery battalions and batteries. The 104th performed well in France and, in early 1941, was available for transfer to Libya, where Erwin Rommel's Afrika Korps needed specialized and heavy artillery support. Boettcher and his men arrived in the spring and were involved in all of the major battles of 1941, including the drive to and siege of Tobruk, and in the English attempts to relieve the fortress (Operations Brevity, Battleaxe, and Crusader, the last of which began on November 17–18, 1941). In the process, Boettcher's tubes blasted more than one British formation to pieces. In the hard, open terrain of the Western Desert, artillery fire inflicted more casualties on both sides than did any other type of firepower, including the combined power of bombers, dive-bombers, and fighter-bombers. Because of the incredible accuracy and efficiency which characterized Arko 104, the Desert Fox developed a healthy respect for General Boettcher and, on November 24, 1941, when he decided to strike for the Egyptian border and into the rear of the British 8th Army, he placed Boettcher in charge of a holding force and ordered him to prevent the British and New Zealanders from raising the Siege of Tobruk. Unfortunately for Boettcher, his force only included the 155th Infantry Regiment, a battalion of the 361st Infantry Regiment, and the 900th Engineer Battalion (all from the 90th Light Division) and part of Arko 104. He faced the bulk of the British XIII Corps, including the excellent 2nd New Zealand Division and the 1st Army Tank Brigade, as well as much of the Tobruk garrison (British 70th Infantry Division, Polish 1st Brigade, and the 32nd Army Tank Brigade), both of which launched major attacks. Karl Boettcher was right between them (Figure 4.4).

Figure 4.4
Operation Crusader—the Dash to the Wire, November 24–28, 1941

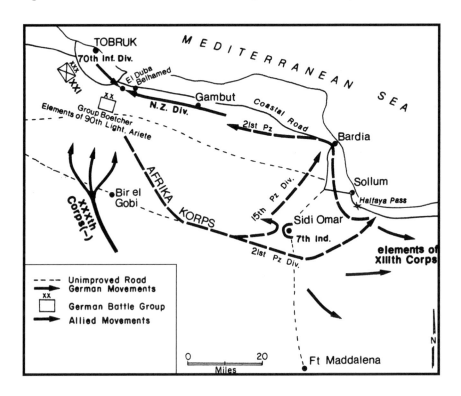

The battle during this period was extremely complicated. "The plot of movements ... resembled the scurrying of ants," the British Official History later recorded. "Neither side had much idea of what was happening."[23] It was clear, however, that Rommel had not left Boettcher nearly enough forces to check the Allies indefinitely. Boettcher, however, put up a magnificent defense against almost overwhelming odds. When Allied resistance did not collapse as he had hoped, Rommel returned to the Tobruk sector with the Afrika Korps on November 27. He found Group Boettcher holding on by its fingernails; only three miles separated the New Zealanders from the garrison's 32nd Army Tank Brigade. Rommel struck immediately and drove off the 2nd New Zealand. The siege continued.

If there was ever any doubt, Boettcher had proven that he could effectively command non-artillery units as well as artillery units. "It was solely due to his skillful leadership and personal action that the enemy breakthrough was prevented until the arrival of the Afrika Korps," his Knight's Cross citation read.[24] When General von Ravenstein was captured on November 29, 1941, Rommel chose Boettcher to replace him. He assumed command of the 21st Panzer on December 1.[25]

On his first day as a divisional commander, Boettcher played a creditable role in checking an advance by the British 7th Armoured Division, while Rommel overran the 4th New Zealand Brigade and smashed the 2nd New Zealand Division. By December 2, however, the Afrika Korps was down to a strength of 80 operational tanks.

On December 4, the fresh British 70th Infantry Division and the 32nd Army Tank Brigade finally defeated the nearly exhausted 21st Panzer Division at El Duda. That night, the 21st Panzer retreated between the garrison and the 4th Indian Division, which was closing in from the south. The Siege of Tobruk was lifted after 242 days. Rommel began his retreat from Cyrenaica during the night of December 7–8.

Boettcher bore no blame for the defeat at El Duda; on the contrary, Rommel recommended him for the Knight's Cross, which he received on December 31, 1941. The following month, he played a supporting role in Rommel's 2nd Cyrenaican campaign, in which the Afrika Korps destroyed two thirds of the British 1st Armoured Division's 150 tanks in a three-day battle. By the time the campaign ended on February 6, 1942, the British had lost 299 tanks and armored vehicles, as well as 147 guns and 935 prisoners. Rommel's total losses were 14 men and three tanks. Karl Boettcher, however, was not a well man. He was 52 years old and had spent almost a year in a combat environment in one of the harshest climates on earth. He reported himself sick on February 18 and was flown back to Europe. He would not be fit for duty for another nine months and did not fully recover until 1944. He received his promotion to lieutenant general in the hospital.

Karl Boettcher did not return to active duty until November 25, 1942, when he assumed command of the *345th Infanterie-Division (mot.)*, which was then in the process of forming at the Wildelecken Maneuver Area in Wehrkreis IX. The 345th Motorized Infantry controlled the 148th Motorized Grenadier Regiment (three battalions), the 152nd Panzer Grenadier Regiment (three battalions), the 345th Panzer Battalion, the 345th Motorcycle Battalion, the 345th Artillery Regiment (two battalions), and the 345th Divisional Support (*Div. Einheiten*) Unit.[26] The division was sent to France, where it was absorbed by the newly forming 29th Panzer Grenadier Division, which was replacing the 29th Motorized Division, a formation destroyed at Stalingrad. Command of the new 29th was given to Walter Fries, a brilliant colonel who had lost an arm and a leg on the Eastern Front. Boettcher was then attached to Army Group D (OB West), which named him deputy commander of the 326th Infantry Division at Narbonne, France, on April 9, 1943. When the commander of the 326th left for another assignment on May 8, Boettcher assumed command of this static division. By the end of the month, however, Boettcher's health apparently betrayed him again. He gave up command of the division on May 31 and was placed in Fuehrer Reserve. The 326th Infantry Division was later smashed in the Normandy campaign, and its commander, Lieutenant General Viktor von Drabich-Waechter—the man who succeeded Boettcher—was killed in action on August 2, 1944.

General Boettcher assumed command of the 347th Infantry Division at Ymuiden, the Netherlands, on October 12, 1943. He was, however, back in Fuehrer Reserve by December 10. On March 10, 1944, he was placed in charge of the 305th Higher Artillery Command (Harko 305), which was part of the 2nd Panzer Army in Croatia. He led it in anti-partisan operations and against the Soviets when the area became part of the Eastern Front. He became commanding general of the 4th Special Purposes Artillery Command on March 10, 1945, and continued to support 2nd Panzer Army on the Eastern Front until the end of the war. He managed to surrender to the British on May 8, 1945.

General Karl Boettcher was released from the POW camps on June 25, 1947. Because his former homes of Thorn and East Prussia were now behind the Iron Curtain—and had been annexed by Poland—he settled in Bad Wimpfen. He died there on February 9, 1975, at the age of 85.

One of the most unusual characters in the Afrika Korps was Major Wilhelm Georg Bach, a Lutheran pastor or "devil dodger," as the German troops often called chaplains. Bach, however, was not serving as a chaplain, but rather as a company and battalion commander in the 104th Motorized Infantry Regiment; in fact, with the possible exception of Baron von Wechmar, he was very likely the best battalion commander in Rommel's panzer group in 1941.

Bach was born in Oberwoesheim, near Bruchsal, Bavaria, on November 5, 1892. When World War I broke out in August 1914, he joined the Imperial Army as a war volunteer in the 109th Reserve Infantry (1st Baden Lifeguards) Regiment and fought on the Western Front from late 1914 until the fall of 1915, when he returned to Germany for officer's training. A year later he returned to the front as a second lieutenant of reserves. Less than two months after that, on October 21, 1916, young Bach was captured by the British and remained a prisoner of war for more than three years until November 1919. After his release, he married, became a Lutheran minister, and raised a family. By 1935, he shepherded the Evangelical Lutheran Church in Mannheim. The following year, however, he was recalled to active duty and was sent to the 14th Infantry Regiment at Konstanz as a 43-year-old second lieutenant. He was promoted to first lieutenant of reserves before the outbreak of the war.

Rev. Bach did well in the 14th Infantry and, after the defeat of France he was transferred to the I Battalion, 104th Motorized Infantry Regiment, as a company commander. A promotion to captain followed. Then, only a few days after the I/104th arrived in North Africa, the battalion was thrown into the Battle of Tobruk, and its commander almost immediately became a casualty. Despite the fact that he was a relatively junior captain, Bach was selected to replace him.

Wilhelm Bach was an amiable Christian gentleman, but also an officer who commanded the respect of his men, just because of who and what he was. His command post was the friendliest and most relaxed in the Afrika Korps—a remarkable place for the German Army in World War II. The tall, graying, cigar-smoking commander with the heavy Baden accent never screamed or swore, but merely expressed his wishes, much in the manner of Robert E. Lee. Like the brilliant, legendary American general, Bach's men (who called him "Papa") loved him, and—unlike the case with Lee—his orders were always obeyed.

In April and May, Bach's battalion fought in the Battle of Tobruk, where all of Rommel's attacks were repulsed. The I/104th was then assigned to Combat Group Herff, which had orders to capture Halfaya Pass on the Libyan-Egyptian border. For more than 100 miles, this was the only place along the Coastal Road where there was a gap in the 600-foot high coastal escarpment, which made it one of the most strategic positions in North Africa. Colonel Herff ordered Bach to spearhead the offensive.

The attack began on May 26. Bach and his men were supported by the heavy (III) battalion of the 33rd Panzer Artillery Regiment, but they faced the elite 3rd Battalion, Coldstream Guards, one of the best units in the British Army, which also had significant artillery and antitank gun support. The Guards promptly pinned down the German grenadiers with very accurate machine gun fire. In temperatures of 130 degrees Fahrenheit, Papa Bach and his men hugged the ground, hiding behind small, impoverished little fortresses made from the local rocks, and in the Qualala Wadi, which was a deep, dried-up river bed. When night fell, however, Bach issued the ancient command: "Fix bayonets!" They surged forward on foot over the rough terrain and soon engaged the British at close quarters. Then, a company of the 15th Motorized Infantry Battalion appeared on the Guards' flank, and they finally broke. The Germans had conquered Halfaya Pass.

Since April, Rommel had been besieging the 9th Australian Division in the fortress of Tobruk but had been unable to take it. He knew that the British would have to retake Halfaya Pass in order to break the siege, so he personally selected Bach to defend it. (One of the secrets to Rommel's success as a commander was his ability to pick the right man for the right job.) Rommel's orders to the reverend were uncompromising: Halfaya Pass was to be held at all costs. He reinforced Bach with a detachment of combat engineers, an Italian battery, four captured 155-mm French artillery pieces, and a battery of five legendary 88-mm anti-aircraft guns, which became the most successful antitank guns of World War II. Bach promptly converted this vital sector into an improvised fortress, complete with trenches, foxholes, strongpoints, dummy positions, and minefields. He expected the enemy to attack across the flat, open plain, between the two wings of the coastal escarpment, so he concentrated his firepower there.

Meanwhile, the British Western Desert Force was reinforced with 135 Matilda II heavy infantry tanks (26.5 tons), 82 Mark IIs (a fast 14-ton cruiser tank, armed with a 40-mm main battle gun), and 21 Mark IV tanks, which weighed only 5.5 tons but were very fast. At 4 A.M. on June 15, 1941, the British commander, Lieutenant General Sir Noel Beresford-Peirse, launched Operation "Battleaxe." His plan called for Major General Sir Michael Creagh's 7th Armoured Division to engage and destroy Rommel's armor in the desert, south of the Sollum-Bardia area; meanwhile, Major General Sir Frank W. Messervy's 4th Indian Division would capture Halfaya Pass, paving the way for the rescue to the Tobruk garrison. Beresford-Peirse planned to resupply the 7th Armoured over the Coastal Road via Halfaya to Sollum; hence, it was essential that Halfaya Pass be captured quickly. For this purpose, he gave Messervy the 22nd Guards Brigade and the heavy tanks of the 4th Armoured Brigade.

Sir Frank spearheaded his attack with the 4th Armoured, which was followed by the foot soldiers of the 11th Indian Brigade. First, however, he started his offensive by pulverizing the Halfaya Pass area with a large artillery bombardment. It was so impressive that many of the

British tankers and Indian infantry mistakenly jumped to the conclusion that the defenders must have been wiped out. They advanced quickly and faced no resistance initially, which confirmed their opinion. Bach and his engineers, however, had constructed a false wadi, which the British guns had totally saturated with high explosive shells. Unfortunately for them, the real Axis main line of resistance was well forward of the decoy position, just beyond the ruins of Halfaya village.

Captain Bach had instructed his men not to fire until he gave the order, and they had camouflaged their guns, including several particularly dangerous 88s, so well that the British had no idea they were even there. As if on parade, the 4th Armoured and 11th Indian walked into the ambush. Bach waited until the Allied troops were literally under the barrels of his guns; then, as the Indian infantry was in the process of detrucking, he ordered them to fire.

All of the German and Italian guns opened up at once. A dozen British and Indian tanks, trucks, and light armored trucks erupted within moments. The confusion was indescribable. More shells hit the surviving British vehicles or blasted the dismounted infantry. It was like drill: rapid fire over open sights! The deadly 88s focused in on the Allied tanks, while the other guns generally concentrated on the trucks or cut holes in the ranks of the infantry. It was a slaughter. Major Pardi's Italian battery of 20-mm guns performed at least as well as its German counterparts.

The British armor fell back to Halfaya village, rallied, and advanced again. This time the attacking force consisted of five Mark IIs, totally unsupported by infantry. (This was so typical of the British Army at this stage of its tactical development. It would not become a true combined arms force until after Montgomery assumed command of the 8th Army in the fall of 1942.) They pushed straight into one of Bach's minefields, and all five were quickly knocked out. Some of the crewmen jumped from the rear of their burning machines and, following the tracks made by their tanks, slowly walked out of the minefield with their hands above their heads, until they reached friendly lines. The German infantrymen, who could have easily killed them all, did not fire. In North Africa, it was not considered proper to shoot helpless men who were trapped in a minefield. Such behavior, so typical in the desert, was virtually unheard of on other fronts in World War II.

The British were nothing if not courageous and persistent. With their first two attacks demolished, they called upon their artillery to blast the Germans out of their positions. Once again, however, their fire fell primarily in the false wadi. Meanwhile, the 22nd Guards Brigade arrived and, with the survivors of the 11th Indian, prepared another attack. It was well after noon before they surged forward out of the ruins of Halfaya village. Once again, the attackers were slaughtered. Now, however, it dawned on the British that the false wadi was a decoy position, and several of Bach's real strongpoints had been identified by the Allied forward observers as they shot down the Indians and Guardsmen. The British artillery and mortars soon opened up again, but this time they focused on actual German positions and inflicted severe casualties on the I/104th. The survivors on both sides were glad to see the sun set on June 15.

June 16 was another day of difficult combat at Halfaya Pass. The temperature rose to more than 130 degrees Fahrenheit. The British and Indian infantry attacked five times. Bach turned them back five times and even launched a few counterattacks of his own. One of them recaptured Halfaya village. By the end of the day, the German and Allied positions remained more or less static.

While Bach checked Western Desert Force's northern thrust, Rommel and the rest of the Afrika Korps dealt with the British 7th Armoured Division. On June 17, the 8th Panzer Regiment of Major General Walter Neumann-Silkow's 15th Panzer Division came up from the Fort Capuzzo sector to the west and plowed into the flank of the 4th Indian Division. Seeing that he had been defeated, Beresford-Peirse gave the order to withdraw. Operation Battleaxe was over. More than 100 British tanks had been totally destroyed or knocked out and left behind when the Western Desert Force retreated. Dozens of others had been damaged or knocked out but had limped or been hauled to the rear, where they were eventually repaired. Rommel had lost about 70 tanks, but only 12 of these were write-offs; the rest were recovered, repaired, and returned to the front. As if to rub salt in the British wounds, a number of their damaged tanks were repaired and incorporated into Panzer Group Afrika.

After Battleaxe, a lull descended on the North African Front as both sides prepared for the next battle. Rommel, who was extremely pleased with Papa Bach's performance at Halfaya Pass, decorated him with the Knight's Cross on July 9 and arranged for him to receive a special promotion to major. Because Halfaya Pass was still the most important position along the coastal escarpment, he saw no need to change his assignment, although he did increase the size of the garrison to 2,100 men.

Bach's major battle for the next several weeks involved simply living in the Sahara Desert. This was not an easy task. British ships and airplanes operating out of Malta sank 17 percent of the supplies sent to Panzer Army Afrika in July. This figure climbed to an incredible 77 percent by November. As a result, the quantity and quality of German rations deteriorated alarmingly. The standard diet consisted of processed cheese in tube containers, tinned sardines, and Italian military-issued tinned sausage, called AM from the stamp on the side. (It stood for *Amministrazione Militare* or Military Administration, but the Italians called it *Arabo Morte*—Dead Arab.) Occasionally, these meager rations were supplemented by *Dauerbrot* (a moist and wholesome bread made from "black" rye or wheat and wrapped in foil), onions, dehydrated legumes, oatmeal gruel, or hard, dry Italian Army biscuits. As the Royal Navy and Air Force continued to tighten their stranglehold on Rommel's supply lines, these supplements became increasingly rare. By fall, the troops sometimes received only one meal a day. Jaundice, amoebic dysentery, and assorted nutritional illnesses soon plagued the troops, as did sand fleas and flies.

Sand fleas were parasites that bore into a soldier's skin until only the tip of its rear end remained exposed; then it sucked his blood until it became a thick, round ball. Many men were infected with them from head to toe. Some were so badly tormented that they went temporarily insane and had to be sent home for treatment.

Flies also made life miserable. "The millions of flies were a real torment," Colonel Hans von Luck recalled later.[27] Wolf Heckmann reported that flies "covered every slice of bread and butter like a black layer."[28] It was impossible to swallow bread with butter and/or jelly without swallowing several flies as well.

The staple of the Halfaya garrison was purified water, which was so filled with chemicals that it tasted like chemical soup. Often it was consumed with reconstituted lemon "juice" or ersatz coffee, which the soldiers called "nigger sweat." Sand vipers and scorpions also caused occasional problems.

Rommel planned to attack Tobruk before the 8th Army[29] could strike him, but because of the supply imbalance, he was unable to do so. The 8th Army attacked on November 17, 1941, and Halfaya Pass was soon cut off from the rest of the panzer group. This was in accordance with Rommel's master strategy. He planned to defeat the British while independent garrisons at Halfaya Pass and the small ports of Sollum and Bardia held out, denying the Allies free access to the Coastal Road. After the British armor was defeated, he would rescue the garrisons, just as he had done in the summer. This time, however, it was the Desert Fox who was defeated. During the night of December 4–5, he abandoned the Siege of Tobruk, which was relieved after 242 days. On the night of December 7–8, he retreated to the west with the remnants of his army. By the end of the month, the garrisons of Sollum, Bardia, and Halfaya Pass were 450 miles behind enemy lines (Figure 4.5).

Meanwhile, Papa Bach and his men continued to hold Halfaya Pass, mainly against Major General I. P. de Villiers' 2nd South African Infantry Division. This time, however, there were few attacks. The British had learned the folly of launching frontal assaults against the

Figure 4.5
North Africa, January 1942

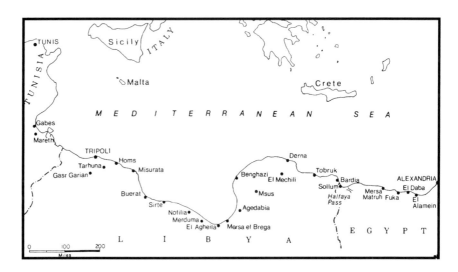

well-prepared defenses of "Hellfire Pass," as they had called it since June 15. They confined themselves primarily to probes, which were always repulsed. After Rommel retreated, they decided to pound the garrison with 25-pounder guns and to starve it into submission.

Christmas Eve that year was somber for the defenders of Halfaya Pass. They had been on half rations for some time and were running out of food and water. There were no presents, no letters from home—not even a Christmas tree. Pastor Bach, however, did pray with them and read to them from the Bible. As a Christmas present, each man was given an extra cup of water. There was no present from the British, however; the shelling never stopped.

Among those cut off when Rommel retreated was the Italian Savona Division. Some of the combat elements under the personal leadership of the division commander, the highly capable and very personable Major General Fedele di Giorgia, had formed a hedgehog position west of Halfaya Pass. Promptly surrounded by the British and South Africans, it had been reduced to less than a thousand men. General di Giorgia signaled the Desert Fox and asked permission to break out of the encirclement and head for Halfaya Pass. Rommel consented, and the courageous Italian general fought his way through British lines and into Halfaya Pass with several hundred brave men.[30] Although they were welcomed by the Germans (who generally liked their Italian counterparts), they put a further strain on the garrison's rapidly diminishing supplies. A week later, they were exhausted.

Bach and de Giorgia finally capitulated on January 17, 1942, after they destroyed all of their weapons.

Rev. Wilhelm Georg Bach never saw Germany again. After his surrender, he was transported to Canada, where he fell seriously ill. He died in Toronto on December 22, 1942, at the age of 50.

The small port of Sollum was garrisoned by the 300th Oasis Reserve Battalion, a two-company unit under the command of Captain of Reserves Ennecerus. Cut off on November 21, the garrison was so small that the South Africans decided it could be taken by assault. This proved to be a mistake. Like the I/104th, the men of the 300th fought like lions. By January 10, 1942, however, Ennecerus had only 70 men left, and their rations were 20 grams of bread, a handful of rice, and a spoonful of currants per man per day. On January 12, the South Africans attacked again, supported by massive concentrations of artillery and mortar fire, which destroyed the last buildings still standing in the gutted town. Again they were beaten back, but German resistance was clearly nearing its end. The South African infantry struck again. Ennecerus and his men fired their last round. The captain now had no choice: he ordered his men to destroy their weapons and break out the white flags. The Sollum garrison surrendered after a siege of 56 days.

The Bardia garrison was commanded by Artur Schmitt. Born at Albersweiler in the Rhineland Palatinate on July 20, 1888, he joined the Bavarian Army as a Fahnenjunker in 1907, and was commissioned Leutnant in the 18th Bavarian Infantry Regiment in 1909. He fought in World War I, where he earned both grades of the Iron Cross. Like so many excellent officers, however, Schmitt was not selected for the 4,000-officer "Treaty Army." Discharged in 1920, he joined the Bavarian State Police, and in 1934 he was promoted to lieutenant colonel of police. The following year, Hitler renounced the Treaty of Versailles, and Schmitt applied to return to active duty. He joined the Reichsheer as a colonel on October 1, 1935.

Schmitt was named commander of the XI Field Ordnance Command in early 1937. He held this post until February 1940, when he assumed command of the 626th Infantry Regiment. This *Stellungs* (positional or static) unit, which was part of the 555th Infantry Division, was made up of *Landesschuetzen*—men from the older age groups—and was considered fourth class (capable of limited defensive missions only). The virtually immobile 626th occupied defensive positions on the Upper Rhine in the spring and summer of 1940, while more mobile German formations with younger soldiers overran France, Belgium, and the Netherlands. After the fall of Paris, the 626th and its parent division moved to Bielefeld. In September 1940, Colonel Schmitt briefly served as acting commander of the 555th Infantry Division, which Hitler had already ordered disbanded.[31] When this process was completed on September 25, Schmitt resumed command of the XI Field Ordnance. He did so well in this post that he was named commander of the 2nd Higher Ordnance Staff on February 19, 1941, and was promoted to major general, effective February 1, 1941.

In the eyes of OKW, Schmitt had proven himself as an ordnance and field ordnance commander. The next step in his logical career progression was to direct a rear area command. He was given Korueck 556—the 556th Rear Area Command, which was subordinate to Panzer Group Afrika. He assumed his new post on September 9, 1941.

Because of British command of the air and sea, Schmitt's difficulties in his new post were insurmountable. The situation became so critical that Hitler transferred the 2nd Air Fleet from the Russian Front to Sicily in November 1941. It was able to relieve the pressure on Rommel's supply lines, but it was too late to help Panzer Group Afrika during Operation Crusader, the major British winter offensive of 1941–42. In addition, Rommel was short of senior German officers, and he did not trust the Italians to defend "the Eastern Sector" (Bardia, Sollum, and Halfaya Pass) to the utmost. He did, however, trust Schmitt to do so. For this reason, the Desert Fox named Artur Schmitt commander of the ad hoc Sector East on November 10. The Allied offensive began seven days later.

Schmitt headquartered at Bardia, where he had previously located his forward ordnance depot and shops. He was cut off when the 21st Panzer Division withdrew on November 26, and he lost effective control of the Sollum and Halfaya Pass garrisons. Shortly thereafter, his ad hoc command was given the designation Division Bardia. It consisted of 4,200 Italians from the Savona Division and 2,200 Germans, mostly from the administrative services. They were besieged by elements of the 2nd South African Infantry Division, the 1st Army Tank Brigade, the Polish Brigade, the artillery of the 2nd New Zealand Infantry Division, and strong elements of the Royal Navy and Air Force.

Despite the fact that he had few combat troops, Schmitt held his positions for more than a month. Then, on about New Years Day, he lost his last water hole and did not have the resources to retake it. He surrendered the garrison on January 2, 1942. When the South Africans entered the city, they liberated 1,100 British prisoners

During the Siege of Bardia, Schmitt found his Italian forces to be of very little use. (The best part of the Savona Division was cut off in the desert with General di Giorgia.) After he surrendered, General Schmitt caused a bit of an international incident by publicly stating that he would have held out much longer if the Italians allies had performed better. The Italian government was highly offended, but Rommel sided with his general. At his recommendation, Artur Schmitt was awarded the Knight's Cross on February 5. It would be some time before he got to wear the decoration, however; at the time, he was on the British transport ship, *Pasteur*, in the Red Sea, headed for Canada.

Even as a prisoner of war, General Schmitt did not stop resisting. He, General von Ravenstein, and Major Bach, among others, developed a plot to seize control of the ship and take it to Singapore, which was then occupied by the Japanese. Unfortunately, the British got wind of the plan, seized the leaders, and placed them in solitary confinement. They even considered throwing the ringleaders into the sea, but fortunately for Schmitt, Ravenstein, and Bach, cooler heads prevailed.

Once they reached shore, Ravenstein and Schmitt temporarily roomed together in a POW camp. This did not work out well for the sophisticated Ravenstein, who disliked the simpler, less-educated, and more dogmatic Schmitt. He was pleased when they were separated.

Hitler and OKH were also obviously unoffended by the outspoken Schmitt's remarks. On January 1, 1943, they promoted him to lieutenant general. After the *Pasteur* incident, Schmitt's time as a prisoner of war was uneventful, and he was released on October 5, 1947. He retired to Munich, where he died on January 15, 1972.

Count Theodor von Sponeck, the commander of the 90th Light Division (1942–43). An early convert to motorized warfare, he was seriously wounded commanding a panzer regiment on the Eastern Front before joining Panzer Army Afrika. He did a brilliant job commanding Rommel's rear guard during the retreat from Egypt. He made no attempt to escape the Tunisian debacle and surrendered to the Allies in May 1943. His brother—also a general—was executed by the Nazis in 1944.

Field Marshal Erwin Rommel, the "Desert Fox."

General of Panzer Troops Ritter Wilhelm von Thoma. A hero of three wars (World War I, the Spanish Civil War, and World War II), Thoma was wounded 14 times in his legendary career. He also served with the Freikorps in "the war after the war" and later helped put down Hitler's Beer Hall Putsch in 1923. He was captured by the Americans in France (1918) and by the British at El Alamein (1942), where he commanded the Afrika Korps. He died in bed.

General of Panzer Troops Gustav von Vaerst. After leading the 2nd Panzer Brigade in Poland (1939), France (1940), Greece (1941), and on the Russian Front (1941), Vaerst was sent to North Africa, where he led the 15th Panzer Division, the Afrika Korps, and the 5th Panzer Army. Seriously wounded in 1942, he nevertheless returned to Africa and was forced to surrender in Tunisia in 1943.

General of Panzer Troops Ludwig Cruewell, commander of the Afrika Korps and deputy commander of Panzer Army Afrika. Considered by many to be Rommel's most capable subordinate, Cruewell played a major role in saving the panzer army south of Tobruk and in smashing the British 8th Army in late 1941. He was captured during the Battle of the Gazala Line in May 1943. He had previously commanded the 11th Panzer Division in the Balkans and on the Eastern Front.

Gustav-Georg Knabe was wounded five times during World War I. Later he fought with the Freikorps and served with the 7th Panzer Division during World War II. In Libya, he commanded the 15th Motorcycle Battalion and the 104th Panzer Grenadier Regiment, and briefly served as commander of the 21st Panzer Division after Baron von Ravenstein was captured. His brilliant career was cut short by an automobile accident in Romania, in which he was critically injured.

Italian Field Marshal Giovanni Messe, the last commander of the 1st Italian-German Panzer Army (formerly Panzer Army Afrika). He succeeded Erwin Rommel on February 23, 1943, and was forced to surrender to the British on May 13. Universally considered the most capable of the Italian commanders, he later joined the Allies as chief of staff of the Royal Italian Army. He had previously commanded the Italian Expeditionary Force on the Russian Front.

General of Panzer Troops Hans-Karl Esebeck was the commander of the 15th Panzer Brigade and the 15th Panzer Division in Libya in May 1941. Seriously wounded in the Siege of Tobruk (1941), he later led the 11th Panzer Division, the 2nd Panzer Division, and the XXXXVI Panzer Corps on the Eastern Front. He was arrested for his part in the anti-Hitler conspiracy and spent the last year of the war in concentration camps.

General of Panzer Troops Hans Cramer, the last commander of the Afrika Korps. Cramer had earlier led the 8th Panzer Regiment in Libya, where he played a major role in capturing Halfaya Pass in May 1941. He was badly wounded in action near Sollum the following month. After a staff tour in Berlin, Cramer served as both acting and deputy commander of the XXXXVIII Panzer Corps on the Eastern Front, before being named commander of the Afrika Korps on February 28, 1943. He surrendered it on May 12.

German troops advancing on the Eastern Front.

Rommel's SdKfz 250/3 "Greif" communications vehicle, in the field in North Africa.

Colonel Maximilian von Herff, the commander of the 115th Panzer Grenadier Regiment and briefly commander of the 15th Panzer Division after General von Esebeck was wounded in May 1941. Later, Herff became a general in the SS and was chief of Himmler's Main Personnel Office. He died in British captivity.

Rommel (*right*), Lieutenant General Alfred Gause (*center*) and Luftwaffe General Christian discuss the situation in early 1944. Gause was Rommel's chief of staff from 1941 to 1944, when they had a falling out. He was later chief of staff of the 5th Panzer Army in France and commanded the II Corps on the Eastern Front.

Field Marshal Albert Kesselring (*left*), the OB South and Rommel's nominal superior during the Desert War. He supported Rommel as best he could, even though they did not always see eye-to-eye on strategic issues or tactical doctrine in North Africa. Later, Kesselring oversaw the ground campaign in Italy (1943–45). The officer on the right in Colonel Gunther von Luetzow, a fighter ace and commander of the 4th Air Division.

Colonel (later Lieutenant General) Fritz Bayerlein, chief of staff and briefly acting commander of the Afrika Korps. He also served as chief of staff of the 1st Italian-German Panzer Army. In 1944–45, Bayerlein commanded the Panzer Lehr Division on the Western Front. His talents as a commander have generally been highly overrated by historians.

A Panzer Mark III, Model J (PzKw IIIj). The main battle tank of the Afrika Korps, this PzKw III boasts a long-barreled 50-mm main battle gun.

The enemy: British Field Marshal Sir Bernard Law Montgomery, commander of the British 8th Army.

Lieutenant General Heinrich Kirchheim, who spent years in German South-West Africa and was considered an expert on tropical and desert warfare. He also earned the *Pour le Merite* in World War I, served in the Freikorps, and led the 169th Infantry Division before being sent to North Africa, where he briefly commanded the Italian Brescia Division and the 5th Light (later 21st Panzer) Division. Rommel sacked him in May 1941.

MG Hans von Ravenstein, the commander of the 21st Panzer Division. A daring and courageous officer, he had also won the *Pour le Merite* during World War I and distinguished himself as commander of the 4th Rifle Regiment in France, the 16th Panzer Brigade in Greece, and the 21st Panzer Division in Libya. His brilliant career was cut short on November 29, 1941, when he ran into an ambush set by a New Zealand lieutenant and was captured.

Erwin Rommel in 1942, shortly after he was promoted to field marshal.

Field Marshal Walter Model meets with Field Marshal Kesselring and his chief of staff, Siegfried Westphal. Westphal served as Rommel's chief of operations and chief of staff in North Africa and briefly commanded the 164th Light Afrika Division. He later served as chief of staff to Kesselring and von Rundstedt, and ended the war as a general of cavalry.

The Desert Fox addressing members of his staff in North Africa, circa 1942.

Adolf Hitler and his press secretary, Otto Dietrich. Because of his lack of rationality, Hitler had an up-and-down relationship with his most talented commanders, including Erwin Rommel.

A British officer inspects a knocked-out Panzer Mark IV, North Africa, late 1942.

A German panzer regiment—probably the 8th Panzer—pauses in the desert.

The surrender in Tunisia, May 1943. The German officers are Major General Fritz Krause, Colonel Joseph Irkens, and Major General Willibald Borowietz. Krause was a great artillery commander and directed Arko 104 (the artillery command of Panzer Army Afrika) before commanding the 164th Light Afrika and 334th Infantry Divisions. Irkens was the last commander of the 8th Panzer Regiment. Borowietz directed the 15th Panzer Division in North Africa. He was killed in an accident in Mississippi in 1945.

Colonel General Heinz Guderian, the "father" of the blitzkrieg. He and Rommel were friends, and several of Rommel's officers served under Guderian's command.

German encampment in the desert. Note the 20-mm anti-aircraft gun in the background.

Major General Georg von Bismarck (*left*), the commander of the 21st Panzer Division, confers with Ludwig Cruewell, early 1942. Bismarck was later killed in action at Alma Halfa Ridge.

Colonel General Rommel (*center*) congratulates General of Panzer Troops Ludwig Cruewell, the deputy commander of Panzer Army Afrika, on his birthday, March 20, 1942. The officer just behind Rommel to the left is General of Panzer Troops Walter Nehring, the commander of the Afrika Korps. Nehring later distinguished himself commanding the XXIV Panzer Corps on the Eastern Front.

Italian troops dig trenches in the desert.

Italian soldiers encamping in an oasis.

The end of Army Group Afrika. A giant prison camp, Tunisia, summer of 1943.

General of Cavalry (and later General of Panzer Troops) Georg Stumme, directing the XXXX Panzer Corps in the Balkans campaign of 1941. Stumme had been Rommel's predecessor as commander of the 7th Panzer Division and succeeded him as commander of Panzer Army Afrika on September 20, 1942. Stumme died of a heart attack during the Battle of El Alamein on October 24, 1942.

Rommel's communications vehicle, stuck in the sand, circa 1941. The Desert Fox's command vehicle can be seen to the rear.

A German convoy moves down the Coastal Road. The Via Balbia (as the Italians called it) was the only paved road of any length in the entire North African theater of operations.

Vehicles of the British 44th Artillery Brigade burn in the desert as the Afrika Korps wins another engagement.

Adolf Hitler, the German supreme commander.

Adolf Hitler, the German supreme commander.

The Afrika Korps in battle, late 1941.

A German gun bangs away, North Africa, circa 1942. Artillery inflicted more casualties on both sides in North Africa than did tanks or infantry.

The desert in flames, Winter Battles, late 1941.

British and South African troops on their way to the POW camps following the fall of Tobruk, June 1942.

CHAPTER V

THE GAZALA LINE AND TOBRUK

Hans Hecker was born in the Meiderich suburb of Duisburg (in the Ruhr industrial district) on February 26, 1895. He entered the service as a Fahnenjunker in the 33rd Field Artillery Regiment on August 2, 1914, but transferred to the engineers in 1915. Seriously wounded in late 1915, he did not receive his commission until July 18, 1917. Young Hecker nevertheless managed to distinguish himself in combat on the Western Front and was awarded the Knight's Cross of the Hohenzollern House Order with Swords in August 1918. He was discharged from the army in early 1919 (an honorary promotion to first lieutenant followed), but returned to active duty as a second lieutenant in the 6th Engineer Battalion at Muenster in 1924. He was promoted to first lieutenant the following year and remained at that grade until after Hitler assumed power in 1933. He remained with the 6th Engineers most of the Reichsheer period, although he also served briefly as engineer officer to the Commandant of Marienburg (1930–31) and with the 1st Engineer Battalion in East Prussia (1931–32). He returned to Muenster as a company commander in the 6th Engineer in 1932. Late that year, he became a tactical/technical officer on the motorization staff.

Promoted to captain in 1933 and to major in 1936, Hans Hecker served as an instructor at the Infantry School in Dresden (1934–36) and then joined the staff of the defense ministry in 1936. He became a staff officer at OKH when the Wehrmacht was created on February 2, 1938.

Major Hecker was named commander of the 29th Motorized Engineer Battalion on November 10, 1938. This was a prized appointment. The battalion was part of the elite 29th Motorized Division (the "Falcon" Division), which was one of the best units in the German Army. Hecker led the 29th Engineers with considerable success in Poland, Belgium, and the

"Drive to the Channel" in May 1940, when Guderian's XIX Corps cut off the British Expeditionery Force, the Belgium Army, and the 1st and 7th French Armies in the Dunkirk Pocket. For his contribution to this victory, Hans Hecker was awarded the Knight's Cross. There was little time to celebrate, however. In June 1940, Hecker and his battalion participated in the conquest of France. After preparing for the invasion of Great Britain, the 29th was transferred to the East, along with its parent division, and fought in the difficult and dangerous battles on the southern sector of the Eastern Front. In late October 1941, however, while his division was driving on Rostov, Major Hecker was recalled to Germany. He was granted a few weeks leave, was promoted to lieutenant colonel (effective December 1, 1941), and was assigned to the Staff, Panzer Group Afrika. After a brief orientation, he was named chief engineer officer (*Pionierfuehrer*) of the panzer group. When Panzer Group Afrika was upgraded on January 30, Hecker became chief engineer officer for a panzer army. To compensate for his relatively low rank, Hans Hecker received an accelerated promotion to full colonel on December 17, 1941. After spending 16 years as a lieutenant, he was a lieutenant colonel for only 17 days.[1]

After Rommel recaptured Benghazi and half of Cyrenaica in January 1942, the British constructed the Gazala Line to block his path to Tobruk and to bar the Germans from further advances to the west. It consisted of a huge series of thick minefields, extending from the Mediterranean coast to Bir Hacheim, a water hole 40 miles to the south. More than a million mines were laid. The line included several isolated, fortified strongpoints called "boxes," which were usually about two miles in diameter and garrisoned by a reinforced brigade. Each box had minefields, entrenchments, barbed-wire entanglements, bunkers, outposts, machine-gun nests, artillery, and antitank batteries, and even tanks—up to a regiment per box. To the rear lay the British operational reserves. Figure 5.1 shows the Gazala Line–Tobruk battlefield.

Rommel was too smart to attack an obstacle this strong, although he deceived the British 8th Army commander into thinking he intended to do just that; meanwhile, he planned to envelope the British southern flank and to cut the British main supply line along the Coastal Road via amphibious assault. He planned to personally lead the main assault force around the southern (desert) flank. Then, when he had defeated the British reserves and was deep in the Allied rear, he would launch his amphibious assault force. It would come ashore near Gabr Sidi Hameida, 20 miles east of Tobruk, cut the Coastal Road, dig in, and hold out until it was relieved by the Afrika Korps. By linking the main assault force with the amphibious force deep in the Allied rear, Rommel would effectively encircle the Gazala Line and Tobruk and cut off the 8th Army from Egypt. Because of his experience in planning Operation "Sealion," Rommel selected Hans Hecker to command his amphibious assault force.

Figure 5.1
The Gazala Line–Tobruk Battlefield

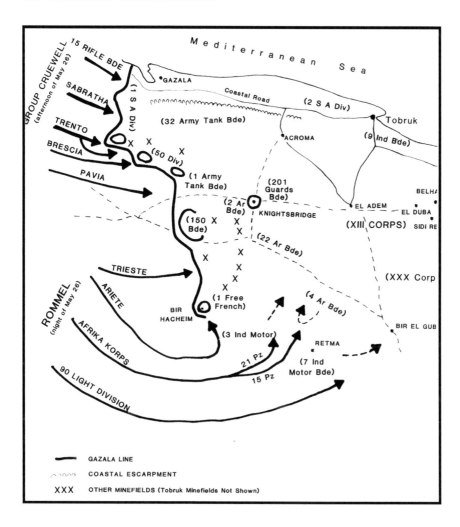

To accomplish his mission, Colonel Hecker was given the 778th Engineer Landing Company, elements of the 33rd and 39th Tank Destroyer Battalions, the Italian 3rd San Marco Marine Battalion, a platoon of captured British tanks, two StuG III assault guns, and the 13th "Brandenburger" Company, which consisted of specially trained commandos who spoke fluent English and/or Arabic. The force included about a dozen antitank guns (most of them captured British weapons), four British trucks, and a mortar battery. Hecker was also given several self-propelled barges and landing craft, as well as operational control of the 6th Minesweeper Flotilla. The German Navy was to cover the landing force with the 3rd Torpedo Boat Flotilla and five submarines, and the Luftwaffe was ordered to provide air support.

Hecker assembled his force at Bomba Bay and, when the Battle of the Gazala Line began on May 26, Rommel ordered him to be ready to commence his landings on May 27. The operation was postponed only after the assault force was fully embarked and ready to put to sea. By this time it was apparent that the Desert Fox had seriously underestimated the strength of the British reserves, and the Afrika Korps was virtually surrounded east of the Gazala Line.

Kampfgruppe (Battle Group) Hecker became part of Group Cruewell's reserve on May 27 and the operation was cancelled altogether on May 28, because it was painfully obvious that Rommel would not be east of Tobruk anytime soon. After Rommel breached the Gazala Line and destroyed the British 150th Infantry Brigade on June 1, Hecker joined the Desert Fox near Bir Hacheim, which was being heroically defended by General Pierre Koenig's 1st Free French Brigade.[2]

Bir Hacheim was a major "box" that defended the southern end of the Gazala Line. As long as it remained under Allied control, Rommel could never safely advance on Tobruk. It was defended by the extremely capable General Pierre Koenig, who had 3,600 men, 26 field guns, 62 antitank guns, 44 mortars, and an anti-aircraft battalion, as well as a battalion of Jews. Rommel had tried to capture it as early as May 26, using elements of the Italian Ariete Armored Division, but failed. On June 2, he ordered the 90th Light Division and the Italian Trieste Motorized Division to invest the fortress; then he tried to blast it into submission using Messerschmitts and Stuka dive-bombers, but this effort also failed. He reinforced the 90th Light and Trieste with Kampfgruppe Wolz (a reconnaissance battalion and Colonel Wolz's 135th Motorized Flak Regiment), but the 88s seemed to have little impact on the fortress.

By June 6, German gains in the Bir Hacheim sector had been minimal, while casualties had been heavy indeed. Two platoons of the 288th Special Purposes Unit (of the 90th Light Division) had only gained 900 yards in eight days of fighting, but had lost two thirds of their men killed or wounded. The Germans had also lost more than 50 airplanes.

Rommel attacked again on June 7, using the 90th Light and Kampfgruppe Wolz. Although they managed to identify several lanes in the minefield and clear them up to a certain point, they were unable to completely breach the minefield or to capture the fortress.

"That accursed Bir Hacheim!" Rommel swore again and again.[3] Twice he had predicted that its fall was imminent, and twice he had been proven wrong. On June 8, he demanded that it be captured that very night. To accomplish this mission, he brought up Kampfgruppe Hecker.

KG Hecker now consisted of large elements of the 33rd Panzer Engineer, 200th Panzer Engineer, and 900th Motorized Engineer Battalions, as well as two infantry battle groups. The 190th Motorized Artillery Regiment and 58 bombers and dive-bombers—escorted by more than 50 fighters—were ordered to support Colonel Hecker. Rommel ordered him to launch a night attack and breach Koenig's minefield, so that the 90th Light Division could finish off the garrison the next day.

The night attack was a partial success. Hecker pushed to within 500 yards of the main French position and overran the Jewish battalion, most of which was captured.

That night, OKW (i.e., Hitler) sent Rommel an order instructing him to shoot the Jews. Not one member of Rommel's staff remembers hearing this order, and no copy of it was found in panzer army files after the war. Like many orders that displeased him, the Desert Fox burned his copy of the order and ignored it. The Jews were treated humanely by KG Hecker and were turned over to the Italians, who treated them like all other prisoners of war.

Hecker attacked again on June 9, but with less success. The colonel himself was wounded when his command vehicle struck a mine. Hecker was thrown into the roof of the vehicle and cut a deep gash in his head. Rommel was furious—but not at Hecker. "This accursed Bir Hacheim has taken a sufficient toll!" he shouted. "I'm going to leave it! We'll attack Tobruk!"

The wounded engineer officer objected, however. He pointed out that he had already captured several strongpoints and that he believed the defenders were weakening. If Rommel would give him one battalion of German infantry, he declared, "I am convinced that we can bring the battle to a victorious conclusion."[4]

Rommel restrained his temper with an effort. After a brief discussion with Colonel Fritz Bayerlein, his acting chief of staff, he ordered Kampfgruppe Baade (the bulk of Lieutenant Colonel Ernst-Guenther Baade's 155th Panzer Grenadier Regiment of the 15th Panzer Division) down from the Cauldron area for another attack on Bir Hacheim.

Hecker was right: French resistance at Bir Hacheim was indeed weakening and, on June 10, the attack of KG Baade almost caused it to collapse altogether. That night, Koenig signaled General Sir Neill Ritchie, the commander of the British 8th Army: "Am at the end of my tether. The enemy is outside my HQ." Realizing that the end was near, Ritchie ordered him to break out and try to reach friendly lines. This the resourceful French general succeeded in doing, along with 2,300 of his men.[5]

After he was treated for his wounds, Hans Hecker resumed his duties as chief engineer officer of Panzer Army Afrika. He played a minor role in the capture of Tobruk and the invasion of Egypt. After Rommel was checked in the 1st Battle of El Alamein, Hecker was responsible for converting the captured British minefields into German minefields, as well as for lifting mines from the Gazala Line and relaying them to protect Rommel's infantry. He also directed the engineer rearguards in the early stages of the retreat from El Alamein, but after a year in the Sahara Desert, Hecker was recalled to Germany. He had been selected to attend a course for future division commanders at OKH.

Hecker's next assignment was not to his liking. While he was attending the Division Commanders' Course his old division, the 29th Motorized, had been cut off and destroyed in Stalingrad. He was ordered to organize a new one, mainly using the 345th Motorized Infantry Division in France. This task was completed by July. The division was redesignated the 29th Panzer Grenadier Division on June 23, 1943, and went on to serve with great distinction in Italy (1943–45). Hecker, however, never led the 29th in the field. He was earmarked to command a panzer division. On July 27, he was sent to the Panzer School at Krampnitz for further training. After this was completed on October 8, he took a rather extended leave and then reported for duty with Army Group C in Italy, where he was named acting commander of the 26th Panzer Division on January 22, 1944. (The original commander, Lieutenant General Baron Smilo von Luettwitz, was temporarily on leave in Germany.)

Like the original 29th Motorized, the original 26th Panzer Division had been destroyed at Stalingrad. Its successor never lived up to the standards of the original, but, under Hecker and his successors, it turned out to be a fairly good combat division. Hecker led it in the Anzio counterattacks, but when Baron von Luettwitz returned, he was named commander of the 3rd Panzer Grenadier Division in March 1944.

The 3rd was another "Stalingrad" unit, which had been formed in the spring of 1943 by absorbing the 386th Motorized Division. The 386th was considered a mediocre formation, but its performance in Italy had exceeded expectations and would continue to do so under Hecker. It fought in the retreat to Rome and was then withdrawn to Florence, from whence it was transferred to the Western Front.[6] It arrived in August—just after the Normandy front had collapsed—and initially engaged the Americans southeast of Paris. The 3rd Panzer Grenadier took part in the withdrawal from France, in the evacuation of Nancy, and in the 1st Battle of Metz. It was still covering the Saar Industrial Region on October 3, 1944, when Hecker was relieved of his command, apparently for reasons of health. (The German personnel files are sometimes very maddening, because they do not always tell whether a commander left his post because of illness or wounds, because he was relieved of his command by a senior officer, or for some other reason.) In any case, he would not receive another command for months.

Hans Hecker did not return to active duty until April 1, 1945, when he assumed command of the 4th Panzer Division. An outstanding unit even by German standards, the 4th Panzer was the most heavily decorated of all of the German tank divisions in World War II. Now, however, it was in tatters and was isolated on the Frischen Nehrung, near the mouth of the Vistula—along with the remnants of the 2nd Army— and was totally isolated by the Red Army. Why Hans Hecker was given this command is not clear, but obviously General of Infantry Wilhelm Burgdorf, the chief of the Army Personnel Office and a strong Nazi, had something against him. Burgdorf was the man who forced Rommel to commit suicide and possibly he held Hecker's former association with the Desert Fox against him. (Burghoff himself committed suicide in Berlin on or about May 2, 1945, so we will never know for sure.) In any case, Hecker was still on the Frischen Nehrung when Hitler shot himself on April 30, 1945. Between then and the surrender of the 2nd Army (and 4th Panzer Division) on May 8, Hans Hecker escaped. Apparently he boarded one of the last boats to carry troops out of the pocket. His division surrendered to the Russians.

General Hecker settled in Muenden after the war. He died there on May 1, 1979.

Rommel's most unusual officer, without question, was Ernst-Guenther Baade.

The son of a wealthy family, he was born in Gut Falkenhagen, in the Ostpriegnitz district of Brandenburg, on August 20, 1897. He grew up on the family's estates and was an experienced horseman before he was a teenager. The family also saw to it that he received an excellent education. (He spoke Italian and was fluent in English and French.) A patriotic young German with a thirst for adventure, Baade joined the Imperial Army as a war volunteer as soon as World War I broke out, two days before his 17th birthday. Naturally, he enlisted in a cavalry outfit—the 9th Ulan Regiment, to be exact.

Baade was promoted to corporal in 1915 and volunteered for officers' training the following spring. After completing a three-month-long Officer Aspirants' Course at Doeberitz, he was transferred to the 9th Replacement Cavalry Squadron of the 9th Dragoon Regiment and was commissioned Leutnant on August 22, 1916. He was, as German enlisted men said, a "90-day wonder."

Baade served with the 9th Dragoons (whose adjutant was Ludwig Cruewell) from March 1916 to March 1917, when he was transferred to the 231st Infantry Brigade. Here he worked as a platoon leader in the 231st Telephone Battalion and later as an orderly officer on the brigade staff. In July 1918, he transferred to the 444th Infantry Regiment. Baade's World War I career ended in late August 1918, when he was caught in a poison gas attack. He spent two months in the 62nd Bavarian War Hospital and was still recuperating when the armistice was signed.

Baade applied for duty with the Reichsheer but was not accepted. He was discharged from the service on May 15, 1920, and spent the next four years as a horse breeder on his own estate in Holstein, northern Germany. He managed to secure an appointment to the Reichswehr in 1924, however, and joined the 14th Cavalry Regiment. He was promoted to first lieutenant the following year, to Rittmeister in 1933, and to major in 1937. In the process, he and his wife earned reputations as international horse-show jumpers. He remained assigned to various cavalry units or schools until August 26, 1939, when his cavalry squadron (part of the 3rd Cavalry Regiment at Goettingen) was redesignated the 17th Reconnaissance Battalion. It fought in Poland as part of the 17th Infantry Division.

Baade was back in the cavalry on December 14, 1939, when he was named commander of the I/22nd Cavalry Regiment. He was promoted to lieutenant colonel on March 1, 1940, and led his squadron in the conquest of the Netherlands and France (1940) and in the invasion of Russia (1941). He was wounded in action on August 15, 1941. When he returned to field duty in Russia on October 15, 1941, he was named commander of the 1st Bicycle Battalion, which was also part of the 1st Cavalry Division. Later, with Baade still in command, this unit was sent back to East Prussia and converted into the 4th Motorcycle Battalion of the 24th Panzer (formerly 1st Cavalry) Division.[7]

With Germany's only cavalry division gone,[8] Baade sought advancement within the motorized branch. He led the 4th Motorcycle on the Eastern Front, performed well, and convinced the powerful Army Personnel Branch that he was capable of commanding a motorized regiment. In April 1942 he arrived in North Africa and, after a brief training period with Staff, 15th Panzer Division, was promoted to full colonel and named commander of the 115th Rifle Regiment.

Baade was a gentleman who believed in chivalry, making him much more suitable for the North African campaign than the Russian Front. He distinguished himself from the beginning. Under the direction of General Hecker, he led the assault that broke the back of the French defense at Bir Hacheim and further distinguished himself at Tobruk.

An idiosyncratic maverick, Ernst Baade definitely marched to his own drummer and soon became a legend in the Afrika Korps by going into battle dressed in a Scottish kilt and carrying a broadsword. In the field, he habitually wore a black beret with a tartan plaid ribbon and carried a huge claymore (a double-edged broadsword formerly used by the Scottish Highlanders) instead of a Luger. Using his perfect English, he often misdirected British artillery fire—or just called up the enemy for a chat. In addition to his eccentricities, Baade proved to be incredibly brave, often leading raids behind enemy lines. Once he was trapped with a British minefield between him and friendly forces. With no time to breach the minefield, he persuaded a captured British engineer sergeant to show him the location of a lane through the minefield. When the sergeant complied and Baade had made good his escape, the colonel let him go.

Although Baade's behavior might have gotten him in trouble elsewhere, it merely provoked amusement tinged with admiration in the Afrika Korps. His men respected him, as did his superiors, because he was an excellent battlefield commander. (Rommel demanded loyalty and efficiency. He demanded nothing else and accepted nothing less.) Baade's unpredictable actions caused anger and irritation at the High Command of the Armed Forces, but it did not ruffle Rommel, who shielded him. Later, he was shielded from Rastenburg's irritation by General of Panzer Troops Hans Valentin Hube (in Sicily) and by Field Marshal Albert Kesselring in Italy. For his part, Baade did not mind irritating the Nazis. Later in the war, OKW signaled OB South and demanded to know if it was true that Baade had signaled the British over their own radio net and wished them a Merry Christmas. Kesselring replied that the rumor was not true. He was lying when he said that: the rumor *was* true.

Baade was decorated with the Knight's Cross on June 27, 1942. Later he would add the Oak Leaves and Swords, making him one of the most decorated soldiers in the history of the Third Reich.

The colorful colonel's exploits in North Africa came to an end on July 28, 1942, when he was seriously wounded during the 1st Battle of El Alamein. He did not return to duty until December, when he was attached to the staff of the German General with Commando Supremo, the High Command of the Italian Armed Forces.

In April 1943, Baade was sent to Sicily, where he formed the ad hoc *Division Kommando Baade* to control march (replacement) battalions bound for Africa. During the first week in May, when it became obvious that Army Group Afrika could not hold out, Baade (acting on his own initiative) stopped sending troops to Tunisia and began organizing the defense of Sicily. From the 46th, 47th, 48th, 50th, and 56th March Battalions, he formed Panzer Grenadier Regiment Palermo, with the I, II, III, and IV Battalions. It was the only German unit in Sicily that was capable of offering even token resistance when General von Arnim surrendered.

Fortunately for Germany, the Allies were not prepared to follow up after "Tunisgrad." OKW and OB South sent Baade some flak units, supply units, and support troops in May. On May 14, Division Command Baade was redesignated Division Command Sicily (*Division Kommando Sizilien*).

Taking advantage of the time the Allies so generously gave him, Baade and his seniors seemingly created a division out of thin air. It included Regiment Ens (two battalions, formed from miscellaneous troops and units); Regiment Koerner (three of the battalions of the former Panzer Grenadier Regiment Palermo); and Regiment Fullriede (three battalions, formed from the former 63rd, 65th, and 67th March Battalions).[9] Later these units became the 1st, 2nd, and 3rd Sicily Grenadier Regiments and then the 104th, 115th, and 129th Panzer Grenadier Regiments, respectively.

Baade also formed a four-battalion Artillery Regiment Sicily, which later became the 33rd Motorized Artillery Regiment. The elements of this regiment came from all over the place. The staff was from the 190th Artillery Regiment, which had been largely destroyed in Tunisia but was reforming in Naples. The I Battalion was the former I Battalion, Hermann Goering Panzer Artillery Regiment (a Luftwaffe unit absorbed by the army). The II Battalion was the former 557th Heavy Artillery Battalion, a GHQ unit. The IV Battalion was the former II/53rd Artillery Regiment, a recently rebuilt Stalingrad unit given to Baade by Field Marshal Kesselring, the OB South. Only the III Battalion was created from scratch. The I Battalion was equipped with heavy guns, the II with three batteries of 170-mm cannon, the III had two light batteries and a mortar battery, and the IV had three light batteries. The new regiment was commanded by Major of Reserves Theodor Simon.

In addition, Division Sicily included the Panzer Grenadier Battalion Reggio (the former 69th March Battalion); Flak Battalion Sicily (later redesignated 315th Flak Battalion), which had three batteries; Division Unit 33 (much of which eventually became the 999th Signal Battalion); and the 215th Panzer Battalion, a GHQ unit supplied by OB South.

The men of the new division were a varied lot. Most of the troops of the 129th Panzer Grenadier Regiment were veterans of the Eastern Front. Most of the 104th Regiment's men were tough survivors of the Afrika Korps, many of whom were now returning to duty after being wounded.

Baade was replaced as divisional commander by Major General Eberhard Rodt on June 9, 1943. Division Sicily was redesignated 15th Panzer Grenadier Division (after the 15th Panzer Division of the Afrika Korps) and went on to distinguish itself on the Italian and Western Fronts. Baade, meanwhile, returned to his liaison duties in Rome. He was not yet through with Sicily, however.

The Allied armies (Patton's U.S. 7th Army and Montgomery's 8th) landed in Sicily on July 10, 1943. Kesselring and General d'Armata Alfredo Guzzoni, the commander of the Italian 6th Army, tried to throw them back into the sea but failed. On July 14, Kesselring concluded that the Axis evacuation of Sicily must be accepted as a matter of long-term strategic policy.

Sicily is separated from Italy by the Strait of Messina, a two-mile body of water that would have to be crossed if the Axis forces on Sicily were to escape. In the meantime, all supplies to Sicily would have to cross the straits. Kesselring sent Hube's Headquarters, XIV Panzer Corps to the island to direct the defense and appointed Colonel Ernst-Guenther Baade "Commandant of the Straits of Messina." Baade, therefore, superseded Luftwaffe Major General Rainer Stahel, the commander of all flak units in Sicily, who was now relegated to coastal defense duties around Palermo. This demonstrates how much faith Kesselring had in Baade, because he had in effect demoted Stahel, who was also a very competent officer and, like Kesselring, was an air force man.[10]

Baade's new command was a very mixed one and included all branches of the service, as well as Italian units. Mainly, it consisted of army ferrying units, Luftwaffe, naval and Italian flak and artillery units, and three naval landing flotillas. Baade controlled units on both the Sicilian and Calabrian (Italian) shores and everything in between.

The distinguished American naval historian, Samuel Eliot Morison, later wrote, "The final episode of the campaign has never received proper attention ... partly because no one on the Allied side has cared to dwell on it. This is the Axis troops' evacuation of Sicily across the Straits of Messina, an outstanding maritime retreat of the war, in a class with Dunkirk, Guadalcanal and Kiska."[11] Another distinguished American soldier, Martin Blumenson, commented that the German ferry service was already operating on July 16. He noted that Baade "ran a cold and efficient, machine-like service entirely apart from the operation conducted by Italian authorities."[12]

To cover the straits, Baade created a "Flak Alley" of 150 German and Italian guns, including four batteries of 280-mm (11.2-inch) guns, two batteries of 152-mm (6-inch) guns and a sizable number of 3- to 4-inch guns, and about 150 German 88-mm and Italian 90-mm dual-purpose guns. As Hube slowly retreated, he reinforced Baade with the II/15th Motorized Artillery Regiment (of the 15th Panzer Grenadier Division), which controlled two batteries of 170-mm guns that had a range of 10 miles. By early August, Baade controlled about 500 guns, including more than 300 anti-aircraft guns, and 134 small naval vessels, excluding minesweepers and patrol boats, which screened the evacuation but did not normally carry troops.

General Hube had four understrength German divisions in Sicily and was facing a dozen British and American divisions, but the mountainous terrain of Sicily was a major combat multiplier for the defenders. He nevertheless ordered Baade to begin evacuating nonessential German units (service support troops) in early August. By August 10, however, he had been pushed into the northeastern corner of the island. That day, he ordered Colonel Baade to commence full-scale evacuations during the night of August 11–12.

Baade's evacuation of Sicily, codenamed Operation "Lehrgang," was a tactical masterpiece. Even the British Official History described it as "brilliantly successful."[13] In all, in six days Baade and his subordinates evacuated 39,569 German troops (including 4,444 wounded), 9,605 vehicles, 94 guns (excluding Baade's own, which were also successfully evacuated), 47 tanks, 1,100 tons of ammunition, and 15,700 tons of other equipment and supplies. In excess of 12,000 German soldiers, 4,500 vehicles, and 5,000 tons of supplies had been sent off before the beginning of Lehrgang. About 70,000 Italians had also been evacuated, mainly by the Italian Navy. The XIV Panzer Corps and its divisions—the 15th and 29th Panzer Grenadier, the 1st Parachute, and the Hermann Goering Panzer—would continue to fight until the end of the war.

Colonel Ernst-Guenther Baade, replete with kilt and claymore, kept his headquarters intact after the evacuation, although his troop units were sent elsewhere. His *Sonderstab* (special staff) remained attached to the XIV Panzer Corps, which used it at various times to direct construction engineer units (used to repair roads, bridges, and facilities damaged by Anglo-American bombing), flak battalions, and *Ostbataillone*: units composed of Ukrainian and White Russian volunteers who had joined the Wehrmacht to fight Communism—or to get out of German POW camps.

On November 27, 1943, Major General Gustav Heistermann von Ziehlberg, the commander of the 65th Infantry Division, was severely wounded in the left arm. Baade was named temporary commander of the division and held it until Heistermann's permanent replacement arrived on December 1, 1943. He then returned to XIV Panzer Corps.

On December 20, 1943, Baade succeeded Major General Carl-Hans Lungershausen as commander of the 90th Panzer Grenadier Division. He led it in the Monte Cassino fighting, in the Gothic Line battles, and in the retreat to the Arno. In the process he proved himself to be an excellent defensive commander and a superb handler of troops, no matter what OKW thought about his unorthodox behavior. Even the Army Personnel Office recognized this and promoted him to major general (February 1, 1944) and lieutenant general (August 1, 1944).

On December 9, 1944, General Baade was shot by a sniper. He was medically evacuated to Germany and placed in Fuehrer Reserve until January 5, 1945, when he attended a two-week commanding generals' course (corps commanders course) in Hirschberg. He was in Fuehrer Reserve for six more weeks and was then given command of the LXXXI Corps on the Western Front on March 1. He fought the Battle of Cologne against the U.S. 1st Army in March and lost the city, although he did manage to blow up all the Rhine River bridges before the Americans could cross them. By now, however, Baade (who had never been particularly careful about what he said) was in trouble because of his anti-Nazi remarks and attitude. Field Marshal Walter Model, the tough pro-Nazi commander-in-chief of Army Group B, ordered him to report to his headquarters. Perhaps sensing a trap, Baade reported himself sick instead and gave up command of the LXXXI Corps on March 13.

Recalled to duty on or about April 18, Baade was named inspector of *Volkssturm*—the last inductees (mostly boys of fourteen or younger and older men of sixty or more). The Afrika Korps veteran, however, was not interested in sacrificing innocents for the lost cause in which he had never believed, so he did little or nothing.

It is not exactly certain what happened to Baade in the last, chaotic days of the war. According to one source, he was threatened by a high-ranking SS man (his own National Socialist Political Officer) in Schleswig-Holstein. Baade shot the Nazi and went into hiding.[14] On or about April 24, near his estate of Neverstaden/Holstein, he was critically wounded by a British fighter-bomber. He was brought to the hospital in Bad Segeberg, where he lingered for two weeks. He finally died on May 8, 1945—the day the war ended.

Walter Kurt Josef Nehring (pronouned *NAIR-ring*) was one of the founders of the theory of the blitzkrieg and (arguably) was the best panzer commander of World War II.

Born in the Stretzin district of West Prussia, Nehring was the descendant of a Dutch family who had fled the Netherlands to escape religious persecution in the seventeenth century. His father was a schoolteacher and reserve officer who moved the family to Danzig while Walter was still a child. Early in life, Nehring decided to become a soldier. He entered his father's regiment, the 152nd Infantry, as a Fahnenjunker on September 16, 1911. Commissioned before the outbreak of World War I, Nehring endured the harsh Prussian training without complaint. He did complain about the low pay, however, and once remarked that Prussian officers served their king and country pretty much at their own expense.[15]

When the Great War began, Nehring was a platoon leader in the 8th Company. The regiment was assigned to the 41st Infantry Division (XX Corps) and was sent east to check the Czar's invasion. Nehring's battalion (the II/41st) was resting in reserve near the village of Waplitz when a large Russian force, which had successfully infiltrated through a hole in the German line, launched a surprise attack. The II Battalion was quickly overrun. Surviving platoons and companies were ordered to fight their way out and rally in the village of Seythen. This Nehring could not do because strong Russian forces blocked his path, so he attacked the village of Meuhlen instead. He captured the place in heavy fighting and was able to reach the nearby German 37th Infantry Division late in the day.

After the Hindenburg-Ludendorff team destroyed the 2nd Russian Army under General Samsonov, they turned against the 1st Army under General Rennenkampf, which was invading East Prussia from the north. They destroyed this army also, but Walter Nehring was not there to see it. He was in the hospital, having been shot in the head and the throat. He partially recovered and was assigned to the regiment's replacement battalion until he was able to return to field duty.

Nehring was attached to the 141st Infantry Regiment and was named adjutant of its II Battalion in late 1914. He returned to action on the Eastern Front (now in Poland) but was almost immediately shot again, this time in the leg. He recovered quickly and rejoined his parent regiment, the 152nd, in early 1915. He was given command of a rifle company shortly thereafter.

In 1915, the Eastern Front bogged down in trench warfare, which Nehring found distasteful. He, therefore, volunteered for flight training, which he began on June 6, 1916—the day he was promoted to first lieutenant. His career as an aviator was destined to be brief. On June 20, he was flying as an observer when his airplane crashed and he suffered a broken jaw. By the time he was discharged from the hospital, his enthusiasm for aviation had waned, and he returned to the infantry. In December 1916, he was named commander of the 1st Machine Gun Company of the 22nd Infantry Regiment on the Western Front.

During the Battle of Mount Kemmel in Flanders, Nehring was shot through the stomach—his third wound of the war. Months in the hospital followed. (Nehring spent more time in the hospital than he did on the Eastern Front.) He was released from the hospital in late September 1918 and assigned to the replacement machine gun company of Wehrkreis XX in East Prussia. He was there when the war ended.

During "the war after the war," Nehring was a member of a Freikorps force, which checked the incursions of Polish irregulars and the Polish Army against Prussia. He was in combat as early as December 1918. Later, after Wehrkreis XX created the 41st Volunteer Infantry Division in the spring of 1919, Nehring became its machine gun company commander and a reconnaissance officer. Later, he was accepted into the Reichsheer and became adjutant of the 20th Infantry Brigade, where he served as one of the liaison officers between the Reichswehr and the Freikorps.

The year 1923 was a big one for young Nehring. He married the daughter of an East Prussian Junker, was promoted to captain, became adjutant of the 2nd Infantry Regiment, took his Wehrkreis exam, and scored so high that he was selected to attend the War Academy in Berlin. As part of the course, he was temporarily attached to the Mobilization and Planning Department in the Reichs Defense Ministry. In accordance with General Seeckt's directive that all Reichsheer officers must have an area of concentration, Nehring chose to specialize in the organization and employment of motorized units. (He was influenced in this decision by Major Heinz Guderian, a member of the department who rapidly became a close personal friend.) This was a pregnant moment in the history of the German Army.

Nehring successfully completed General Staff training and returned to the field army as a training officer with the 6th Motorized Battalion. This gave him a chance to put into practice some of the theories that he had been developing. His ideas concerning tank and armored reconnaissance tactics proved to be so successful in the autumn maneuvers of 1929 that the Reichsheer ordered all other motorized battalions to be trained along the same lines.

In 1931, Nehring's career took another giant leap forward when General Oswald Lutz was named inspector of motorized units.[16] (In 1935, he was simultaneously named chief of army motorization.) With Guderian as chief of staff of the inspectorate and Nehring as chief of operations, a triumvirate was formed that revolutionized not only the German Wehrmacht but the very nature of warfare in general. Both Guderian and Nehring wrote extensively and were tireless advocates of armored and motorized warfare.

In 1933, Nehring went to Italy and studied Mussolini's tank forces. He then came home and worked on the blitzkrieg theories that would shake the world just a few years later. (Many senior German commanders opposed these ideas, including General Ludwig Beck, the chief of the General Staff. Nehring was more diplomatic in advancing his theories than his friend Guderian.) Nehring's theories included the use of dive-bombers as flying artillery for the panzer units because they could launch pin-point attacks, as opposed to standard bombers, which could be used effectively only against area targets.

By now considered an international expert on armored warfare, he studied the Soviet Army. Via extensive research and interviews with officers returning from the secret German tank training facility in Russia, he was able to calculate the output of Soviet tractor factories, which would no doubt be converted to tank production if there were a Russo-German war. He determined that the Soviet military-industrial complex had the capacity to produce more than 1,000 armored fighting vehicles per month. Guderian presented this information to

Hitler and was met with scorn and disbelief, but Nehring's predictions were accurate.[17]

Walter Nehring also worked on panzer unit organization and became a strong advocate for the creation of antitank units. (Eventually, almost every division in the German field army had an antitank battalion.) Together with Lutz and Guderian, Nehring was responsible for inventing blitzkrieg warfare. (Guderian has received the lion's share of the credit and deservedly so, but he neither invented nor advanced the concept all by himself. The less forceful Lutz and the less visible Nehring also deserve a considerable amount of credit.)

In 1936, Nehring was selected to organize the shipment and resupply of men and equipment (including tanks) to the Condor Legion and the German military mission in Spain. Then, he attended a course for officers earmarked for the highest levels of command. In the spring of 1937, at the invitation of the Swiss government, he went to Switzerland and lectured their army on modern warfare, including armored warfare. He then returned to Germany and on October 1, 1937, was named commander of the 5th Panzer Regiment at Wuensdorf, Wehrkreis III. (This unit later became part of the Afrika Korps and was eventually destroyed in Tunisia. It was part of the 3rd Panzer Division in 1937.)

While Nehring was gaining command experience at the regimental level, war clouds gathered over Europe. Very much aware that their theories might soon be put to the ultimate test, Heinz Guderian—who was now commander of the XIX Motorized (later Panzer) Corps—arranged for his number one assistant to be transferred to the XIX Motorized as chief of staff. The transfer took place on July 1, 1939. The corps crossed into Poland on September 1.

Guderian's panzer tactics shocked the world in both Poland and France, which were conquered in campaigns of five and six weeks, respectively. At one point in France, Nehring took his theoretical operations plans, changed the dates, and sent them to the units without further modification. They worked perfectly. The best units of the French Army were destroyed in Belgium and northern France, and the British Expeditionary Force escaped via Dunkirk after abandoning its remaining vehicles, guns, tanks, and other heavy equipment.

On June 1, 1940, Nehring became chief of staff of Panzer Group Guderian, which controlled three motorized corps. France surrendered three weeks later. Nehring, meanwhile, was promoted to major general and, on October 25, was given command of the 18th Panzer Division, which was officially activated in Leisnig, Wehrkreis IV, the next day.

The 18th Panzer was formed mainly from elements of the 4th and 14th Infantry Divisions. It consisted of the 18th Rifle Brigade (52nd Rifle Regiment, 101st Rifle Regiment, and 18th Motorcycle Battalion); the 18th and 28th Panzer Regiments (two battalions each); the

88th Artillery (later Panzer Artillery) Regiment; the 98th Panzer Engineer Battalion; and the 88th Signal, Reconnaissance, and Antitank Battalions.[18]

Almost as soon as Nehring took charge of his division, he received orders to join Panzer Group Afrika.[19] These orders were rescinded, however, apparently because someone changed his mind. No doubt Cruewell (who had served with Nehring in the 3rd Panzer Division) wanted him as one of his divisional commanders, and he had a great deal of influence with Rommel, who probably requested Nehring's services. Others at OKH (and possibly Hitler as well) wanted him for an even more important operation—the invasion of the Soviet Union. In any case, Walter Nehring remained with the 18th Panzer, at least for the moment.

Nehring spent the next few months bringing the 18th Panzer up to speed. He was not, however, able to make good all of its equipment deficiencies. In early June 1941, it was given a large shipment of captured French tanks and other vehicles. Although they were completely unsuitable for the Russian Front, they were all Nehring and his men could get, so they resolved to do the best they could with them.

In March 1941, the 18th Panzer Division redeployed to Prague. On June 22, it crossed into the Soviet Union, with Walter Nehring in the lead vehicle. As part of Guderian's 2nd Panzer Group (later Army), the 18th played a major role in the battles of encirclement at Minsk, Smolensk, Kiev, and others, and swept across the northern Ukraine. It was heavily engaged in the battle of encirclement at Bryansk, in which several Soviet armies were destroyed. Casualties and mechanical failures severely weakened the division, however, and its combat strength had been reduced by 70 percent by November 23.

The harsh Russian weather and Stalin's Winter Offensive of 1941–42 caused even further losses to the 18th Panzer; however, on January 7, 1942, it received orders to rescue the 216th Infantry Division, which had been surrounded at Ssuchinitshy. Nehring began this rescue operation on January 16 and smashed through the Russian encirclement. Despite high snow drifts and awful weather conditions (which Nehring later said caused more problems than the Reds), the 18th Panzer reached the perimeter of the 216th Infantry within a few days. It managed to bring off the division, including 1,000 wounded men.

On January 26, 1942, Nehring handed command of the division over to Major General Baron Karl von Thuengen-Rossbach and returned to Germany. He was promoted to lieutenant general and given command of the Afrika Korps.

In Libya, Nehring was confronted by the British 8th Army, which was well entrenched behind the Gazala Line. Rommel planned to outflank it to the south and then turn north, behind the minefields, and push on to the Coastal Road, defeating the British armored reserves and encircling the infantry divisions of the 8th Army in the process. Nehring expressed concern that British counterattacks during the northward push could trap the Afrika Korps east of the Gazala Line and cut it off from its supply depots to the west. Rommel, however, overruled his objections.

The operation began on May 26, and Figure 5.2 shows the initial advance. Panzer Army intelligence had badly underestimated the strength of the British armored forces, which—as Nehring feared—counterattacked

Figure 5.2
The First Attack on the Gazala Line, May 26, 1942

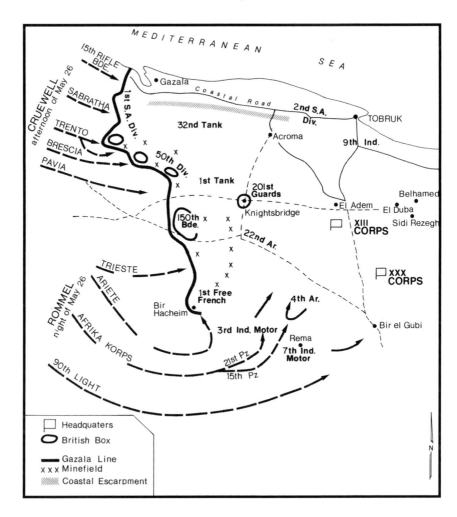

on May 27. Worse still, they struck with American Grant tanks, which were superior to any German tank in the desert at that time. Also, a new and previously undetected British antitank gun, the six-pounder (roughly equivalent to the German 75-mm gun) blasted the German armor. Both of Nehring's panzer regiments suffered heavy casualties. By late afternoon, the Afrika Korps was almost surrounded, the Grants were continuing their relentless attacks, the Afrika Korps' transport was fleeing from them, and the situation was critical.

"It was one of those situations in which catastrophe overtakes an entire army," Paul Carell wrote later. "Alternately they can be moments when a single bold decision can turn defeat into a victory. The man who conceived such a bold idea and enriched military strategy with a new tactic was General Walter K. Nehring. The man who executed the idea was [Luftwaffe] Colonel Alwin Wolz."[20]

Alwin Wolz was the commander of the 135th Motorized Flak Regiment. "A flak front!" General Nehring cried. "Wolz, you've got to build up a flak front to act as a flank defense with all available guns!"

Wolz—personally assisted by Erwin Rommel—built a flak front nearly two miles in length just before about 40 Grants pushed into the waivering flank of the Afrika Korps. They were instantly engaged by the 16 long-range 88-mm heavy anti-aircraft guns, which all opened fire at the same moment. Several Grants were hit and some of them exploded. The British, however, realized that they had a chance to destroy Rommel's army, so they pressed their attack in spite of their casualties. It did them no good. By late afternoon, two dozen Grants lay burning, wrecked by the 88s. As the British armor retreated, the 8th Army's artillery opened up on the exposed flak batteries. A number of gun crews were completely wiped out. Fortunately for the Germans, a ghibli (huge sandstorm) sprang up, and neither side was able to fight for the rest of the day.[21]

After the capture of General Cruewell, Walter Nehring became, in effect, Rommel's second-in-command. He went on to play a conspicuous role in the Battle of the Cauldron, where the Afrika Korps and the Italian Ariete Armored Division held off the 8th Army; in beaching of the Gazala Line; in the destruction of the 8th Army's armor and Knightsbridge; in the Battle of Tobruk, where the 1st South African Infantry Division was destroyed; in the pursuit across eastern Libya and into Egypt; in the Battle of Mersa Matruh; and in the 1st Battle of El Alamein, where the panzer army was finally checked. In late August 1942, the supply imbalance between Panzer Army Afrika and the 8th Army became so great that the Desert Fox felt compelled to stake everything on one last change offensive. Because of fuel shortages, he struck at Alam Halfa Ridge and found Montgomery waiting on him with nearly overwhelming forces. Nehring and Bismarck spearheaded the attack on the night of August 31–September 1. Georg von Bismarck was killed at the head of his division. Walter Nehring was also in serious trouble. A new Allied device, the "Christmas Tree" flare, lit up the battlefield for the Royal Air Force, and one of their pilots spotted Nehring's command vehicle. Despite heavy German machine gun fire, the fighter-bomber pressed on with its attack and dropped a bomb right beside Nehring's vehicle. Several officers were killed in the blast. General Nehring was badly wounded in the head, the arm, and the torso. He had to be evacuated back to Europe.

Rommel was finally defeated at El Alamein and began to retreat to Libya on November 4. Four days later, the Anglo-American 1st British Army (General Kenneth A. N. Anderson) landed in French North Africa and drove for Tunisia to take Rommel in the rear. Before they could do this, however, the Tunisian capital of Tunis had to be taken. Field Marshal Kesselring, the commander-in-chief South (OB South), summoned Walter Nehring from the hospital and ordered him to prevent this. Despite the fact that his arm was still not healing properly, Nehring accepted the challenge. He was given command of the XC Corps (which had not yet been formed) and flew to Tunis. Initially, Nehring had only himself, his aide, and his driver. A day or so later, he had elements of Kesselring's headquarters company. He established an ad hoc transport unit by confiscating Tunisian taxicabs. Meanwhile, U.S. General Dwight D. Eisenhower (whose army group controlled both Anderson and Montgomery) had 130,000 men in Algeria and Morocco alone. On November 11, Kesselring flew the elite 5th Parachute Regiment to Tunis. Nehring immediately sent it to the west, where he rapidly established a front.

Eisenhower should have won the race for Tunis, but he did not because of Nehring's skillful defense, the prompt reaction of Kesselring, who rushed reinforcements to the sector, the actions of the Luftwaffe's II Air Corps (which attacked Allied supply lines and slowed their advance), and because of the winter rains, which turned western Tunisia into a sea of mud. By the end of November, the 10th Panzer Division was in Tunisia, and other German and Italian divisions were either in the country or on their way. Walter Nehring, however, openly questioned the wisdom of defending Tunisia at all. He foresaw that Anglo-Saxon air and naval power would one day cause the collapse of Axis supply lines, which would lead to the destruction of the XC and Panzer Army Afrika. No moral coward, Nehring frankly presented his view to the Nazis and OKW. He was promptly branded a defeatist by Hitler and was denounced by Dr. Goebbels with special fervor.

Since the Nazis took power, Walter Nehring had been promoted rapidly: to lieutenant colonel (September 1, 1934), colonel (March 1, 1937), major general (August 1, 1940), lieutenant general (February 1, 1942), and general of panzer troops (July 1, 1942)—six promotions in eight years. After Tunisia, there would be no more promotions. On December 3, 1942, Hitler placed all Axis forces in Tunisia under the newly created Headquarters, 5th Panzer Army. He gave the new command to Hans-Juergen "Dieter" von Arnim, along with a promotion to colonel general. Walter Nehring left North Africa on December 9, never to return. His career was ruined.

In April and May 1943, Nehring's predictions came true. Axis supply lines collapsed and Army Group Afrika (5th Panzer and Panzer Army Afrika, which was now designated 1st Italian-German Panzer Army) was destroyed.

Nehring was only unemployed for just over two months. Although he would never receive another advancement in rank, he was (like Erwin Rommel) simply too good a commander to leave on the shelf permanently. Meanwhile, the German 6th Army surrendered at Stalingrad and, to the north, XXIV Panzer Corps had been smashed. Its last three commanding generals had been killed. General of Artillery Martin Wandel was reported missing in action on January 14, 1943, never returned, and is missing to this day. His successor, Lieutenant General Arno Jahr, was killed in action on January 20. He was replaced the same day by Lieutenant General Karl Eibl. The very next day, at Nowy-Georgijewskija, northwest of Stalingrad, Eibl was killed when some Italian soldiers mistook his command vehicle for a Russian armored car and blew it up with hand grenades. Eibl was replaced by the senior surviving officer at corps headquarters. His name was Otto Heidkaemper, and he was a colonel![22]

Walter Nehring assumed command of the XXIV Panzer on February 10, 1943, and directed it in the retreat to the Don and to the Dnieper, where it managed to hold a bridgehead east of the river in spite of fierce Soviet attacks. Meanwhile, Field Marshal Erich von Manstein, the brilliant commander-in-chief of Army Group South, was able to stabilize the front and assume the offensive, which ended in the recapture of the important city of Kharkov. The exhausted XXIV Panzer Corps was then allowed to withdraw from the front, rest, and partially rebuild.

Hitler's last offensive, Operation "Citadelle," began on July 5, 1943. Manstein, who directed the southern prong of the attack, held Nehring's corps in reserve. According to the plan, Army Group South was to break through the Russian lines; then XXIV Panzer Corps would drive north through the breach and link up with Colonel General Walter Model's 9th Army, which was advancing from north to south. The plan did not work, however, and there was no breakthrough to the south. Instead, Nehring's corps was forced to redeploy south to the Mius River sector, where the Red Army was about to break out. Nehring checked the Russians but was wounded again for the fifth time in his career. He was awarded the Wounded Badge in Gold.

Nehring's corps was used as a fire brigade on the southern and central sectors of the Eastern Front. He was proud of the fact that, although the Red Army broke through north and south of him, the front of the XXIV Panzer Corps was never breached. It was encircled, along with Hans Valentin Hube's 1st Panzer Army, in the spring of 1944 but (along with Hube) managed to fight its way out. The XXIV Panzer was then sent to Galicia, where Nehring assumed temporary command of the 4th Panzer Army on July 2, 1944. Here he checked a major offensive by the 1st Ukrainian Front.

Although Nehring did well as an acting army commander, Tunisia had not been forgotten. He was sent back to command XXIV Panzer Corps on or about August 8. He fell ill at this time, however, and did not resume command of his corps until mid-October, by which time it was in Slovakia. That fall and early winter, Nehring helped Colonel General Gotthard Heinrici, the commander of the 1st Panzer Army, check the 4th Ukrainian Front's efforts to break through to the west. Then XXIV Panzer Corps was transferred north to the flatlands of Poland and was placed in Army Group A's reserve.

In central Europe, January 12, 1945, was a snowy day, characterized by cold and poor visibility. West of the Vistula River, the Red Army had established the Baranow bridgehead. It was defended by General of Panzer Troops Baron Maximilian von Edelsheim's XXXXVIII Panzer Corps on the south and west, while General of Infantry Hermann Recknagel's XXXXII Corps held the northern face. In all, they controlled seven veteran infantry divisions, which meant that they were all severely depleted. Edelsheim's corps, for example, had no tanks, only about 12 assault guns per division, and only enough infantry to post one man every 15 yards of front. In most places along their 30 miles of front, Edelsheim and Recknagel could not form a continuous line; instead, they established strongpoints and covered the intervening terrain with patrols. Opposite them, the 1st Ukrainian Front concentrated five armies, two tank armies, more than 1,000 tanks, and thousands of artillery pieces.

The Soviets opened up a heavy artillery bombardment before dawn. They concentrated an estimated 420 guns *per mile* of front. The barrage was awesome, and it lasted three hours. Then it shifted to the rear, while the Russian infantry moved out. By noon, there were gaps in the German front large enough for the Soviets to commit their armor.

The two panzer divisions of Walter Nehring's XXIV Panzer Corps lay about 10 miles behind the front. They were ordered to counterattack, but the Red advance was so rapid that for once they caught Nehring in his assembly areas. Many of his units were overrun before they could react. By nightfall, the Russians had reached the Nida River and were a dozen miles into the rear of Fritz-Hubert Graeser's 4th Panzer Army. The XXXXVIII Panzer and XXXXII Corps had been smashed, and the remnants of Nehring's XXIV Panzer were digging in around Kielce, trying desperately to halt the juggernaut. Both frontline corps had already lost half their men, and Nehring's losses were also severe.

During the night of January 12–13, General Nehring regained his balance. On January 13, he conducted a skillful defense of the Kielce-Chmielnik sector and significantly slowed the Soviet advance. This did not suit Marshal Konev, the commander of the 1st Ukraine. On January 14, he committed his reserves. That day, Nehring's two divisions were attacked by three full armies: the 13th, the 4th Tank, and the 3rd Guards. The next day, the defense of the XXIV Panzer finally broke, and Nehring fell back to the west. By now the weather had cleared, and the Red Air Force pelted the retreating Germans with hundreds of fighter-bomber and bomber sorties, while the Luftwaffe (now a broken force) was hardly seen.

All along the front, Army Group A collapsed. On Nehring's north flank, General Recknagel tried to rally the XXXXII Corps, but he was killed by a Soviet shell on January 15 and the remnants of his corps scattered in disorder. To the south, XXXXVIII Panzer Corps had largely ceased to exist. By January 17, Nehring was miles behind the Red Army's frontlines and was surrounded by a dozen Russian armies.

Most other generals would have been finished at this point. Walter Nehring, however, called upon all his skill and experience to master a most desperate situation. He formed a "floating pocket" and maintained his perimeter as he retreated to the northwest, picking up stragglers, shattered divisions, intact units, and civilians as he went.

The civilians were justifiably terrified. The Reds were robbing, murdering, and raping at will. Often they would gang rape daughters in front of their horrified parents, then kill the daughters, and then torture the parents to death. Rape victims included 12-year-olds and grandmothers in their 70s. Seeking to save themselves and their families from this fate, tens of thousands of panic-stricken civilians turned to Walter Nehring to save them. Not one was turned away. (Nehring understood what they were going through. His own home had been destroyed in an Allied air raid, and his family was somewhere to the west—homeless refugees.) Before long, there were more civilians within the floating pocket than there were soldiers on the perimeter.

The Communists had more armies attacking the floating pocket than Nehring had divisions to defend it. He was attacked by several armies every day. He turned back every attack. Simultaneously, to the west and northwest, the Red Army blew up the bridges spanning the rivers to Nehring's front, thinking this would stop him. It did not. Meanwhile,

General of Panzer Troops Dietrich von Saucken, another incredibly brave man, advanced toward Nehring from the west with his Grossdeutschland Panzer Corps. He was also promptly surrounded, but he continued pressing east. On January 22, he linked up with XXIV Panzer Corps and immediately placed himself under Nehring's command. Nehring now commanded the XXIV Panzer, Grossdeutschland Panzer, LVI Panzer, and XXXXII Corps, with the 291st, 88th, 72nd, 342nd, 214th, and 17th Infantry Divisions, as well as the 45th and 6th Volksgrenadier, the 16th and 17th Panzer, and the 20th and 10th Panzer Grenadier. Stalin ordered the floating pocket destroyed. Despite odds of more than 7 to 1 in their favor, this was something the Red Army could not do.

Without resupply and in the depths of winter, Nehring kept his "Wandering Pocket" moving northwest and held his perimeter intact. He finally fought his way through to the Oder and reached German lines at the end of January—an incredible feat of military genius. He had covered 150 miles straight through the middle of the Red Army. "Generals Nehring and von Saucken performed feats of military virtuosity during these days that only the pen of a new Xenophon could adequately describe," Heinz Guderian exclaimed in admiration.[23] James Lucas cited Nehring's own account of the event: "Little or no rest coupled with shortages of ammunition and fuel but with frost and snow in abundance, along frozen roads, against a stronger and more speedy enemy, traversing difficult country and crossing rivers which had no bridges ... none of these could stop our determination to succeed and to defeat the enemy wherever he was met."[24] In my opinion, this campaign proves that Walter Nehring was the best panzer commander in the German Army in World War II—including Guderian and Rommel. I realize that this is a minority opinion, but that is what I believe.

Even Hitler was thrilled by Nehring's accomplishment. He personally decorated the panzer general with the Swords to his Knight's Cross, while Saucken (who already had the Swords) received the Diamonds. Hitler even let Nehring out of the professional doghouse, at least to a degree, and gave him command of the 1st Panzer Army in Upper Silesia. (He assumed command on March 20.) Nehring, however, did not receive (and never did receive) his promotion to colonel general.

General Nehring knew, of course, that the war was lost. His main objective now was to hold his line and allow as many civilians to escape to the west as possible; then he hoped to escape to the west with his army.

The last Soviet offensive began on April 16. It was too powerful and the Red Army was too fast for Nehring to accomplish everything he wanted to do. Most of 1st Panzer Army was trapped at Deutsch

Brod (now in the Czech Republic) and was forced to surrender to the Soviets. Nehring's army headquarters and a handful of units were at Tabor when the end came and managed to surrender to the Americans.

Walter Nehring was released from the POW camps in 1947 and retired to Duesseldorf, where he lived in a modest apartment. Shunning publicity, he died in Duesseldorf on April 20, 1983.

Hans-Lewin von Barby was born in Berlin on July 25, 1899. He joined the army as a Fahnenjunker in 1917 and fought in World War I. Discharged as a second lieutenant of reserves in 1919, he joined the state police. By 1936, he was a captain of police in Duesseldorf. Later that year, his police company was inducted into the Wehrmacht, and he found himself commanding the 4/77th Infantry Regiment. In late 1938, he was promoted and given command of the I Replacement Training Battalion of the 33rd Infantry Regiment. Five days before the war began, he was named commander of the newly formed 474th Infantry Regiment of the 254th Infantry Division in Muenster. He led this battalion in the Western campaign of 1940, where he was wounded in the leg.

Barby was given command of the III/255th Infantry Regiment at Munsterlager on December 1, 1940. He took this unit to North Africa in early April 1941. That summer, he was promoted and given command of the 361st Afrika (later Infantry) Regiment, which included many former Foreign Legionnaires. When Rommel approached their camp, he always instructed his driver: "Lock up the spare tire. We're coming to the 361st."

The 361st was part of the 90th Light Division and was initially short of motorized transport. It was therefore assigned to the Siege of Tobruk. In the fall and winter of 1941, it took part in several successful defensive battles. On November 30, 1941, Lieutenant Colonel von Barby attacked the British at Sidi Rezegh and prevented a relief force from linking up with the Tobruk garrison. For this he was awarded the Knight's Cross and promoted to colonel.

Barby spearheaded Group Cruewell's diversionary attack against the Gazala Line on May 26, 1942. Unfortunately, he got too close to the action and was badly wounded. He succumbed in the Derna Hospital the next day.[25]

CHAPTER VI

THE STAFF

Alfred Gause served Erwin Rommel for almost three years—longer than any other of his World War II subordinates. (Rommel did not make long-lasting professional associations, in part because he made very few close personal friendships. He also tended to physically wear out subordinates very quickly.) Gause was a solid but not brilliant General Staff officer who, unfortunately, left us no written memoirs and did not speak extensively of his experiences after the war. More than anything else, he was a professional soldier, not given to conspiracy or "office politics." His goal was to serve Germany and the commander(s) appointed above him. He was loyal, long-suffering, and efficient—which is why the Desert Fox retained him as long as he did.

Gause was born in Koenigsberg, East Prussia, on February 14, 1896. He joined the Imperial Army as a Fahnenjunker on March 14, 1914, five months before World War I began. He was commissioned Leutnant in the 18th Engineer Battalion on January 15, 1915. Except for two brief periods when he attended courses of instruction at the Infantry School at Lokstedter Lager (January–February 1918) and the Engineer School at Jemmont (late February–April 6, 1918), Gause spent the entire war with the 18th Engineers. He fought in the battles of Flanders and Champagne, on the Somme, at Cambrai, and on the Marne. He was wounded several times in the process.[1] He became battalion adjutant on October 9, 1918, and was promoted to first lieutenant nine days later—three weeks before the armistice.[2]

After the war, Gause (who was already known for his dry sense of humor) returned to East Prussia, where he was named adjutant of the 1st Engineer Battalion. This was followed by a tour of duty with the staff of the 1st Infantry Division, which—like the 1st Engineers—was headquartered in his home town of Koenigsberg (1921–22). He was then sent back to the 1st Engineers (1922–25) and did another tour as battalion adjutant (1924–25). Gause spent a year with the 1st Artillery Regiment (1925–26), which was also stationed in the East Prussian capital, before undergoing yet another tour with the 1st Engineer Battalion (1926–27). He did the first of the his two recorded tours as a commanding officer in 1927 when he was named commander of the 2nd Company, 1st Engineer Battalion, but this assignment only lasted from February 1 to 28. Meanwhile, his career took a giant leap forward when he scored in the upper 15 percent of his class in the Wehrkreis exam and was selected as a candidate for the General Staff. He immediately began training in Koenigsberg. He was promoted to captain on November 1, 1927, attended a secret training course under the chief of the Troop Office (as the clandestine General Staff was called) from October 1930 to September 1931, and was granted admission into the General Staff on October 1, 1931. (He would not, however, be able to wear the distinctive red strips on his trousers until after Hitler renounced the Treaty of Versailles in 1935.) By now, Gause was on the staff of the 5th Infantry Division in Stuttgart.[3]

Alfred Gause spent the next six years in Wuerttemberg. He was posted to the staff of Wehrkreis V in 1934, and from October 15, 1935, to October 12, 1937, was Ia (chief of operations) of Wehrkreis V, which doubled as V Corps. He was promoted to major on May 1, 1934, to lieutenant colonel on October 1, 1936, and to full colonel on April 1, 1939.[4]

Colonel Gause was assigned to the extremely important Armed Forces Office of the War Ministry in October 1937 and remained there after February 4, 1938, when the ministry became the High Command of the Armed Forces (OKW) under Wilhelm Keitel. Unlike his chief, Gause was not taken in by the Nazis; he was, however, not an anti-Nazi either. He was a simple, highly efficient East Prussian General Staff officer and would remain so until the end of the war.

Gause spent the first two months of World War II in Berlin and did not directly participate in the Polish campaign. On November 1, 1939, however, he was named chief of staff of Lieutenant General Christian Hansen's X Corps, which was then in the process of moving from Warsaw to the Lower Rhine. He directed the staff of this unit in the conquests of Belgium and France in 1940.

After the fall of Paris, Hitler decided to demobilize several divisions of *Landwehr* (older age) troops, and Gause was named chief of the Demobilization Branch in the General Army Office of the High Command of the Army (OKH). Here, he worked closely with Colonel General Franz Halder, the chief of the General Staff. In the middle of this task, he served a three-month period on detached duty on the coast of the English Channel as chief of staff of the XXXVIII Corps, which was then commanded by Erich von Manstein, who is considered by many authorities to be the most brilliant German commander to emerge from World War II. He returned to Zossen (a town south of Berlin, where OKH headquartered) at the end of January 1941.

Colonel Gause remained at OKH until late May 1941, when he was named chief of the German liaison staff to the Italian High Command in North Africa. Here—according to General Halder—Erwin Rommel, the upstart commander of the Afrika Korps, was running amuck. (In his diary, Halder referred to Rommel as "this soldier gone stark mad.") Gause's staff was sent to Libya with very vague instructions. It was not to report *to* Rommel or be subordinate to him; rather, it was to report *on* him to Zossen. In short, Gause's mission was to be a liaison officer and a glorified spy. Possibility to cement Gause's loyalty, OKH promoted him to major general on June 1.

Halder badly underestimated his man, for Alfred Gause had no intention of "playing politics" in Italian North Africa. Almost as soon as Gause arrived in Libya, Rommel "locked his heels." The Desert Fox let him know in no uncertain terms that he alone commanded all German Army forces in Africa—including Gause and his staff. Gause's response was to submit completely. (He also believed in the military principle of unity of command and recognized the danger of a divided command structure.) Gause officially became chief of staff of Panzer Group Afrika on September 1, 1941.[5]

Initially, Gause had to adjust himself to Rommel's unorthodox leadership style. Like many panzer leaders of his day, Rommel often led from the front; unlike his peers, however, he liked to carry his chief of staff *with him* on his visits to the front. This made Gause's job much more difficult and dangerous and did not lead to any commensurate benefits for Rommel, Gause, or Panzer Army Afrika. Also, with Rommel and Gause absent at the front, very junior officers such as Lieutenant Colonel Siegfried Westphal were often left in charge at army headquarters. Such field grade officers were at a distinct disadvantage when dealing with senior Italian generals, who tended to turn up from time to time. In addition, by accompanying Rommel at the front, the chief of staff was much more likely to be killed or wounded than would normally be the case. This fate finally overtook Alfred Gause on June 1. During the Battle of Got el Ualeb (in which the British 150th Infantry Brigade Group was destroyed), a British antitank round almost hit General Gause. He was hurled backward through the air by the force of the blast, landed against the side of a panzer, and suffered a serious brain concussion, in addition to shrapnel wounds. He was out of action for weeks. He was temporarily replaced by Fritz Bayerlein.

Luftwaffe Field Marshal Albert Kesselring, the OB South, visited Gause at the German military hospital at Derne, on the Mediterranean Sea. "My dear Gause … things can't go on like this," Kesselring declared. "Rommel must not cruise about the front line. He's no longer a divisional or corps commander. As an army commander, it must be possible to reach him. You must make him see this."

Perhaps the Luftwaffe marshal expected some degree of sympathy from Gause or Colonel Westphal, who had also been wounded and was in the bed next to Gause. "Herr Feldmarschall," Gause replied, "the colonel general [Rommel] cannot be restrained.... But how could he lead here in Africa from the rear? This is the type of warfare where everything has to be decided from the front." Westphal agreed with the chief of staff.

"One day it might have disastrous consequences, gentlemen," Kesselring concluded.[6]

Because of their loyalty and efficiency, Gause, Westphal, et al. gradually won Rommel over. He realized he needed a General Staff to properly handle his army, and his suspicion and distrust of General Staff officers gradually melted away; in fact, something like friendship developed between Gause and the Desert Fox, although Rommel took care that he did not grow too close to any of his subordinates. He also continued to carry his chief and often other General Staff officers with him to the front. They might become casualties, of course, but Rommel felt that no man was indispensable; they could always be replaced.

While he was recovering in Europe, Alfred Gause actually received a handful of personal letters from Erwin Rommel. When he returned to North Africa in August, he found Panzer Army Afrika in Egypt, only 60 miles from the Nile but stalemated at El Alamein. The Gause who returned was not at his best, because he experienced constant headaches and had obviously not fully recovered from the wounds he had suffered during the Battle of the Gazala Line. In September, he had to return to Europe to take a cure. At the same time, Rommel's deteriorating health also forced him to take a furlough. He was temporarily replaced by General of Panzer Troops Georg Stumme while Westphal replaced Gause.

Rommel returned to North Africa in time to fight in the Second Battle of El Alamein, during which Panzer Army Afrika was finally decisively defeated. On November 8, 1942, the Anglo-Americans launched Operation "Torch," and landed an entire army in the German rear. Instead of abandoning North Africa, however, Hitler decided to establish a second Axis army in Tunisia. On December 7, Gause was named chief of Special Staff Libya and Tunisia in Rome. His job was to furnish Rommel and Colonel General Hans-Juergen von Arnim, commander of the newly activated 5th Panzer Army in Tunisia, with all of the troops and supplies they needed. This task was impossible from the beginning but grew more difficult as the Allied ring tightened on Rommel and Arnim. Meanwhile, Headquarters, Army Group Afrika was created in

Tunisia. Gause became its chief of staff on March 1, 1943, and was promoted to lieutenant general on April 1.

Rommel was recalled to Europe on March 9, 1943, and was sent on involuntary leave. Gause remained behind as Arnim's chief of staff. He performed as well as could have been expected under the circumstances. By May 1943, however, Army Group Afrika's supply lines had collapsed and Axis resistance was crumbling. Arnim, meanwhile, had developed a respect and appreciation for Alfred Gause. Rather than allow his talented chief to fall into enemy hands, Arnim sent him back to Europe on a pretext in early May. Shortly after he departed, Eisenhower launched his final offensive and Axis lines collapsed altogether. The last remnants of Army Group Afrika surrendered on May 12.

As the army group died, Hitler summoned Rommel to Fuehrer Headquarters and admitted that Rommel had been right about North Africa, and that he had been wrong. Germany's strategic problem now became where to defend against the next Allied blow in the Mediterranean. To defend Italy, Hitler entrusted Kesselring's OB South/Army Group C to hold Sicily and southern Italy. He also established a special staff under Field Marshal Rommel to defend northern Italy if the Allies landed there. Rommel naturally picked Alfred Gause as his chief of staff. The staff was upgraded to Headquarters, Army Group B on July 19, 1943.

The Allies landed in Sicily on July 10, 1943, and on the mainland on September 3. The main Allied invasion of Italy began on September 9. By the onset of winter, it was obvious that the Anglo-Saxons had committed themselves south of Rome, and Army Group B's presence in the north was unnecessary. Hitler, therefore, found another job for his erstwhile favorite. Rommel and his staff were ordered to conduct an inspection of the Atlantic Wall. To the Fuehrer's surprise, Rommel and Field Marshal Gerd von Rundstedt, the commander-in-chief, West (OB West), petitioned him to place Army Group B under the command of OB West and give it a sector of the Atlantic Wall to defend. Hitler reluctantly agreed, and Erwin Rommel received his last assignment.

Along with Rommel, Gause and his staff prepared the coasts of France, Belgium, and the Netherlands for the Allied invasion. Meanwhile, Gause's home in East Prussia was destroyed in an Allied bombing raid, so Frau Rommel invited Frau Gause to share her home in Wuerttemberg with her. Unfortunately, Frau Gause was not as submissive to Lucie Rommel as Albert was to Erwin. The two women were soon fighting, which led to a permanent break between the two families. As a result, Gause was placed in Fuehrer Reserve on April 15, 1944. He was replaced by Lieutenant General Hans Speidel.

Rommel was not completely through with Albert Gause. He tried to get his former chief of staff command of a panzer division. This could not be arranged; however, on June 15, 1944, Gause returned to France as acting chief of staff of Panzer Group West. Earlier that week, the headquarters was flattened by an Allied bombing raid, and its chief of staff was killed. It was withdrawn from the Normandy sector and sent to a location near Paris, where it had to be completely rebuilt. Albert Gause was primarily responsible for this task, because the commander of the panzer group, General of Panzer Troops Baron Leo Geyr von Schweppenburg, was recovering from wounds he received during the air raid. Once the job was completed, Panzer Group West returned to the Western Front. It was redesignated 5th Panzer Army on August 5.

During the summer and fall of 1944, General Gause worked under the command of Geyr, General of Panzer Troops Heinrich Eberbach, and SS Colonel General Joseph "Sepp" Dietrich. On September 14, 1944, Dietrich assumed command of the 6th Panzer (later SS Panzer) Army, which was withdrawn to Germany to prepare for what became known as the Battle of the Bulge. When he left for his new post, Dietrich took Gause with him. Then, on November 20, 1944, General Gause was relieved of his duties. Apparently, his previous loyalty to Rommel made him a suspect in the anti-Hitler conspiracy; in any case, Dietrich had another man in mind for the chief of staff position and did not fight to retain him. Gause was without an assignment until January 1945, when he attended a corps commanders' training course. He graduated on January 31 but remained in Fuehrer Reserve until April 1, when he was named commander of the II Corps.

The II Corps was isolated in the Courland Pocket in western Latvia. It was obvious to virtually all of the generals that Germany would soon lose the war. It was equally obvious that the soldiers who would have the least chance of escaping Soviet captivity were those in the Courland Pocket. Someone in the Army Personnel Office obviously had it in for General Gause because of his previous association with the Desert Fox. This was probably General of Infantry Wilhelm Burgdorf, who had offered Rommel a cyanide capsule on October 14, 1944. In any case, Alfred Gause's only command during World War II was an isolated corps far behind Russian lines. He never received his promotion to general of panzer troops and commanded a step above his grade of rank until May 10, 1945, when the II Corps marched into Soviet captivity.

Alfred Gause was not released from prison until October 10, 1955. With his East Prussian home at Koenigsberg now part of Russia, he retired to Karlsruhe, West Germany, where he lived quietly and showed little inclination to tell his story to historians. He died in Bonn on September 30, 1967.

Siegfried Westphal was born in Leipzig on March 18, 1902, the son of an army officer. He graduated from Berlin-Lichterfelde (the foremost cadet academy in Germany) and entered the service at age 16 as a Fahnenjunker in the 12th Infantry Regiment on November 10, 1918. Germany signed the armistice the next day. Westphal remained in the service, however, and was commissioned second lieutenant in the 11th Cavalry Regiment in 1922. In 1932, he was assigned to the War Academy as General Staff candidate. He graduated in August 1935 and was assigned to the operations branch of the General Staff of the army. By 1938, he was a major, commanding a squadron in the 13th Cavalry Regiment at Lueneburg, Wehrkreis X. Just before World War II began, he was named Ia of the 58th Infantry Division, which was immediately sent to the Saar on the Western Front.[7]

As a General Staff officer, Siegfried Westphal had a reputation for both brilliance and arrogance. Certainly he was good at what he did—and knew it. He was named chief of operations of the XXVII Corps on the Lower Rhine on March 5, 1940. His corps fought in Belgium and France in 1940, and he was then posted to eastern France on occupation duty.[8] Westphal, however, was attached to the Franco-German Armistice Commission in August and was engaged in this duty on January 30, 1941, when he was promoted to colonel.[9]

In the summer of 1941, Westphal was sent to North Africa, where he became Ia of Panzer Group Afrika on June 15. He fought in all of the major battles in North Africa from the Siege of Tobruk until the Battle of the Gazala Line. Because of Rommel's command methods, he often had responsibilities that exceeded his rank and position. On November 24, 1941, during the Winter Battles, for example, Rommel struck toward the Egyptian frontier with the entire Afrika Korps, believing that this move would cause the collapse of the British 8th Army. General Sir Alan Cunningham, the army commander, was ready to retreat, but General Sir Claude Auchinleck, the commander-in-chief, Middle East, was not. He fired Cunningham, replaced him with Major General Sir Neil Ritchie, his own chief of staff, and ordered Ritchie to regroup and advance toward Tobruk again, despite Rommel's move, which was later dubbed "the Dash to the Wire."

On November 25, the 2nd New Zealand Division was attacking the weak Group Boettcher at Belhamed. That afternoon, the New Zealand 4th Brigade took the airfield at Gambut, while the 22nd Guards Brigade joined the 2nd New Zealand and mauled Group Boettcher.

Rommel had carried General Gause, his chief of staff, with him as he rode off to the east, leaving Westphal the senior officer at panzer army headquarters. The colonel realized that Boettcher could not hold out indefinitely, and that a major defeat was inevitable if reinforcements were not brought up immediately. The only force available for this task was the Afrika Korps. Westphal was unable to contact Rommel, Gause, or General Cruewell via radio despite multiple attempts. Showing considerable moral courage and placing his career squarely on the line, Westphal signaled General von Ravenstein, reversed Rommel's orders (without indicating this fact to Ravenstein), and ordered the 21st Panzer Division to return to the Tobruk sector. "All orders given to you hitherto are cancelled," the order read. "Twenty-first Panzer Division is to break through the Indian line in the direction of Bardia."[10] The division was 19 miles inside Egypt at the time and headed for a British supply depot, 50 miles to the east.

Rommel did not learn that the 21st Panzer had turned around until Ravenstein reported to him in Bardia. Even then, he thought that the British must have broken the German code. There was nothing to be done about it now, however. He ordered Ravenstein's division to refuel in Bardia and, with the 15th Panzer, personally headed back to the Tobruk sector. When he finally arrived back at army headquarters on the evening of November 27, he found himself in an unexpected confrontation with Westphal. Even though he was furious, Rommel did not say anything; he simply turned on his heel and went to bed. Perhaps he realized that in his anger he might say something he would regret later. The next morning he emerged completely rested, and— much to the relief of his staff—forgave Westphal. He even admitted that the Ia's course of action had been the correct one.[11]

Like everyone else, Westphal found that working for demanding and Spartan Rommel was a difficult business. He nevertheless grew to admire his chief. "The man grew immensely in stature in proportion with his task," he recalled after the war.[12]

Rommel and Westphal had another disagreement on May 31, 1942, and this one almost cost the colonel his life. During the Gazala Line battles, he had gone forward with Rommel in an armored car to make a reconnaissance of the Got el Ualeb Box, to make sure that the Stuka dive-bombers were attacking it correctly. Westphal disagreed with Rommel about a minor point, and Rommel responded with a sharp remark. They were observing the situation from the soft-skinned portion of the armored car when they came under British artillery fire. Rommel dove for cover in the armored part of the vehicle and shouted for Westphal to do the same. The chief of operations, however, was still sulking and did not obey, acting as if he had not heard the general. Suddenly, there was a huge explosion. Siegfried Westphal flew through the air like a bird and landed on the desert floor with a large piece of shrapnel in his upper thigh. Rommel's driver, meanwhile, took off. Fortunately for Westphal, he was picked up by a Kuebelwagen (the German equivalent of a jeep) and taken to headquarters, from which he was sent to the hospital at Derna. He was medically evacuated back to Europe shortly thereafter. He was temporarily replaced by F. W. von Mellenthin, who was by now a close personal friend.

Westphal returned to duty on August 31, 1942. He fought in the 2nd Battle of El Alamein and in the subsequent retreat into Libya. Meanwhile, in October, Westphal was named chief of staff of Panzer Army Afrika (which was redesignated 1st Italian-German Army) to replace Alfred Gause, who had gone to Europe to take a cure. Westphal held this appointment only a short time. On December 1, 1942, Major General Carl-Hans Lungershausen temporarily stepped down as commander of the 164th Light Afrika Division. To his great pride, Westphal was named acting commander. He led it until December 29. Then Lungershausen returned, and Westphal himself reported ill. He never saw North Africa again. Rommel, meanwhile, had recommended him for the Knight's Cross. He received the award on November 29.

Siegfried Westphal returned to duty on February 1, 1943. Now he was working for Luftwaffe Field Marshal Albert "Smiling Al" Kesselring, the commander-in-chief of OB South and Army Group C, who named him chief of operations. Kesselring was much more amiable than Rommel, and Rome was certainly a better environment in which to work than was the Sahara Desert. Also, Westphal's promotion path in North Africa was blocked by Alfred Gause, who would be Rommel's chief of staff until the spring of 1944. Now, working at a higher level (i.e., army group as opposed to army), Westphal had scope for advancement. He was promoted to major general on March 1, 1943.

Westphal became chief of staff of OB South on June 15, 1943. He continued in this post through the invasions of Sicily, Sardinia, Corsica, and Italy, at Salerno and Monte Cassino, and during the Anzio landings. Finally, after a protracted struggle, the Allies broke through the German line and it was questionable whether the German 10th Army would be able to escape. It did, but Rome had to be evacuated. The city fell on June 4, 1944. The next day, Siegfried Westphal (a lieutenant general since April 1, 1944) finally suffered a physical breakdown. He collapsed and had to be evacuated back to Germany. He did not return to duty until September 9.

Westphal's new (and last) assignment was as chief of staff of OB West, a term that referred to the commander-in-chief, West, or his headquarters. Westphal's new boss was 68-year-old Field Marshal Gerd von Rundstedt, who rarely left his luxurious headquarters. Westphal helped the old marshal direct the battles of the Siegfried Line, the Ardennes Offensive, and the subsequent retreat to the Rhine and was by all accounts a better chief than his predecessor, General of Infantry Guenther Blumentritt. Westphal, however, was one of the best General Staff officers in the history of the Wehrmacht. Rundstedt was certainly pleased with his chief of staff and recommended Westphal for promotion. He became a general of cavalry on February 1, 1945.

When the Americans captured the Remagen Bridge on March 6, 1945, Hitler retired Rundstedt for the fourth and final time and replaced him with Kesselring, who was more optimistic, more pro-Nazi, and more energetic than Rundstedt. There was little he could do, however. The U.S. Army encircled and destroyed Army Group B in the Ruhr Pocket in April 1945, and all of Kesselring's efforts to continue the war were doomed. Hitler committed suicide in Berlin on April 30, and Kesselring and Westphal surrendered shortly thereafter.

After the war, Westphal wrote *Defeat in the West*, which was published in 1952. He also worked for the U.S. Historical Branch in Europe and was senior author of a number of manuscripts, mainly about the Italian campaign. He lived to the age of 80, finally succumbing at Celle on July 2, 1982. He was one of the last senior generals of the Wehrmacht to pass into history.

Alfred-Ingemar Berndt was born in Bromberg on April 22, 1905. His natural gift for writing was reinforced by a fine local education. He joined the Nazi Party in 1923 (at the age of 18) and became a Brownshirt by 1925. Meanwhile, he made his living working as a freelance journalist. By 1932, he was a party press leader in Berlin and was deputy editor of Goebbels's party newspaper, *Der Angriff* (The Attack). He joined the staff of the Propaganda Ministry in 1936 as a *Ministerialrat*, became a *Ministerialdirigent* in 1938, and was promoted to *Ministerialdirektor* (a high rank in the Nazi civil service) in 1941. Berndt, meanwhile, received a commission as a second lieutenant of SS reserves in 1934. He briefly served on the staff of Reichsfuehrer-SS Heinrich Himmler and later was on the staff of the *Reichssichheitshauptamt* (*Rishauptamt*)—the Reich Security headquarters, which was headed by the notorious Reinhard Heydrich.

Shortly after the war broke out, Berndt joined the army as a reserve sergeant, stating that no one who had not served at the front had any right to call himself a propagandist. He served in France in 1940, was commissioned second lieutenant of reserves in August 1940, and joined the Afrika Korps when it formed in February 1941 as Ic-Propaganda. He became Goebbels's representative to Panzer Group (later Army) Afrika in August 1941 and to Army Group Afrika in February 1943.

Rommel had an American sense of public relations and used Berndt's talents and contacts to full advantage. The Nazi writer often served as his representative to Berlin or to Fuehrer Headquarters as the occasion demanded it. Using Berndt also made it possible for Rommel to bypass the normal military chain of command and to influence powerful Nazis in his favor. The Desert Fox, meanwhile, used his influence with his friend, Lieutenant General Rudolf Schmundt, the powerful head of the Army Personnel Office, to have Berndt promoted rapidly. He became a first lieutenant in 1942 and a captain in 1943.

For his part, Berndt did much to cultivate and advance the legend of the Desert Fox. The term itself was coined by the British, but the Nazi Propaganda Ministry seized upon it and gave Rommel the maximum possible positive exposure in Germany and the occupied territories. Rommel's friend Goebbels even stated that Rommel would make an excellent commander-in-chief of the Army after the war. Goebbels's diaries are full of references to Rommel and Berndt. His prominence led to an honorary promotion to SS-Brigadefuehrer for Berndt in April 1943.

Berndt remained with Rommel until March 9, 1943, when the Desert Fox was recalled to Europe and was placed in Fuehrer Reserve and, in effect, was relieved of his command. Berndt then returned to the Propaganda Ministry as deputy Reich press chief, rather than returning to Tunisia where the front was collapsing. (Army Group Afrika surrendered on May 12, 1943.)

Alfred Berndt left Berlin in September 1944 and transferred to the SS as a *Hauptsturmfuehrer der Reserve* (SS captain of reserves). Rommel, meanwhile, was forced to commit suicide on October 14, 1944, for his part in the July 20, 1944 attempt to assassinate Hitler and overthrow the Nazi regime. Curiously, in early 1945, Berndt visited Rommel's widow and told her that Keitel and Jodl were responsible for forcing the Desert Fox to kill himself—and that Hitler did not learn of their actions until later. Why Berndt would tell such a lie is not known.

In early 1945, SS Captain Berndt was given command of the II Battalion, 5th SS Panzer Regiment, which was then fighting on the Eastern Front. He was killed in action at Veszprem, Hungary, on March 28, 1945.

The intelligence officers who served Erwin Rommel were, generally speaking, very good. They all had the same training and, according to Hans-Otto Behrendt, the deputy Ic (chief intelligence officer) of Panzer Army Afrika for most of the war, "They were used to sizing up the facts clearly, to estimating enemy strength without illusions, and to depict it objectively and without undue pessimism." While not perfect, they could "acquire an insight into the enemy's intentions without drifting into the realms of fantasy ... and there was little if any exaggeration evident in their reports...."[13]

The first Ic of the Afrika Korps was Major von Plehwe (February–March 1941). He was succeeded by Captain Count Wolf von Baudissin, an excellent officer who, unfortunately, was shot down on a reconnaissance flight near Tobruk on April 5, 1941, and spent the rest of the war in Allied prison camps. He was succeeded by Captain Roestel.

Rommel's most famous intelligence officer was Major Friedrich Wilhelm von Mellenthin, who was Ic of Panzer Group (later Panzer

Army) Afrika from August 15, 1941 until May 30, 1942. After he temporarily moved up to chief of operations (after Siegfried Westphal was wounded), Captain Hans-Otto Behrendt served as acting Ic until Major Ernst Zolling (the chief intelligence officer of the Afrika Korps) replaced Mellenthin as Ic of the panzer army in August.

Captain Roestel replaced Count von Baudissin after he was captured at Tobruk.

Born on June 17, 1910, he was commissioned Leutnant in the 3rd Engineer Battalion. He began attending the War Academy on November 3, 1938, and was attached to the Operations Branch of the High Command of the Army during the Polish and French campaigns. In late 1940, he was named Ic of the XXXIX Motorized Corps, which was then on occupation duty in southwestern France, and in April 1941, he became chief intelligence officer of the Afrika Korps.[14]

With limited resources and inadequate maps, Roestel was unable to give Rommel an adequate picture of the Tobruk defenses. Partially as a result, the Desert Fox attacked some of the stronger sectors of the perimeter and was unable to crush the garrison. Neither Rommel nor Roestel were able to obtain much cooperation from the Italians, who had constructed the defenses before 1941. During Operations "Brevity" and "Battleaxe," however, Roestel was able to give Rommel a reasonably accurate picture of British dispositions and intentions. He was a good Ic, although not as good as Zolling, his eventual successor. Rommel, however, was satisfied with his performance and had him promoted.

Major Roestel reported himself ill on October 10, 1941, and was sent back to Europe. Two months later, on December 15, he returned to active duty and became Ic of the Guderian's 2nd Panzer Army, a definite promotion. He labored at this post for a year and a half, serving on the central sector of the Eastern Front. He was promoted to lieutenant colonel on May 1, 1943.

After a brief period of service on detached duty at OKH in Zossen, and as Ia of Wehrkreis XI (August 1–31, 1943), Roestel was named Ic of the 18th Army, effective October 25, 1943. His intelligence estimates predicted that the Soviets would launch a major offensive to break the Siege of Leningrad and turned out to be all too accurate. The 18th Army was smashed and had to retreat into the Baltic States. Colonel Roestel, meanwhile, was recalled to Berlin in late February 1944.

After receiving an orientation on the situation in the Balkans, Roestel was named Ia of the Wehrmacht Military Mission to Romania, which was headed by General of Cavalry Eric Hansen.[15] The mission was "taken in" by the Romanian generals, who averred loyalty to the Third Reich, while secretly planning to defect at the earliest opportunity. The mission also did not appreciate the fact that the Red Army was about to attack the German and Romanian forces in overwhelming strength.

Roestel was still in this position on August 20, 1944, the "Black Sunday" of the German Army in World War II. On that day, Soviet Marshal Timoshenko attacked the Axis forces in Romania with 920,000 men, 1,400 tanks, 1,700 airplanes, and 16,000 guns, rocket launchers, and mortars. Colonel General Johannes Friessner's Army Group South Ukraine met the attack with 46 understrength divisions—half of them Romanian. The total strength of his German formations was 360,000 men, supported by fewer than 60 tanks, 280 assault guns, and 232 airplanes. The Romanian units promptly dissolved and went home or—in many cases—simply joined the Russians and turned their guns on their former Allies. The Reds poured through the gaps in the Axis line. The German 6th Army was overwhelmed, along with sizable parts of the 8th Army. Among the 250,000 Germans who disappeared during this offensive was Colonel Roestel. He was last heard from in Bucharest on August 31, 1944, the day Stalin's legions entered the city.

Friedrich Wilhelm ("F. W.") von Mellenthin (pronounced *Fon Mell-enn-teen*) was born in Breslau, Silesia (now Wroclaw, Poland) on August 30, 1904. His father, a professional army officer from Pomerania—the most Prussian of the Prussian provinces—could trace his ancestry back to 1225. His mother, Orlinda von Waldenburg von Mellenthin, was a great-granddaughter of Prince August of Prussia and a great-grandniece of Frederick the Great. His family looked upon military service as a calling, not a job. Naturally, F. W. was raised from the crib to be an officer. This traditional Prussian upbringing was continued by Orlinda even after her husband—Lieutenant Colonel Paul Henning von Mellenthin—was killed in action while directing artillery fire on the Western Front on June 29, 1918.[16] F. W. later referred to his mother as his "guiding star."[17] Two of her three sons became generals.[18]

F. W. grew up on the family estates of Mellenthin and Lienichen in Pomerania. He graduated from high school (*Real-Gymnasium*) in Breslau and enlisted as a *lancer* (private) in the 7th Cavalry Regiment, because there were no officer slots available in the 100,000-man or "Treaty" army. Although F. W. later recalled the next 11 years were the best of his military life, the first four (when he was an enlisted man) were tough. After 18 months, he was promoted to corporal, and, as a Fahnenjunker, was sent to officers' training courses at the Infantry School at Ohrdruf and the Cavalry School at Hanover. Finally, on February 1, 1928, he was commissioned second lieutenant in the 7th Cavalry. He spent the next seven years with his regiment.

Although he was short—only 5' 6"—F. W. von Mellenthin was slim, intelligent, urbane, and full of energy. He was a fine equestrian and won many golden trophies for horse racing, steeplechasing, and dressage. Even as an octogenarian, he spent at least two hours a day on horseback.

On March 2, 1932, he married Ingeborg von Aulock, the daughter of a major. She would give him two sons and three daughters.

Mellenthin was very happy in the 7th Cavalry, but nevertheless accepted an appointment to the War Academy on October 1, 1935, where he began his General Staff training. (Along with more than 1,000 other officers, he had taken the week-long Wehrkreis qualifying examination and had finished in the upper 15 percent that were selected for General Staff training. About two thirds of these survivors were cut before the course was completed.) He finished the two-year course in the fall of 1937 and, as a captain, was assigned to the staff of Wehrkreis III in Berlin. Its commander was General of Infantry Erwin von Witzleben, of whom Mellenthin was very fond. Shortly after his posting, Mellenthin became his Ic. He was also involved in several special events, such as military parades and ceremonies put on to honor various foreign dignitaries. He also served for a few weeks as army liaison officer to Konrad Henlein, the leader of the Sudeten Germans. After the annexation of the Sudetenland, Mellenthin returned to Berlin, where he was largely responsible for planning a parade honoring Hitler's 50th birthday. By now, "I was tired of running a military circus," the young Prussian recorded.[19] He arranged to return to a line unit and was ordered to report to the 5th Panzer Regiment of the 5th Light Division on October 1, 1939. Unfortunately, World War II began on September 1, and his transfer was cancelled.

Mellenthin served as III Corps Ic during the Polish campaign and during its redeployment to the Western Front near Saarbruecken. That winter, he was sent back to what had been Poland, where (as a major) he became Ia of the 197th Infantry Division, then training at Posen. This division was later transferred to the Western Front, where it was assigned to Army Group C, which performed a purely secondary role in the French campaign of 1940. After France surrendered, the 197th was send to Breda, the Netherlands, where it performed occupation duties.

After a few weeks duty in Holland, which he thoroughly enjoyed, von Mellenthin was transferred to the 1st Army Headquarters in Lorraine, where he was named chief intelligence officer. His commander was his old boss, Erwin von Witzleben, who was now a field marshal, and who no doubt arranged his transfer. Mellenthin lived in a Gothic castle in Nancy and again very much enjoyed his assignment. He noted in his classic book, *Panzer Battles*, that "It is a matter of regret that Gestapo officials soon raised a barrier between the occupation troops and the civil population." He found that many prominent

Frenchmen held "a genuine desire" to co-operate in the establishment of a United Europe but were soon alienated by the Nazis.[20]

In the winter of 1940–41, Mellenthin worked on plans for the rapid occupation of Vichy, France, which was connected to the plan to rapidly send German forces to Spain, so that they could occupy Gibraltar. Generalissomo Franco, the Spanish dictator, would have none of it, however, so Mellenthin arranged to have a brief period of temporary duty with an Italian cavalry regiment at Genova. In late March 1941 he was named Ic of the 2nd Army, which was then assembling in Austria for the invasion of Yugoslavia.

The Germans invaded Yugoslavia and Greece on April 6, 1941. Although the Greeks (who were aided by the British) put up stiff resistance, the Yugoslavian forces collapsed almost immediately. Belgrade fell on April 12 and the Yugoslavs surrendered five days later. Mellenthin called the operation "virtually a military parade."[21]

After the capitulation, Mellenthin was named German liaison officer to the Italian 2nd Army, which was on occupation duty along the Dalmatian coast in the Balkans. Here, F. W. was amazed by the obsolete equipment of the Italian Army, as well as the low standard of training he found among the junior officers. This new job did not last long, however; at the end of May, he was ordered to report to Munich. Here he joined the Gause's special staff, which was then forming in Bavaria, where he was the new Ic. (Later, this became Staff, Panzer Army Afrika.) En route, he took a short leave and visited his ancestral estates, where his wife had moved along with their five children, to get them away from the bombing of Berlin. On June 11, Mellenthin, along with General Gause and Lieutenant Colonel Siegfried Westphal, the Ia of the panzer group, flew from Rome to Tripoli. On the trip over, they got a view of things to come: several times they were forced to avoid British airplanes by flying at sea level. Then they met with Erwin Rommel.

Mellenthin had met Rommel in Berlin in 1938, but he was in no way prepared for what he faced working for the Desert Fox: "Rommel was not an easy man to serve; he spared those around him as little as he spared himself. An iron constitution and nerves of steel were needed to work with Rommel, but I must emphasize that although Rommel was sometimes embarrassingly outspoken ... once he was convinced of the efficiency and loyalty of those in his immediate entourage, he never had a harsh word for them."[22] Rommel was by every account a hard man for whom to work. He could be very rude to his staff and scathing to senior commanders (especially Italians), but never so to enlisted men or prisoners of war. His men (including lower-ranking Italians) loved him, but this was not always the case with his staff and immediate subordinates. Mellenthin, however, recalled that "I was to learn to love and honor [him] as one of the outstanding generals of our times, the Seydlitz of the panzer corps, and perhaps the most daring and thrustful commander in German military history."[23]

Mellenthin served Rommel for 15 months, from June 1941 to September 15, 1942. "He was the toughest taskmaster I've ever known. He spared no one, least of all himself," von Mellenthin recalled.[24]

During the actual fighting, Rommel was often out of touch with his staff for days. When he did return to headquarters, "He would arrive from the field covered with dust and grime, burst into the command post, and gruffly demand, 'Wie ist die Lage?'" [What is the situation?] To which Westphal and I would instantly respond with a crisp 5-minute summary." It would take Rommel no more than 30 seconds to analyze the facts and issue standing orders for an entire week. "Very seldom did these need to be modified," Mellenthin marveled.[25]

Mellenthin fought in all of the battles of Panzer Army Afrika from the Siege of Tobruk to the 1st Battle of El Alamein. He and his staff badly underestimated the strength of the British 8th Army before the Battle of the Gazala Line, largely because of British aerial parity (which limited the effectiveness of Luftwaffe reconnaissance aircraft), excellent camouflage techniques, commendable radio security (alas vastly superior to that of the American army, even today), and armored car superiority, which prevented the German reconnaissance battalions from gaining a true picture of the situation. Panzer Army intelligence also failed to detect the presence of a large number of Grant tanks (which were superior to any German tank in the desert in 1942), underestimated both the length and depth of the British minefields, failed to note the existence of the Knightsbridge box (and its garrison, the 201st Guards Brigade), and failed to locate and identify two armored and three infantry brigades, including the 3rd Indian Motor Brigade, southwest of Bir Hacheim. Mellenthin later noted that perhaps this was fortunate because had he known the true strength of the 8th Army, even Rommel might not have attacked it. Rommel did not hold any of these failures against von Mellenthin, however, and promoted him to chief of operations on June 1, 1942, after both Gause and Westphal had been wounded. With Rommel's approval, Mellenthin was promoted to lieutenant colonel on April 1, 1942.

Mellenthin more than redeemed himself during the 1st Battle of El Alamein. The British commander, General Sir Claude Auckinleck, abandoned the Qaret el Abd box on the southern part of the front to lure Rommel into committing his armored reserve to that sector. For once, Rommel fell into the trap. On July 9, 1942, he concentrated the 21st Panzer and 90th Light Divisions for an attack on the British left (southern) flank, as well as the Littorio Armored, one of the best Italian divisions. Naturally, being Rommel, he went with them and carried his chief of staff with him, leaving Mellenthin in charge at army headquarters. Then, on July 10, the 9th Australian Division launched a major attack against the Italian Sabratha Infantry Division, on the panzer army's northern (coastal) flank. Sabratha soon collapsed altogether.

Panzer Army Headquarters was behind the Axis northern (coastal) flank, i.e., right behind Sabratha. Mellenthin watched with alarm as hundreds of Italians fled past him to the rear. He soon learned that all of the Italian artillery had been captured. His first inclination, of course, was to move the headquarters to the rear as well, saving its valuable documents and irreplaceable equipment. Mellenthin, however, realized that there was nothing in reserve and that the coastal road had to be blocked or the entire panzer army would be threatened with annihilation. He organized the staff into an ad hoc battle group and reinforced it with some nearby anti-aircraft guns, as well as some German infantry replacements who were passing by. With this improvised unit, the chief of operations managed to check the Australian attack, although valuable personnel were killed in the process. (Among them were Lieutenant Seebohm and most of his Wireless Intercept Unit.)

Before the Australians could reorganize and launch another attack, Rommel rushed up from the south with his personal battle group (the *Kampfstaffel*) and a battle group from the 15th Panzer Division and struck them in the rear. Although he was checked and the Australians managed to inflict heavy casualties on the Trento Infantry Division, the main body of the German 382nd Infantry Regiment of the 164th Light Afrika Division arrived that afternoon, and the panzer army was saved. In his *Papers*, Rommel praised Mellenthin by name for halting the Australian attack, something he rarely did.[26]

Colonel Siegfried Westphal returned from the hospital during the night of August 30–31 and resumed his duties as Ia. Mellenthin was now an excess officer and was no longer essential to the staff of Panzer Army Afrika, as Major Zolling had replaced him as Ic (see below). Additionally, Mellenthin had been suffering from amoebic dysentery for months and was by now a very sick man. (This disease is often fatal, even today.) The medical officer had already recommended that he return to Europe. On September 9, he reported "off duty" to Rommel and left North Africa as few days later. He never saw Erwin Rommel again.

To Lieutenant Colonel von Mellenthin, who had just spent 15 months in the Sahara Desert, the next several in the hospital at Garmisch in the Bavarian Alps seemed like heaven. The German Tropical Institute had developed excellent methods for combating the amoebas, and F. W.'s health soon improved. The situation on the Eastern Front, however, was deteriorating. The German 6th Army under General of Panzer Troops Friedrich Paulus bogged down in street fighting in Stalingrad, and on November 19, 1942, the Red Army launched a huge counter-offensive aimed at encircling the 6th. The Reds brushed aside Paulus's reserve, the XXXXVIII Panzer Corps, and the Russians surrounded 240,000 German and Romanian soldiers in the Stalingrad pocket on November 23.

With a moderate degree of justification, Adolf Hitler held the commander of the XXXXVIII Panzer, Lieutenant General Ferdinand Heim, responsible for the disaster.[27] He relieved Heim of his command on November 20 and had him thrown into prison without a trial. Colonel Werner Friebe, the chief of staff, was also sacked.[28] They were replaced by General of Panzer Troops Otto von Knobelsdorff and Lieutenant Colonel Friedrich William von Mellenthin, respectively.[29]

Mellenthin fought in most of the major battles on the southern sector of the Russian Front from November 29, 1942, until September 14, 1944. He performed brilliantly in desperate fighting under Knobelsdorff and his successor, General of Panzer Troops Hermann Balck, and left us a wonderful account of these battles in his classic book, *Panzer Battles*, which has been in almost continuous print since the University of Oklahoma Press first published it in 1956. He served as acting commander of the 8th Panzer Division during the Battle of Brody (July 1944) and was chief of staff of the 4th Panzer Army under Balck from August 15 to September 14, 1944. When Balck was named commander-in-chief of Army Group G in September 1944, he took Mellenthin with him to the Western Front.[30] Mellenthin was promoted to colonel on May 1, 1943.

Balck and Mellenthin led Army Group G (with the understrength 1st and 19th Armies) brilliantly during the Lorraine campaign in the Vosges against the U.S. 7th and 3rd Armies and the French 1st Army. Army Group G had been severely mauled during the retreat from France. The 19th Army, for example, lost 1,316 of its 1,480 guns during the retreat, and only 10 of its tanks survived. Balck and his chief of staff were able to hastily rebuild it (and least partially) and were greatly aided by OB West, whose chief of staff was Siegfried Westphal, Mellenthin's old friend from Africa. Despite odds stacked heavily against them (some of their panzer divisions were down to five operational tanks), they managed to hold their lines—in part because of Allied supply difficulties. They even checked Patton in the 1st Battle of Metz, delayed the Allied attack on the West Wall for months, and were largely responsible for enabling OB West to launch the Ardennes Offensive on December 16, 1944. They were unable to hold off the Allies forever, however, and could not prevent Patton from taking Metz (on November 21) or the French from taking Strasbourg (November 24).

Meanwhile, Colonel General Heinz Guderian, the "father" of the blitzkrieg, had been acting chief of the General Staff since July 21, 1944.

In late November, he sent an emissary to Headquarters, Army Group G, with some gratuitous advice on how to employ artillery. Compared with the Americans and their allies, however, Army Group G had only a few guns, and they had only a few rounds each. Mellenthin did not appreciate the interference. "Our problem that late in the war was not how to employ artillery, but where to get the guns and ammunition.... We were critically short on everything."[31] He spoke bluntly—too bluntly—to the OKH representative, who returned to Zossen and complained to Guderian that Mellenthin had insulted and then ignored him.

Now Guderian was upset but, unlike Mellenthin, he had the power to do something about it. He summoned the Pomeranian to Zossen on November 28, gave him a thorough tongue-lashing, and placed him under house arrest.

"I said nothing in my own defense, absolutely nothing," Mellenthin recalled.[32] He knew that Guderian was famous for his explosive temper and, if he said anything at all, it would only make the situation worse. Ironically, Mellenthin's last promotion—to major general—had already been approved. It became effective on December 1, 1944, while he was still locked up. He was then sacked as chief of staff of Army Group G. He returned to Balck's headquarters on December 5, 1944, but only to hand over his duties to his successor, Major General Helmut Staedke.

In *Panzer Battles*, Mellenthin implied (but did not explicitly state) that Hitler was to blame for his relief, dismissal from the General Staff, and arrest. He told the whole story to U.S. Lieutenant Colonel Verner R. Carlson when that officer flew to South Africa just to visit with him in the late 1980s. Although he did not lie in *Panzer Battles*, he did not tell the entire truth either. Why is not known.

Mellenthin's arrest turned out to be a blessing in disguise. He had the opportunity to visit his family (now living in the Warthegau) and spent Christmas with them—the only Christmas of the war he got to spend at home. Then he got them out of there because the Red Army was not far off. Three weeks later, it broke through the thin German line and overran the Warthegau and much of Silesia and East Prussia, leaving countless tales of rape, murder, and horror in their wake. Mellenthin meanwhile relocated his wife and five children to temporary quarters with friends north of Berlin.

After Guderian cooled down, he decided to reemploy Mellenthin. This was probably because of Guderian's long-standing friendship with Hermann Balck, who had served as a regimental commander under Guderian when he broke the back of the French Army in 1940. (Guderian speaks very highly of Balck in his autobiography, *Panzer Leader*.) Balck was dismissed as C-in-C of Army Group G because of a

Himmler intrigue in mid-December 1944, and Guderian managed to obtain another command for Balck—6th Army on the Eastern Front. Although we have no details, the issue of Mellenthin must have arisen when the two old comrades met in December 1944. In any case, Guderian was not yet ready to restore Mellenthin to the General Staff, but gave him command of a regiment in the 9th Panzer Division instead. He reported to Headquarters, Army Group B on the Western Front on December 28 and took command of his regiment the next day. He found that it only had about 400 men left.

Mellenthin led his new command in the Battle of Houffalize and in the final stages of the Battle of the Bulge, during which he beat off several American attacks. His unit formed the rear guard of the 5th Panzer Army, and Mellenthin's experiences in Russia proved invaluable, as he knew much more about retreating through ice and snow than did his opponents. By the end of the battle, Mellenthin was out of Guderian's "dog house." Meanwhile, General of Panzer Troops Baron Hasso von Manteuffel, the commander of the 5th Panzer Army, was transferred to the Eastern Front. He was replaced by Colonel General Joseph Harpe. Mellenthin was picked to be Harpe's chief of staff. He took over on March 5.

Mellenthin's account of the last days of the war is thin, in large part because he did not care to remember that bitter episode of his life. Army Group B (composed of the 5th Panzer and 15th Armies) was surrounded in the Ruhr Pocket on April 1. Resistance collapsed relatively quickly. On April 15, Field Marshal Walter Model ordered the army group to break into small bands and to try to escape to the east. He discharged older and younger men from the service on April 17 and ordered everyone to cease fighting, in effect dissolving the army group. He committed suicide the next day.

F. W. von Mellenthin was not yet ready to go into the POW camps. With a handful of other officers, he broke out of the pocket and headed east, traveling by night and hiding by day. It was too late, however. Hitler committed suicide on April 30, and Mellenthin was captured by American soldiers at Hoexter Wesel on May 3.

Mellenthin spent the next two and a half years as a prisoner of war. When he was released, his estates in the East and all of his wealth were gone. He spent the next three years as a homeless refugee in West Germany, which was now a land of little or no opportunity. In 1950, he emigrated to South Africa, where prospects were better. He at least had family there, as his wife's grandfather had moved there in 1868. In his late 40s—an age in which most people start thinking about retirement—F. W. von Mellenthin started over in the business world. Three years later, with little aviation experience or background, he started his own airline, Trek Air, which later became Luxavia. He managed to capture a sizable portion of Lufthansa's market, so much so that Lufthansa hired him as its regional director. Trek Air, meanwhile, became very profitable. He later commented that success in the airline business—indeed any business—was "really only a matter of good staff work and selecting the right people."[33] Using his General Staff principles and his talent for picking the right person for the right job, Mellenthin retired a rich man.

The short ex-general with the pale blue eyes continued to work almost until his death. He rode his horses two hours every day and spent eight hours a day at his desk as an unpaid consultant to various charities. He also consulted for NATO and the U.S. Army, spoke to various Western war colleges, and maintained contact with his extended family. Once a year he flew to West Germany and attended a dinner with his old regiment, the 7th Cavalry. (These reunions were held in Wiesbaden, West Germany, because Breslau had been taken over by Poland and renamed Wroclaw.) Finally, he went the way of all mortals and died at Johannesburg, South Africa, on June 28, 1997, at the age of 92.

Ernst Zolling succeeded Friedrich Wilhelm von Mellenthin as chief intelligence officer of Panzer Army Afrika.

Zolling was born on July 26, 1903, and joined the Reichsheer. He was commissioned in the artillery and was on the staff of the II Battalion, 59th Artillery Regiment as a captain in 1936. He passed his preliminary (Wehrkreis) General Staff examination in early 1937 and began his training at the War Academy on October 5, 1937. His formal training ended on August 26, 1939, when he was assigned to the staff of Arko 27 (the 27th Artillery Command). This new staff controlled the artillery of the newly formed XXVII Corps, which helped guard the lower Rhine in 1939 when most of the Wehrmacht was busy overrunning Poland.

On February 5, 1940, Zolling became Ic of the VIII Corps, which was in the Eifel (the German Ardennes) as part of the 4th Army. Now a major, Zolling discovered that he liked military intelligence and remained in that area of specialization virtually for the rest of his career. Meanwhile, the German Army invaded France and the Low Countries on May 10, and Zolling played a part in the battles of Liege, Arras, and Calais. The VIII Corps remained in Army Group B's reserve, while the bulk of the German Army completed the mopping up operations in France in June.

Ernst Zolling, meanwhile, had completed his probationary period and was admitted to the General Staff on July 20, 1940.

For the next several months, VIII Corps prepared for the invasion of the United Kingdom—an invasion that never came. It remained on the coast of the English Channel until the end of 1940, when it was transferred to Bialystok in German-occupied Poland. It crossed into the Soviet Union on June 22, 1941, and fought in all of the major battles of 9th Army, Army Group Center, until November 1941. By this point, even the corps units had taken severe casualties, and the VIII Corps was sent back to Paris to rebuild and recuperate. The VIII later returned to Russia and was destroyed at Stalingrad. Zolling was not with it, however. He had been transferred to the desert and arrived in North Africa on December 21, 1941. After six weeks on the staff of Panzer Army Afrika, he became Ic of the Afrika Korps on February 15, 1942.

According to Hans-Otto Behrendt, the deputy chief intelligence officer of the panzer army, Mellenthin assessed Allied intentions on the basis of a "realistic intuition," whereas Zolling made his deductions from "logic."[34] He proved to be better than Mellenthin at sorting out the enemy's strength and order of battle. To do this, he relied primarily (but not entirely) on what the Germans called the "Good Source"—items cabled by the American Military attaché in Cairo, Colonel Bonner Frank Fellers, to Washington. In August 1941, the Italian Military Intelligence Service (SIM) had succeeded in persuading a clerk in the U.S. Embassy in Rome to open a safe containing the top secret American Military Attaché Code (called the "Black Code"), to photocopy it and the relevant code-key tables, and to replace both without being discovered or arousing suspicion. The German *Abwehr* (the Military Intelligence Branch at OKW in Berlin) was able to intercept Fellers' coded telegrams, translate them, and have them in the hands of Rommel's intelligence officers within a day. As a result, the Axis had a source of the utmost strategic, operational, and even tactical importance.

Zolling was also excellent as a counterintelligence officer. The British soldier had been well trained on how to act if he was captured. Every British soldier was given an excellent pamphlet entitled "The Answer to this is Silence." It instructed the British prisoner on what questions a German or Italian interrogator was likely to ask and which questions to refuse to answer—which was most of them. Before Zolling, the German leadership had preferred not to dwell on the possibility that a German or Italian might be captured and had no such guidance. Axis POWs were, therefore, revealing far too much, and British intelligence officers were harvesting an intelligence bonanza. Zolling corrected this glaring omission. He had "The Answer to this is Silence" modified and translated into an instructional leaflet, which every German soldier was ordered to keep with his paybook. When interrogated, the German soldier was to give his name, rank, date of birth, place of birth, and place of residence. All other questions were to be answered: "I cannot answer that." He knew that the British would respect this response. He also warned the *Landser* that if they were captured, the British were fond of placing hidden microphones in areas where prisoners might converse freely. They were also good at placing agents in POW camps or collection points. Disguised as fellow prisoners of war, they could discreetly pump a real prisoner for information and were an excellent source of military intelligence.[35] The Abwehr and SIM were, of course, doing the same thing.

Friedrich Wilhelm von Mellenthin was an excellent General Staff officer, and every historian of this era owes him a huge debt for his classic book, *Panzer Battles*; it seems evident, however, that he was not as effective an intelligence officer as was Ernst Zolling. Very few were. Unfortunately for Rommel, this excellent officer was forced to leave North Africa with amoebic dysentery during the retreat from Egypt. He was temporarily succeeded by Hans-Otto Behrendt.

Zolling was placed in Fuehrer Reserve on November 23, 1942, and it would take him six months to regain his health. While still seriously ill, he was promoted to lieutenant colonel, effective January 1, 1943.

Ernst Zolling returned to active duty on May 15, 1943, as Ic of Field Marshal Albert Kesselring's OB South, which was then headquartered in Rome. Once more he did an excellent job and remained at this post until September 10, 1944, when he became Ic of OB West under Field Marshal Gerd von Rundstedt. Promoted to colonel on November 1, 1944, he was "inherited" by Kesselring when he became OB West in March 1945. He surrendered to the Americans at the end of the war.

Captain Hans-Otto Behrendt was the acting Ic until November 25, 1942, when Captain (later Major) Leibl arrived. He held the post until May 1943, when the panzer army (now dubbed the 1st Italian-German Panzer Army) surrendered in Tunisia.

Another officer who could not stand the rigors of the harsh desert climate indefinitely was Dr. Walther Asal, the chief medical officer of the panzer army.

Asal was born in Bruchsal on June 14, 1891, and served in World War I and the Reichsheer. He was promoted to *Oberstarzt* (colonel in the medical service corps) in 1932 and was stationed in Dresden as a member of the medical staff of the 4th Medical Battalion when Hitler came to power. Later, he was named chief medical officer of the 4th Infantry Division (also in Dresden) and served with that unit during the invasion of Poland.[36] In March 1940, he was named chief medical officer of the XI Corps and served with that unit during the invasion of Belgium and the Dunkirk campaign. Later the XI was earmarked for participation in Operation "Sea Lion," the invasion of Great Britain, which never came. The corps performed occupation duties in western France until the spring of 1941. In March 1941, the XI Corps was attached to the 12th Army and took part in the invasion of Yugoslavia the following month. After briefly commanding occupation forces in Serbia, the XI was sent to the Russian Front in July 1941, and, as part of the 11th Army, penetrated the Pruth River line, en route to its ultimate destruction at Stalingrad. Asal, meanwhile, had been recognized as a highly competent medical officer and administrator. He was sent to North Africa and, on August 13, 1941, assumed his new post as chief medical officer of Panzer Group Afrika. A promotion to *General-arzt* (major general in the medical service corps) followed on October 1, 1941.[37]

Dr. Asal did as well as anyone could have in North Africa, conducting preventative medicine (insofar as was possible), tending to wounded, and conducting medical evacuations. He even supervised an early vitamin program that, although primitive by today's standards, was considered revolutionary in its day and led to charges by the Allies that the "Nazis" were trying to create supermen. This was not true, but Asal was making every effort to take care of the troops of Panzer Army Afrika, who had to subsist in a harsh environment and on an inadequate diet. Asal and his staff also took care of the wounded during the Siege of Tobruk, the Winter Battles of 1941–42, the retreat from Cyrenaica, the recapture of Benghazi, the Battle of the Gazala Line, the capture of Tobruk, the drive into Egypt, and the 1st Battle of El Alamein. It is to his credit that wounded Allied troops who fell into his hands received exactly the same care and treatment as wounded German and Italian soldiers. Once again, Rommel was served by a highly competent and responsible subordinate. The tremendous responsibilities of his job, coupled with the relentless heat of the Sahara, finally took their toll on Dr. Asal, however. He fell sick and had to be evacuated to Germany. He was placed in Fuehrer Reserve on September 12, 1942.

It took Walther Asal almost two years to recover. When he finally reported fit for duty, he was immediately named commandant of the Military Medical Academy, a post he assumed on August 1, 1944. Two months later, on October 1, he was promoted to *Generalstabsarzt* (lieutenant general of the medical service corps), the second highest rank one could achieve in his branch. Asal continued to run the academy until 1945, when it was overrun by the Allies. When the Soviets and Americans joined hands in April 1945, cutting the Third Reich in two, Asal was named chief of medical affairs of the Armed Forces Staff North (*Wehrmachtsstab Nord*). Hitler committed suicide a few days later, on April 30, 1945, and was succeeded by Grand Admiral Karl Doenitz, who headquartered in Flemsburg, northern Germany. The Doenitz government was liquidated on May 23, and Dr. Asal surrendered to the British.

Many German physicians disgraced themselves by committing inhumane (and indeed inhuman) acts during World War II and were later tried as war criminals. No such charges, however, were ever leveled against Dr. Walther Asal. The British released him from the POW camps and he returned to private practice. He died on April 21, 1987, at the age of 95.

Dr. Hans-Joachim Barnewitz was another noted medical officer. Like Walther Asal, he had no special training for directing medical services in the desert. Unlike Asal and almost every other officer described in this book, Barnewitz never showed any particular interest in a military career.

He was born in the Charlottenburg suburb of Berlin on August 18, 1892. Instead of volunteering for military service in World War I, as did the vast majority of his peers, young Barnewitz opted for a university education and then medical school. After launching a promising career in private practice and in medical administration, he was inducted into the German Army on March 1, 1938, largely because Hitler's rapidly expanding military needed physicians. Because of his education and experience, Barnewitz was awarded the rank of *Oberfeldarzt* (lieutenant colonel in the Medical Service Corps). Initially, he was assigned to the staff of the Army Hospital in Koenigsburg, East Prussia. In August 1939, however, he was named chief medical officer (CMO) of the 228th Infantry Division.

The 228th Infantry was a Landwehr unit, composed mainly of older-age reservists. It was officially created on August 16, 1939, and was mobilized only 10 days later. It played a minor role in the Polish campaign and was then assigned to Frontier Guard Command Center, where it performed occupation and security duties in the Warsaw area until May 1940.[38] Dr. Barnewitz, meanwhile, was "promoted." On February 5, 1940, he was named CMO of the 6th Infantry Division, a regular army unit then stationed on the Mosel and preparing for the invasion of Belgium.

As was the case with all German divisional chief medical officers, Barnewitz's command included medical aid and evacuation stations, a fully motorized ambulance unit, and a divisional hospital. The 6th Infantry crossed the frontier on May 10, 1940, and was involved in heavy fighting in Belgium and in the Battle of Dunkirk. It took part in the subsequent conquest of France and in the preparatory phases of Operation "Sealion," the invasion of Britain. After this operation was cancelled, Barnewitz and his unit remained in France on occupation duty. He was promoted to Oberstarzt on March 1, 1941.

Colonel Dr. Barnewitz was transferred to Libya in June 1941 as German Medical Officer to the Italian High Command in Africa. Four months later, on October 13, 1941, he became CMO of the Afrika Korps. Dr. Barnewitz now had an extremely difficult medical challenge, for there were many problems in the DAK. With the Royal Navy and Air Force strangling Rommel's supply lines, the diet of the average soldier was totally inadequate. This, coupled with wounds, the tremendous exertions of combat operations, sand fleas, and the long-term strain of the harsh environment of the Sahara Desert all combined to take their toll on the men of the Afrika Korps—and on Colonel Barnewitz, who was twice the age of the average "African," as the German soldier in Libya called himself. Barnewitz nevertheless served during the Siege of Tobruk, in Operations "Battleaxe" and "Crusader," the retreat from Tobruk, the recapture of Benghazi, the Gazala Line battles, the capture of Tobruk, the pursuit into Egypt, and the 1st Battle of El Alamein. During all of these battles, wounded Allied soldiers who were captured—including "non-Aryans"—were treated just as well as wounded Germans.

Finally, on September 5, 1942, Dr. Barnewitz had to report himself sick and was relieved of his duties for medical reasons. He was evacuated back to Germany, where it took him nine months to recover his health.

On May 10, 1943, as the Afrika Korps was surrendering in Tunisia, Hans-Joachim Barnewitz returned to active duty in a less demanding role as commander of the Military Hospital at Thorn. He remained here until late 1944, when Soviet military advances forced the evacuation of the hospital. Barnewitz's performance, however, had convinced the Army's Medical Branch that he could do an excellent job under increasingly difficult circumstances. In the final weeks of 1944, Barnewitz was appointed *Korpsarzt* (corps CMO) of Wehrkreis XII.

Wehrkreis XII—the XII Military District—was headquartered at Wiesbaden and included the Eifel, the Palatinate, and the Saar.[39] Barnewitz was thus soon involved in the treatment and medical evacuation of German casualties (and wounded American prisoners) during the Battle of the Bulge. During the middle of this difficult and confusing campaign, his assignment as CMO of Wehrkreis XII was made permanent. He was promoted to *Generalarzt* (major general of the Medical Branch) on March 1, 1945.

General Barnewitz continued at his post until the Americans overran the Saar, the Palatinate, and captured Wiesbaden. He then headed east with the remnants of Wehrkreis XII and did not surrender until May 1945. (Apparently he joined the 11th Army in the Harz but without a formal appointment.) He was freed from the POW camps in 1946—a very early release date for a German medical general, given the horrors of the Holocaust and the inhuman Nazi medical experiments that were then shocking the world. Barnewitz's early release suggests an assumption on the part of the Western Allies—that no Afrika Korps doctor would have anything to do with anything like that! This assumption was, in fact, absolutely correct.

General Barnewitz returned to northern Germany and resumed private practice in Holstein. He showed no interest in resuming his military career when the West German Army (the Bundesheer) was established in 1955; indeed, this author has never unearthed any evidence that Dr. Barnewitz ever showed the slightest interest in a military career, other than a fervent desire to perform his duties at the highest possible level of competence and efficiency. He seems to have accomplished that, as evidenced by the fact that he became a major general after only seven years of military service.

Dr. Hans-Joachim Barnewitz died at Luebeck on April 19, 1965.

Andreas Buechting was Rommel's chief signals officer from the beginning of the desert war until the Second Battle of El Alamein.

He was born in Danzig, East Prussia, on January 17, 1896. He joined the Imperial Army as a Fahnenjunker in the 3rd Telegraph Battalion when World War I broke out and remained with this unit throughout the conflict, during which he was promoted to second lieutenant. Not selected for the Reichsheer, he was given an honorary promotion to first lieutenant when he was discharged on October 12, 1919. The next day, young Buechting joined the state police in Kattowitz.

Buechting spent the entire pre-Hitler years in the police, serving in Frankfurt/Main, Glatz, Goerlitz, Barmen, Bonn, and Breslau. In the process, he made himself a communications expert. He rejoined the army as a captain on October 1, 1935, and was immediately given command of a signals company. Two months later, he was promoted to major and was named commander of the 46th Signal Battalion at Muenster, Wehrkreis VI. He was promoted to lieutenant colonel effective New Year's Day, 1939. Early the following year, he was assigned to the 222nd Signal, which was then expanding from a company to a battalion. After the campaign in France, he was given command of the 570th Signal Regiment in Poland. This unit was the signals command for Field Marshal Gerd von Rundstedt's Army Group A, which would invade Russia as Army Group South on June 22, 1941. Buechting would not be with them, however. On October 1, 1940, he was promoted to colonel and on April 29, 1941, was named commander of the 580th Higher Signal Command (*Hoeherer Nachrichtenfuehrer 580*) in Libya.

Buechting commanded the 580th in all of the campaigns of Panzer Group (later Army) Afrika. Rommel never complained about his performance, and OKH—which was also impressed—earmarked him for further promotion. Meanwhile, in September 1942, Rommel fell ill and returned to Europe. He was replaced by General of Panzer Troops Georg Stumme.

The Second Battle of El Alamein began on October 23, 1942, when Montgomery's British 8th Army unleashed a massive bombardment, with 1,200 guns concentrating on a five-mile sector on the northern flank of the panzer army. The German 164th Light Afrika and 90th Light Divisions held their positions, but the Italian 62nd Infantry Regiment was routed. By dawn the following day, the British were attacking with four infantry and two armoured divisions (700 tanks), and the northern flank was in danger of collapsing. The Allied bombardment had also disrupted land-line communications between army headquarters and those of the light divisions. That morning, General Stumme and Colonel Buechting drove toward the headquarters of the 90th Light. Stumme stopped to observe the enemy's advance, but got too close to the action. A bullet struck the colonel in the head. The general jumped on the running board of the car as the driver sped away. He then had a heart attack and fell off the running board without the driver noticing.

Andreas Buechting died later that same day. He was posthumously promoted to major general, effective October 1, 1942.

Baron Heinrich von Behr was the commander of the 475th Panzer Signals Battalion and the chief communications officer of the Afrika Korps.

He was born in Roennen, in the Courland (Kurland) district of the Baltic state of Latvia, on June 26, 1902. Too young to fight in World War I, Behr enlisted in the Latvian Freikorps/Libau Cavalry Regiment in January 1919, in order to fight the Soviets, who were threatening to overrun the entire Baltic region. Behr apparently volunteered without the permission of his influential family. They promptly secured his discharge (whether he wanted it or not) three weeks after he signed up.

After the Soviet threat subsided, the Allies forced the German Army and Freikorps volunteers to leave the independent nation of Latvia, and the ethnic Latvians put pressure on their *Volksdeutsche* citizens (people of German blood and heritage) to follow them. The von Behrs did so about 1920. Meanwhile, Heinrich completed his education and, on April 1, 1922, enlisted in the 16th Cavalry Regiment. He became an officer cadet in 1925 and was commissioned second lieutenant in the 6th Cavalry Regiment in December 1926. He remained with the 6th Cavalry until 1934; in the meantime, he became interested in signal communications. He commanded the signals platoon of the regiment from 1929 until 1934, when he became adjutant of the Higher Signals Officer of the Cavalry Inspectorate. In 1937, he became a course director at the Army Sport School at Wuensdorf and a trainer in the modern pentathlon. He was promoted to first lieutenant in 1926 and to Rittmeister (captain of cavalry) in 1935.

Two days after World War II began, Behr was transferred to the 81st Panzer Signal Replacement Battalion at Weimar as a company commander. A month later he was promoted to major and assumed command of the 198th Signal Battalion of the 98th Infantry Division, which was then forming in the Grafenwoehr Maneuver Area of Wehrkreis XIII (northern Bavaria). The division was transferred to the Saar Front in December. In April 1940, however, Behr was given command of the 39th Panzer Signal Battalion of the Berliner 3rd Panzer Division. He fought in Belgium and France in May and June 1940, and accompanied his battalion back to Germany in July. In 1941, he took part in the invasion of the Soviet Union, fighting in the battles of encirclement at Smolensk and Kiev, among others. In October 1941, Behr received a promotion of sorts when he was named commander of the 424th Panzer Signal Battalion of the XXIV Panzer Corps, also on the Eastern Front. On December 16, however, Behr was sent back to Germany. He took a month's leave and arrived in North Africa on January 15, 1942, where he assumed command of the 475th Panzer Signal, the communications battalion of the Afrika Korps. He was promoted to lieutenant colonel on March 1.

Behr led the 475th Panzer Signal through the fierce battles of the Gazala Line, Tobruk, Mersa Matruh, the 1st and 2nd Battles of El Alamein, and the first stages of the retreat to Tunisia. He did a fine job commanding a mobile signals battalion in the fast moving tank battles, and the High Command decided that he was capable of more. After a long furlough, he was transferred to the Panzer School at Wuensdorf and educated as a panzer grenadier regimental commander. He was detached to the 26th Panzer Division for further education and on-the-job training in May 1943. On July 1, 1943, he was named commander of the 200th Panzer Grenadier Regiment of the 90th Panzer Grenadier Division. He fought in all of the major battles on the Italian Front and was promoted to colonel on February 1, 1944.

After Baade was wounded in action on December 9, Lieutenant General Count Gerhard von Schwerin replaced him for about two weeks. He, in turn, was replaced by Baron von Behr, who assumed command of December 27, 1944, and led it for the rest of the war. Behr was promoted to major general on April 1, 1945, and surrendered the remnants of his division on April 28.

Heinrich von Behr was in prison until the fall of 1947. He worked in the civilian sector until 1956, when he was offered a position in the army of the Federal Republic of Germany (West Germany). Behr accepted and was named brigadier general in the Bundesheer—major general under the old (Third Reich) rank structure. Behr was charged with the task of forming the 5th Panzer Division in early September.

There were many volunteers and by October 1 the division was formed. He was promoted to major general (two-star general under the American system) in 1957.

Behr commanded the 5th Panzer Division until late 1959, when he was named commander of the corps troops of the I Corps in Muenster. This was his last appointment. He retired on September 30, 1962, and settled in Bonn. He died there on August 14, 1983.

Another of Rommel's highly capable staff officers was Paul Diesener, who was a member of the staff of the Afrika Korps and Rommel's liaison officer with the Italian XXI Corps during the Siege of Tobruk, during the Winter Battles, during the Second Cyrenaican campaign, and in the planning phases of the Gazala Line campaign.

An older officer, Diesener was born in Berlin on April 27, 1882. He joined the Imperial Army as a Fahnenjunker in early 1902 and was commissioned second lieutenant in the 6th Grenadier Regiment in 1903. He fought in World War I and rose to the rank of captain, but was not selected for retention by the Reichswehr. Discharged as an honorary major in late 1920, he returned to his chosen profession as a "retread" in late 1933, working as a training officer at Deutsch Krone on Germany's eastern border. Initially, Diesener was an "E" or territorial officer and did not have the same prestige or scope for promotion as did regular officers. He nevertheless worked hard and earned a promotion to lieutenant colonel in 1938.

When World War II began, Diesener was named commander of the 52nd Frontier Guard Regiment at Deutsch Krone, Wehrkreis II, in Pomerania, on Germany's border with Poland. He became commander of the 75th Infantry Replacement Regiment in November 1939 and took charge of the 25th *Landesschuetzen* Regiment (an infantry/security unit made up of older men) in April 1940. He was named acting commander of the Woldenberg Recruiting Area in the autumn of 1940.

It was not until April 1, 1941, that Paul Diesener returned to active troop officer status. Not coincidentally, he was promoted to full colonel that same day. He was given command of the 693rd Infantry Regiment of the 339th Infantry Division on June 20, 1941, then located on the demarcation line between Vichy France and German-occupied France.

Colonel Diesener served as regimental commander for only about five weeks, then he was transferred to the staff of the Afrika Korps. Normally, only younger officers were sent to Africa and, at age 60, Diesener was probably the oldest German soldier in the entire theater. Rommel, however, selected him to serve as liaison officer with the Italian XXI Corps, which was besieging Tobruk. Diesener did an excellent job and helped to stabilize the sometimes-unreliable Italians in all of the battles from August 1941 through April 1942. Finally, however, he was relieved of his duties. At age 61, he was undoubtedly too old for duty in the harsh climate of the Sahara Desert, and further service here could easily have permanently damaged his health. Diesener, however, had proven his usefulness in dealing with the Italians. He was named chief of the German liaison staff with the Italian 2nd Army in the Balkans on May 21, 1942. He held his post until June 9, 1943, when he was named commander of the 5th Railroad Security Staff in the same area. This, of course, was a very difficult assignment and became more difficult as time passed, because it became more obvious that Germany would lose the war. As a result, the guerrilla movement in Yugoslavia grew. Finally, on October 27, 1944, as the Eastern Front reached Serbia, the special staff became superfluous and was dissolved. Colonel Diesener was placed in Fuehrer Reserve and was never reemployed. As a reward for his many years of service, however, he was promoted to major general on April 1, 1945.[40]

General Diesener was captured by the Allies on May 2, 1945, but no war crimes charges were ever filed against him, unlike many German generals who served in Yugoslavia. He was released on February 28, 1946, and retired to Hildesheim, where he died on May 22, 1970, at the age of 88.

Karl Buelowius succeeded Hans Hecker as chief engineer officer of Panzer Army Afrika.

Born in Koenigsberg, East Prussia on March 2, 1890, young Buelowius joined the Imperial Army as a Fahnenjunker in the 1st Engineer Battalion (*Pionier-Bataillon 1*) on November 27, 1907, attended the War School at Glogau, and was commissioned Leutnant in 1909. He spent two years as a student at the Military Technical Academy before becoming a platoon leader in the 1st Battalion when World War I began. In late 1914, he became commander of a mortar company in the I Corps, and later served as adjutant to the chief engineer officer of the I Corps. He was promoted to first lieutenant in 1915. In August 1916, he became commander of the 213th Engineer Company, and a year later was sent to Palestine, where he commanded the 205th Engineer Company. Recalled to Germany, he was promoted to captain in May 1918, took an abbreviated General Staff course (July–August 1918), and was given command of a third engineer company (the 14th), which he was leading when World War I ended.

Buelowius was discharged from the service in 1920 but returned to active duty as a company commander in the 1st Engineer Battalion at Koenigsberg in 1924. He remained in this post until 1928, when he was attached to the staff of the Commandant of Insterburg. In late 1930, he was posted to the staff of the Infantry School at Dresden (1930–34). He was promoted to major in 1934.

Karl Buelowius spent virtually the rest of his career in engineer assignments. He commanded the 11th Engineer Battalion (1934–35), the 6th Fortress Engineer Staff (1936–39), was commander of the X Fortress Engineer Inspectorate at Breslau, Silesia (1939), and became commander of the X Higher Engineer Construction Command when World War II began.

Buelowius was named chief engineer officer of the 8th Army at the end of the Polish campaign and became chief engineer officer of the 9th Army on May 15, 1940, during the French campaign. He continued in this capacity during the Russian campaign and was promoted to lieutenant colonel (1936), colonel (1939), and major general (April 1, 1942).

On October 25, 1942, during the Battle of El Alamein, General Buelowius was named chief engineer officer of Panzer Army Afrika. He did what could be done to try to save Rommel's defensive line at El Alamein, but this proved to be impossible. Then, as Rommel retreated across Egypt and Libya and into Tunisia, Buelowius proved himself a master defensive engineer, materially delaying Montgomery's 8th Army with his minefields, demolitions, dummy positions, and booby traps. As a reward, Buelowius was named engineer general of Army Group Afrika.

In April 1943, Buelowius was given his only command of the war. General Hasso von Manteuffel, the commander of the ad hoc Division von Manteuffel, was wounded, and Buelowius took his place. The division's mission was to hold its positions in the hills of Tunisia, so it was certainly an appropriate command for a skilled combat engineer. Buelowius could do little, however, to influence the overall situation in Tunisia, where the supply lines had collapsed and Army Group Afrika was on the verge of annihilation. The front crumbled the following month, and General Buelowius surrendered to the Americans on May 9, 1943.

During the course of duty on the Eastern and North African Fronts, Karl Buelowius had reportedly developed a serious drinking problem. His sanity deteriorated in captivity, and he became depressed and paranoid. On March 27, 1945, in the hospital at Camp Forrest, Tennessee, he committed suicide.

Roland von Hoesslin is a symbol of what was best in Nazi Germany in 1944. This is why he had to die.

He was the descendant of an old Bavarian family that had served the kings of Bavaria for centuries. Roland was born in Munich on February 2, 1915, while his father, Hubert von Hoesslin, was serving on the Western Front.[41] (Hubert later became a lieutenant general during World War II).[42] At age 17, Roland joined the 17th Cavalry Regiment at Bamberg in 1933 as a Fahnenjunker and formed a lifelong friendship with then-Lieutenant Count Claus von Stauffenberg.

Hoesslin was commissioned in 1936 and promoted to first lieutenant in 1939. He took part in the military annexations of Austria and the Sudetenland in 1938. On September 1, 1939, the day World War II began, he was adjutant to the commander of the 10th Reconnaissance Battalion of the 10th Infantry Division (later 10th Panzer Grenadier Division). He fought in Poland and was then posted to the School for Panzer Troops at Potsdam-Krampnitz, where he underwent tank training and stayed on to instruct panzer *Fahnenjunkern*. He thus missed the French campaign. In March 1941, he was posted to the Afrika Korps as an orderly officer. Soon he was an assistant operations officer. Rommel liked and admired the enthusiastic young lieutenant, but there was a shortage of trained and experienced reconnaissance officers in the Afrika Korps. When two of the three company commanders in the 33rd Panzer Reconnaissance Battalion became casualties, Rommel reluctantly transferred him to the unit, where he became commander of the 3rd Company on August 20, 1941.

Young Hoesslin fought in all of the major engagements of the Afrika Korps from March 1941 to July 1942. He was promoted to captain in early 1942 and was awarded the Iron Cross, Second and First Class for his actions in the Battles of El Adem and Trigh Capuzzo in June 1942. A few days later, he took command of the battalion.

On July 15, 1942, during the 1st Battle of El Alamein, the Italians lost an important strongpoint. Captain von Hoesslin led an immediate counterattack and retook the position. In the process, however, he was seriously wounded. Rommel saw to it that he received the Knight's Cross while he was in the hospital at Mersa Matruh.

Hoesslin was evacuated back to Germany and spent the next nine months in various hospitals. When he returned to active duty, he was sent to Insterburg, East Prussia (now Chernyakhovsk, Russia), where he attended the Panzer Reconnaissance Battalion Commanders' School. He remained in Insterburg as commander of the 24th Panzer Reconnaissance Replacement Battalion.

In April 1944, he met with his old comrades from the 17th Cavalry, Peter Sauerbruck[43] and Count Claus von Stauffenberg. Stauffenberg was now a colonel and chief of staff of the Home Army (also called the Replacement Army). The Count, who had lost an arm and an eye in Tunisia, informed Hoesslin that he was leading a plot to assassinate Adolf Hitler and overthrow the Nazi regime. Hoesslin joined the conspiracy immediately. It was decided that he would use his three companies to seize important buildings in Wehrkreis I (East Prussia). The plot, however, did not go as planned. Stauffenberg placed a bomb under the Fuehrer's table on July 20, 1944 and Hitler was wounded in the blast but survived. He was also very angry. Shortly before midnight on July 20, Count von Stauffenberg was executed on the orders of Colonel General Fritz Fromm, the commander-in-chief of the Replacement Army, who was trying to get rid of witnesses who might testify to the fact that he knew about the conspiracy, wanted it to succeed, and allowed it to proceed.[44]

On August 1, 1944, Hoesslin was transferred to Meiningen, Thuringia and—ironically—was promoted to major. Twenty-three days later, however, he was arrested by the Gestapo. Quickly dishonorably discharged from the army by the so-called Court of Honor, he was hauled before Judge Roland Freisler's People's Court on October 13, 1944. He was convicted and hanged the same day (although one source stated that he was not hanged until the next day, October 14.) He was 29 years old.

The name of one General Staff officer of Rommel's Afrika Korps will surprise many people: Guenther von Kluge. He was the son of Field Marshal Guenther Hans "Clever Hans" von Kluge, who became Rommel's hated enemy in Normandy. Although they became united in purpose and glossed over their differences, they had spoken such harsh words to each other that the enmity between the two never completely evaporated.

The younger Kluge was born on December 15, 1910, when his father was a lieutenant. An artillery officer like his father, he joined the 3rd (Prussian) Artillery Regiment at Frankfurt/Oder as a Fahnenjunker in the late 1920s and was named adjutant of the 31st Artillery Regiment at Halberstadt in Brunswick on October 6, 1936. He was selected for General Staff training at the War Academy in 1939, got his first taste of combat in Poland, but had to quickly return to the Reich, because his classes began on September 19—less than three weeks after the invasion began. Less than two weeks later, Kluge was transferred to the staff of the General of Artillery at the OKH. He did not resume his training until April 7, 1940. By now, the General Staff course had been greatly reduced in length and was located in Dresden. It was concluded on June 14.

Immediately after finishing his War Academy course, Kluge was briefly attached to the staffs of the 16th and 12th Armies, in order to give him some familiarization with the workings of higher field headquarters. On July 10, 1940, as a probationary member of the General Staff, he was named Ib (quartermaster) of the Franconian 15th Infantry Division. Six months later, he was laterally transferred to East Prussia as Ib of the 1st Infantry Division.

Major von Kluge was transferred to the staff of General Streich's 5th Light Division on February 1, 1941, and was promptly named Ic of the division. He seems to have had no particular gift for military intelligence but, unlike Streich, he did not bring Rommel's wrath down upon himself, either. He and Rommel developed no personal relationship. Guenther was just another hard working General Staff officer and a probationary member at that—the kind of man the Desert Fox would tolerate as long as he did his job.

On August 15, 1941, the younger Kluge became Ib of the 21st Panzer Division. This was a promotion of sorts and now he reported directly to General von Ravenstein. He only held his new post six weeks. As was not at all unusual, several months in the Sahara Desert had caused his health to deteriorate, and he was sent back to Germany on sick leave at the end of September. He never returned to North Africa.

Kluge had done well enough in Africa to be admitted to the General Staff. On December 28, 1941, having survived both his probation and his illness, he was assigned to the 8th Panzer Division as its Ib. (Kluge seems to have had the most talent for supply and logistical positions.) The division fought in the Volkhov sector and helped Army Group North check Stalin's winter offensive of 1941–42. On June 5, 1942, Kluge was promoted to Ia of the XXXIX Motorized (later Panzer) Corps, which was then part of Army Group Center, commanded by his father. Later, on March 1, 1943, he was named Ia of the 18th Panzer Division, which was in the process of being converted into a motorized artillery unit. Field Marshal von Manstein had high hopes for this experiment, but it was not judged a success and the division was dissolved in 1944. Guenther von Kluge was nevertheless considered a successful General Staff officer and he was promoted to lieutenant colonel on May 1, 1943.

Kluge continued to fight on the Eastern Front until the summer of 1944. His father, meanwhile, had become commander-in-chief of Army Group Center, which was facing Moscow. He was seriously injured in an automobile accident in October 1943, and did not return to duty until July 1944. When he did, Hitler named him OB West (Supreme Commander, Western Front). The field marshal arranged for his son to be transferred to his staff as a special duties officer. Ironically, he arrived on July 20, 1944, the day Colonel Count von Stauffenberg detonated a bomb under Hitler's conference table. The Fuehrer was wounded by the blast. When he regained his senses, he began screaming for revenge.

Field Marshal Hans von Kluge had been on both sides of the anti-Hitler conspiracy. He had sympathized with the plotters and had conspired with them, but he had lacked the civil courage to act against the Nazi dictator, and had accepted a huge "bonus" from him. Now he was under tremendous pressure. The Gestapo was investigating him and the Western Front was on the verge of collapse. He could only "prove" his loyalty to the Fuehrer—and keep his head—by checking the Allied invasion.

After Rommel was critically wounded on July 17, Field Marshal von Kluge appointed himself commander-in-chief of Army Group B in Normandy. He used his son as a special messenger. In late July, he named Guenther OB West's permanent representative to Headquarters, 7th Army. This army was led by SS Colonel General Paul Hausser, whom the elder Kluge considered incompetent. (They had attended the cadet school at Gross Lichterfeldt together at the turn of the century and had developed no close friendship then.) With considerable justification, Kluge held Hausser responsible for the American "Cobra" breakout of July 25–26. Kluge, however, was afraid to sack the SS general and Hitler appointee for political reasons, but he did relieve his chief of staff, and had his son report of 7th Army's activities on a daily basis.

As the Americans—spearheaded by Lieutenant General George S. Patton's 3rd Army—broke out of Normandy, Hitler prevented Field Marshal von Kluge from conducting a timely withdrawal. By the second week of August, a salient was forming around Falaise. The 7th Army was on the west side and 5th Panzer Army held the line to the north, but there was little to the south to check Patton. Hitler thought he saw an opportunity to restore the situation by breaking through American lines to the sea and cutting off Patton's 3rd Army to the south. The task of implementing this plan and directing the counterattack fell to General of Panzer Troops Baron Hans von Funck's XXXXVII Panzer Corps.

Funck launched his impossible attack during the night of August 6–7 and actually made considerable progress. Starting 20 miles from the sea, he broke through American lines at Mortain and gained a few miles before the American fighter-bombers appeared. Then, the strike divisions of XXXXVII Panzer were crushed by American Thunderbolts, Mustangs, and Lightnings, supported by British rocket-firing Typhoons. Funck lost 81 tanks and hundreds of other vehicles and promptly called off the attack.

Hitler, of course, was furious at the failure, which he blamed on Field Marshal von Kluge. He immediately ordered the creation of an ad hoc Panzer Group Eberbach, under the command of General of Panzer Troops Heinz Eberbach, to assume command of the counteroffensive. Eberbach until that moment had been commanding 5th Panzer Army, which he was forced to hand over to SS Colonel General Sepp Dietrich—much to his disgust, for he considered Dietrich incompetent.

The staff of Panzer Group Eberbach was an emergency organization that was completely unnecessary. HQ XXXXVII Panzer Corps was much better prepared and equipped to renew the attack. Panzer Group Eberbach was also inadequate for its task. It had only three radio stations and two of these were usually out of order. Because of the deteriorating military situation and the Anglo-Saxon air domination, parts of the staff never even arrived. It was only able to function at all because of help provided by Headquarters, 7th Army. Eberbach himself "repeatedly reported this fact and requested to dissolve my staff as worthless and without any meaning."[45] Hitler nevertheless ordered Panzer Group Eberbach to resume the attack on August 11, using six panzer divisions.

Eberbach never resumed the offensive. Patton was in the German rear and was driving north toward Falaise, and the entire Army Group B was in danger of being encircled. On August 11, a despairing Field Marshal von Kluge finally took matters into his own hands and committed the panzer group against Patton north of Alencon. Panzer Group Eberbach, however, was not able to prevent most of the army group (including the entire 7th Army and most of the 5th Panzer Army) from being encircled on August 16.

About 100,000 German troops were surrounded in the Falaise Pocket, which was about 35 miles long and 15 miles wide. Led by their generals, they launched an immediate breakout attempt, and about half of them escaped. Some 10,000 were killed and about 40,000 were captured. They also lost 334 tanks, self-propelled guns, and armored vehicles; 252 towed artillery pieces; 2,447 motorized vehicles; and huge amounts of other equipment. The German losses were ruinous: France could no longer be saved, and the survivors of the once proud army group headed for the German border, most of them as rapidly as they could.

Meanwhile, Adolf Hitler fired Field Marshal von Kluge.

As early as 1941, the elder Kluge had been a vacillating member of the anti-Hitler conspiracy, but he could never actually bring himself to act against the Fuehrer. On July 20, Colonel Count Claus von Stauffenberg had placed a bomb under Hitler's conference table and the ensuing explosion narrowly missed killing the dictator. It did not take the Gestapo long to determine that Kluge was implicated in the plot. On August 14, Kluge went to the front and disappeared. He was pinned down by Allied fighter-bombers until nightfall and all of his vehicles—including his communications truck—had been destroyed. The ever-suspicious and paranoid Adolf Hitler, however, decided that he must have been secretly negotiating with the Allied generals. On the evening of August 15, he appointed Field Marshal Walter Model OB West and commander-in-chief of Army Group B. SS General Hausser was named acting commander of the army group, until Model could arrive from the Eastern Front. (Hitler was not aware that Hausser had been seriously wounded in the Falaise breakout.) Field Marshal von Kluge was ordered to report to Berlin. The politically sensitive officer knew exactly what that meant.

On August 18, the car carrying Kluge neared Metz on the German border, the scene of some of his World War I battles. Here he spread out a blanket and quietly committed suicide by biting a cyanide capsule. Two days later, a depressed Lieutenant Colonel von Kluge was sent to Germany with the body of his father.

One of the older Kluge's last acts was to write a letter to Adolf Hitler, calling upon him to end the war. As a result, the Fuehrer ordered that he be buried quietly, with military pallbearers but without military honors or fanfare. His cause of death was officially announced as a cerebral hemorrhage.

After he buried his father, young Kluge returned to the front. Panzer Group Eberbach had been dissolved, and Eberbach himself was captured by the British on August 31. On August 25, meanwhile, Colonel von Kluge was attached to the staff of the XXXXVII Panzer Corps, under the command of General Baron von Funck. The Headquarters was pulled back to the German border, where, on Hitler's orders, General von Funck was sacked on September 4. Kluge and the rest of the staff were effusive in their thanks to the general for his courtesy and years of service. He was succeeded by Lieutenant General Baron Heinrich von Luettwitz, the erstwhile commander of the 2nd Panzer Division.

Kluge was only with the corps another day or so. On September 10, he became Ia of the 87th Infantry Division, which was fighting for its life on the northern sector of the Eastern Front. Kluge, however, only held this post two weeks. By now, the Gestapo knew of the late Field Marshal von Kluge's deep involvement in the plot to overthrow the Fuehrer, and they also knew that he must have confided in his son, who also had no love for the Nazis. On September 25, 1944, Guenther von Kluge was placed in Fuehrer Reserve and was never reemployed. His uncle Wolfgang (Field Marshal von Kluge's younger brother) was dishonorably discharged from the service later that year.[46]

Friedrich Wilhelm von Homeyer was born in Berlin on October 16, 1899, the son of a major of police. Young Friedrich (as he was called) was educated in the cadet academies of Wahlstatt and Gross Lichterfelde (also called Berlin-Lichterfelde) and joined the 10th Light Cavalry at Angerburg as a Fahnenjunker at age 16. He fought in World War I, earned both grades of the Iron Cross, and was commissioned in 1917.

During "the war after the war," von Homeyer fought in the Baltic States. He was discharged from the service in 1920 and became a journalist. Eventually, he served as press attaché at the German embassy in Cairo. He also became president of the Transoceanic Society in 1936.

When World War II began, Homeyer was a Rittmeister (cavalry captain) of Reserves. In early 1940, about the time Erwin Rommel arrived, he was assigned to the 7th Panzer Division as an assistant operations officer. The future Desert Fox was pleased with his performance in Belgium and France. When Rommel was summoned to command the

Afrika Korps, he no doubt recalled talking with Homeyer about the latter's days in Egypt. In any case, Rommel (who needed officers with desert experience) took the reserve captain with him to Libya in early 1941.

Captain von Homeyer stayed with Rommel until the latter part of 1941. Then he joined the 90th Light Division and organized the 580th Motorized Reconnaissance Company, which became a battalion with three squadrons (companies) in the spring of 1942. Homeyer did a fine job commanding the 580th Reconnaissance and Rommel told him so. On July 3, during the 1st Battle of El Alamein, just as Captain von Homeyer was preparing to lead his men on a reconnaissance mission near the Quattara Depression, Rommel turned up and told him that he had recommended him for the Knight's Cross. The Army Personnel Office acted swiftly and he was approved for the decoration on July 6. Homeyer never wore it, however; on July 3, 1942, shortly after he left Rommel, a British artillery shell exploded near his vehicle and killed him.

CHAPTER VII

EL ALAMEIN

Georg Stumme, who succeeded Erwin Rommel as commander of Panzer Army Afrika, was a man who fully enjoyed all of the pleasures of life. Short of height and full of energy, his men called him "Fireball." He had a notable fondness for luxurious living, especially in the realm of food and drink, but also an instinctive ability for recognizing tactical opportunities and the courage to seize them. Like Rommel, he was a practical and pragmatic field officer, not the academic General Staff type like Halder or General Beck. Stumme habitually wore a monocle even when he was a lieutenant, and, as a senior officer, his face seemed to be permanently flushed because of his high blood pressure.

He was born in Halberstadt on July 29, 1886, and entered the service as a Fahnenjunker in the 57th Field Artillery Regiment in 1906. Commissioned second lieutenant the following year, he transferred to the cavalry branch shortly thereafter and spent much of his career on horseback. He fought in World War I, served in the Reichsheer, and was a lieutenant colonel when Adolf Hitler took power. Stumme rose rapidly under the Nazis, receiving promotions to colonel (1933), major general (1936), and lieutenant general (1938). On October 10, 1938, he was named commander of the 2nd Light Division, which he led in Poland the following year.

Stumme's new command was quite formidable, except for its tank battalion, which was equipped only with the very poor Panzer Mark I and II light tanks. The Panzer Mark II had only a very light 20-mm main battle gun, whereas the Panzer Mark I had no main battle gun at all—only machine guns. The rest of the division, however, was much better equipped, and the 2nd Light performed better than any of the light divisions in Poland. As part of the German 10th Army (Hitler's spearhead), it fought its way through the Polish frontier defenses (September 1–3, 1939), helped overrun the Warta district, and pushed on to the suburbs of Warsaw. It was then recalled to the west to help crush the only significant Polish counteroffensive of the campaign. The 2nd fought in the Radom encirclement (September 8–12), where much of the Polish Army was destroyed. It then drove north to the Bzura and turned east again, pushing on to the Vistula and taking part in the Siege of Warsaw. After the Polish capital capitulated on September 27, the division returned to the Reich and its home station of Gera (in Thuringia or Wehrkreis IX), where Stumme was given the task of reorganizing the 2nd Light into as a panzer division. It was officially redesignated 7th Panzer Division on October 18, 1939, although the actual reorganization took considerably longer.

During the reorganization, the newly formed staff of the 25th Panzer Regiment joined the division in late October, along with its newly created I and II Battalions. The division's original panzer battalion (the 66th) became the III/25th Panzer Regiment. Headquarters, 7th Reconnaissance Regiment was disbanded, while I/7th Recon became 7th Motorcycle Battalion and II/7th Reconnaissance became the 7th Recon Battalion. The 6th and 7th Cavalry Rifle Regiments were now redesignated 6th and 7th *Schuetzen* (motorized or rifle) Regiments.

Despite some improvements, the tank units of the new division remained poor. The regiment was partially reequipped with Panzer 38 (t), a Czech tank, manufactured at the Skoda plant, which Germany took over in 1938 after Hitler occupied the Sudetenland. The division was not given any of the Panzer Mark III—the best German tank of the day. It did receive 23 modern Panzer Mark IVs, but they were armed with short-barreled 75-mm guns, which seriously limited their effectiveness. There was little Stumme could do about this, however.

In late 1939, Stumme redeployed his division to the Western Front, where it prepared for the invasion of France. Here, on February 15, 1940, he turned command of the 7th Panzer Division over to Major General Erwin Rommel. Stumme himself had been transferred to Luebeck, Wehrkreis X, where he had been given command of the XXXX Corps, which was then in the process of organizing.

Stumme's new corps included the following organic units: 128th Artillery Command (Arko 128), the 440th Corps Signal Battalion, the 440th Corps Supply Unit, and the 440th Corps Field Replacement Battalion. After the main Allied armies had been defeated in Belgium and northern France, XXXX Corps was sent to the south, where it joined 6th Army and played a minor role in the subsequent "mopping up" operations in central and southern France, directing three "marching" infantry divisions. The corps was back in Germany by July. It became a motorized corps on September 15, 1940, and a panzer corps on July 9, 1942.

Meanwhile, Georg Stumme was promoted to general of cavalry on June 1, 1940. He and his headquarters were transferred to Field

Marshal Fedor von Bock's Army Group B in Poland in September and remained there until January 1941; then they were sent to Romania and later to Bulgaria. In April and May 1941, XXXX Corps played a major role in the conquest of Greece, directing the 9th Panzer Division, the 73rd Infantry Division, and the SS Motorized Division "Leibstandarte Adolf Hitler." This campaign convinced Stumme that his future lay with the mobile branch. On June 4, 1941, he arranged to have his rank changed to general of panzer troops. Later that month, he and his command were sent to Austria.

The XXXX Motorized Corps did not take part in the initial invasion of the Soviet Union, but joined Army Group Center in August. It was assigned to 9th Army and fought in the Toropez sector (where it directed two infantry divisions), but in September it was transferred to General Hoepner's 4th Panzer Group (later Army), where it was given the 2nd Panzer, 10th Panzer, and 258th Infantry Divisions. Here Stumme really came into his own. His corps formed the southern pincher of a vast double envelopment that encircled six Soviet armies (55 divisions!) in the Vyazma sector. The battle began on September 30 and the pocket was surrounded on October 7, but the fighting did not end for another ten days. The trapped Reds launched several desperate breakout attempts and at one time there was close quarter fighting in Stumme's advanced command post. In the end, however, the Russians had no choice but to surrender. Including the three Soviet armies destroyed at Bryansk, a few miles to the south, Stalin lost 663,000 men in the Battle of the Vyazma-Bryansk Pocket.

Stumme and his men quickly redeployed for the decisive drive on the Soviet capital. They advanced along both sides of the Moscow Highway and pushed to within 40 miles of the Kremlin before they were stopped by the Russian mud. Once the ground froze, Stumme and his corps surged forward again. The 2nd Panzer Division, in fact, came closer to Moscow than any other unit (within six miles), and its reconnaissance battalion could actually see the Kremlin before it was thrown back.

During the final stages of the Battle of Moscow, XXXX Motorized Corps was transferred to 4th Army to the south, where Stumme directed the 19th Panzer Division and a couple of infantry units during the retreat of 1941–42. Then, Stumme and his staff were sent to Army Group South, where they began preparing for Operation "Blue," the drive to Stalingrad and the Volga. At this point, Georg Stumme's career was suddenly ruined.

On June 19, 1942, the general was at his headquarters—a villa near Kharkov, which had been confiscated from a commissar. He and his three division commanders—Major General Hermann Breith of the 3rd Panzer, Major General Baron Hans von Boineburg-Lengsfeld of the

23rd Panzer, and Major General Max Fremerey of the 29th Motorized—were feasting on various delicacies and washing them down with Crimean champagne. Also present was Lieutenant Colonel Gerhard Franz, the corps chief of staff, and several other officers. The atmosphere was cordial and extremely relaxed, until the news arrived that a Fieseler Storch reconnaissance airplane carrying Major Reichel, the chief of operations of the 23rd Panzer Division, was missing and had probably crashed, possibly behind Soviet lines.

Stumme turned pale. With his permission, Reichel had carried a memorandum and a map outlining the plan for Operation "Blue." Worse yet, there were strict regulations—dictated by the Fuehrer himself—forbidding any officer from putting this kind of information in writing. The party was definitely over. The general immediately ordered a full-scale search for the aircraft.

The Storch had indeed crashed in Soviet territory. Elements of the 336th Infantry Division had seen it go down. A patrol was quickly sent out and found Reichel and his pilot—both dead. Reichel's mapboard and briefcase were missing. Stumme and Franz now had no choice but to report the incident to General of Panzer Troops Friedrich Paulus, the commander of the 6th Army. Paulus reluctantly passed the news on to Field Marshal Fedor von Bock at Army Group South that same day, June 20. A dispatch outlining the incident arrived at Fuehrer Headquarters at Rastenburg that same day.

The subsequent investigation was conducted by no less a personage than Field Marshal Wilhelm Keitel, the commander-in-chief of OKW. Known throughout the officers' corps as Hitler's lackey, Keitel naturally recommended what he believed Hitler wanted: a court-martial. But this time he was right: sensible regulations had been disobeyed, security had been grossly violated, and a major offensive had been compromised. Stumme and Franz were relieved of their duties on June 26, and Boineburg was sacked on July 20. Stumme and Franz were hauled before a special court-martial.[1] The presiding officer was Reichsmarschall Hermann Goering, the commander-in-chief of the Luftwaffe.

The trial lasted one day. Both officers were convicted. Stumme was sentenced to five years' fortress detention, while Franz got two. Goering, however, was extremely impressed with the comportment of the two officers. "You argued your case honestly, courageously, and without subterfuge," he declared as he shook hands with them after the trial. "I shall say so in my report to the Fuehrer."[2] Field Marshal von Bock also made a personal appeal to Hitler on behalf of the two men at their next meeting. As a result of their appeals, Hitler remitted their sentences after they had spent only four weeks in prison and recalled them to active duty. They were both sent to Africa: Stumme as deputy commander of Panzer Army Afrika and Franz as chief of staff of the Afrika Korps.

When Stumme arrived in Egypt on September 16, 1942, Erwin Rommel was a very sick man. The Desert Fox returned to Europe for treatment on September 25, and left Stumme in charge of the army.

The military situation in North Africa was desperate. The Royal Navy and Air Force had virtually cut Rommel's supply lines and the panzer army was stalemated at El Alamein, unable to disrupt Montgomery's build-up and awaiting his attack. Stumme was outnumbered 2 to 1 in men, guns and antitank guns, and 2 1/2 to 1 in tanks. The situation was, in fact, much worse, because many of the Italian units were demoralized and their equipment was next to worthless. If only Germans were considered, Stumme was outnumbered 4 to 1 in men, 5 to 1 in tanks, 4.5 to 1 in artillery, 3 to 1 in antitank guns, and 4 to 1 in serviceable aircraft.[3]

Because of Panzer Army Afrika's fuel shortage, neither Rommel nor Stumme had much choice about their plan for fighting the 2nd Battle of El Alamein. One issue of fuel was required to move one panzer 100 kilometers (62.5 miles). When Rommel left, the army had eight issues per tank, but very little fuel arrived during the four weeks. (Rommel later implied that Stumme did not restrict fuel usage strictly enough, and there seems to be some justification to this charge.) On October 23, the panzer army had only three issues per tank. Rommel estimated that it would need 30 issues per tank in the upcoming battle.

Without fuel, Stumme had no choice: since the El Alamein line was the only defensive position for a thousand miles that could not be outflanked, and since he could not conduct mobile warfare, he constructed a defensive line 2,000 to 3,000 yards in depth (behind a minebelt of 1,000 to 2,000 yards) and ordered the troops to hold it at all costs.

At 9:40 P.M. on October 23, Montgomery's 8th Army opened up with 1,200 guns, pounding a five-mile sector of the front. They concentrated against Stumme's northernmost division, Major General Karl Hans Lungershausen's 164th Light Afrika, which was pulverized. Entire units were buried alive or simply disappeared and an Italian infantry regiment broke and ran. Then, at 1 A.M. on October 24, Montgomery attacked with four infantry divisions.

Like many German generals in World War II, Georg Stumme practiced the philosophy of leading from the front. With the northern flank on the verge of collapse, he rushed to the scene of the action. While he was observing the Allied advance, an enemy machine gun suddenly opened up on him and a bullet struck one of his officers in the head. Stumme jumped on the running board of his car as his driver sped away. In the excitement, General Stumme disappeared. Apparently he had fallen off the running board without the driver's noticing. He was missing for several hours.

Lieutenant General Ritter Wilhelm von Thoma, the commander of the Afrika Korps, took command of Panzer Army Afrika, ordered patrols out to find General Stumme, and signaled Berlin that he was missing. On the evening of October 24, Hitler personally telephoned Rommel and asked him to return to Egypt. By the time he arrived shortly before midnight on October 25–26, Georg Stumme's body had been found. He had suffered a fatal heart attack. He was hastily buried near the place he fell.

Gerhard Franz was convicted and sent to prison with his commander, Georg Stumme. Like Stumme, he was given the chance for a professional comeback in Africa. He was, however, more successful than Stumme.

He was born in Bobeck, in the Roda district of Thuringia, on February 26, 1902. Unlike most future officers in the Wehrmacht, Franz began his military career as an enlisted man. In 1917, at the age of 15, he became a student in the *Unteroffiziers-Vorschule* (Non-commissioned Officers' Preparatory School) at Northeim. He remained there until April 1919, when he was transferred to the regular N.C.O. School, also at Northeim. Finally, in September 1919, he completed his training and was sent to the 21st Infantry Regiment at Nuremberg as a corporal. He was transferred to the 17th Infantry Regiment at Brunswick in early 1921 and was promoted to sergeant in 1922.

Even before Franz became a sergeant, he had increased his goals and was taking officer preparation courses, first in Brunswick, then at Potsdam, and finally at Ohrdruf. He was promoted to *Faehnrich* (senior officer cadet or ensign) in 1923 and was commissioned Leutnant in the 17th Infantry Regiment on December 1, 1924. Except for six months in 1929, during which he did combat engineer training with the 6th Engineer Battalion, he remained with the 17th Infantry until 1933.

Without wealth or important contacts, Gerhard Franz obtained everything he got via his native intelligence, hard work, and deliberately educating himself through hard study. In 1933, as a first lieutenant, he passed the Wehrkreis General Staff examination in the upper 15% of those tested. On October 1 of that same year he began his secret General Staff training in Berlin. (Under the terms of the Treaty of Versailles, the German General Staff was illegal. The German Army did not officially acknowledge that Franz and his classmates were undergoing General Staff training at the War Academy until after March 16, 1935, when Hitler renounced the Treaty of Versailles.) He was promoted to captain on July 1, 1934.

In 1935 to 1937, Franz continued his training with the commandant of Schweidnitz and with the General Staff of the Army in Berlin. In late 1935, he was transferred to Army Service Depot 4 at Schweidnitz as a probationary member of the General Staff. Again successful, he became a full member of the General Staff on January 8, 1937.

In November 1938, because of his lack of command experience, Franz was transferred to the 5th Motorized Infantry Regiment at Stettin, where he assumed command of the 9th Company. After a successful command, he was promoted to major on April 1, 1939, and two months later was named chief of operations (Ia) of the elite 29th Infantry Division, which was motorizing at that time. It was redesignated 29th Motorized Division on August 24, 1939.

The 29th Motorized fought in Poland, where it was part of the main German attack in 1939. Transferred to the west, it played an extremely prominent part in the French campaign of 1940. It fought in Luxembourg, in the drive across Belgium (protecting the flank of the "Panzer Corridor"), at Dunkirk, and later at Belfort in the French Alps. On garrison duty in eastern France until January 1941, it was transferred back to Germany and crossed into Russia with Guderian's 2nd Panzer Group on June 22, 1941. It played a conspicuous role in the battles of encirclement at Minsk, Smolensk and Bryansk, and in the Battle of Tula during the Moscow campaign. Franz, meanwhile, had been promoted to lieutenant colonel, effective April 1, 1941.

In late 1941, Franz was taken out of the battle and sent to Poland (the *Generalgouvernement*) as chief of staff of Corps Command XXXV, a special purposes unit that was in the process of upgrading into a regular corps HQ under 9th Army. When this task was completed on January 20, 1942, Franz became chief of staff of the XXXV Corps. He was not in this post long, however. In April 1942 he was sent on leave, and on May 10, Gerhard Franz joined General Stumme as chief of staff of the XXXX Corps. He was given an accelerated promotion to colonel on July 1. Twenty-five days later he was relieved of his duties. Along with Georg Stumme, he was court-martialed for the security violation described above and was sentenced to two years' imprisonment.

Fortunately for Franz, Hermann Goering was impressed with him, so he was given another chance. He was sent to Egypt, where he was attached to the staff of the Afrika Korps. On December 7, 1942, he became chief of staff of the DAK, and held this post throughout the retreat from El Alamein. Four years of active campaigning in Europe, the snows of Russia, and the Sahara Desert—not to mention the stress of a court-martial and a short prison sentence—finally caught up with Franz, however, and he reported himself sick on February 2, 1943. He did not return to active duty for six months.

On August 1, 1943, Gerhard Franz took up his new assignment as chief of staff of the XXXXII Corps in Crimea on the Black Sea. At the time, the commander of the XXXXII Corps (Lieutenant General Anton Dostler) was simultaneously Military Commander, Crimea. This post was far behind the Eastern Front and, with its excellent climate, it have seemed to be a good assignment for Colonel Franz. Unfortunately for him, the Eastern Front moved steadily to the west, and the defense of the Crimea was turned over to Colonel General Erwin Jaenecke's 17th Army. The XXXXII Corps was shifted north and was involved in the highly demanding defensive battles on the southern sector of the Eastern Front. Colonel Franz fought at Kharkov, in the retreats to the Dnieper and the Dnestr, and in the Battle of Vinniza, before the XXXXII was encircled—along with the XI Corps—in the Battle of Cherkassy. Here, in February 1944, the pocket commander General of Artillery Wilhelm Stemmermann was killed, and it was every man for himself. Franz and his men had to swim a Russian river (in February!) to reach safety. Perhaps half of the corps escaped. The remnants of the XXXXII were sent back to Kovel and then to Poland to rebuild. In May 1944, the Staff, XXXXII Corps was incorporated into the I Cavalry Corps HQ and a new XXXXII Corps was created in Wehrkreis XIII for use in Poland.

By the late summer of 1944, the Wehrmacht's military machine was in full reverse, officer losses were very high, and experienced commanders were desperately needed for the new divisions being produced by the Replacement Army. After serving as chief of staff for three different corps—the last two of which were successful—Gerhard Franz had at last worked his way out of the OKH doghouse. After a week's leave, Franz attended the Division Commanders' Course from August 8 to 31, 1944. After graduation, he was at once sent to the Higher Troop Leadership Course for Panzer Troop Officers. Why he attended this second course is a complete mystery. As soon as he graduated, he was immediately given command of *Divisiongruppe 256* of Corps Detachment H, which was very much a non-motorized formation.

Franz's new unit had been created as the 256th Infantry Division in the fall of 1939 but had suffered such heavy losses at Vitebsk in 1944 (as part of 3rd Panzer Army) that it had been downgraded to Division-gruppe or regimental status. OKH, however, had decided to rebuild it as a *Volksgrenadier* (people's infantry) division and it had been taken out of the line shortly before Franz assumed command.

Gerhard Franz joined his new command in the Koenigsbrueck Maneuver Area in Silesia in September. It initially consisted of the 456th and 481st Regimental Groups. Shortly thereafter, however, it absorbed the understrength and only partially formed 568th Grenadier Division on September 17, 1944. With these partially trained inductees, as well as new recruits and returning wounded, Franz was able to organize the 256th VG into an infantry division with three grenadier regiments (the 1162nd, 1163rd, and 1164th), each with two battalions, and the 1568th Reconnaissance, Signal, Engineer, and Antitank companies.

After it was officially activated on September 17, 1944, the 256th was sent to Groningen in Schleswig-Holstein, where it completed its training under Wehrkreis X of the Replacement Army. In October, it was sent to Army Group B on the Western Front and fought at Tilburg in November. The 256th Volksgrenadier fought in eastern France, in the northern Alsace, in the battles of the Siegfried Line, at Bitche, in the Saar-Moselle Triangle, and in the defense of the middle Rhine. The division performed very well for a Volksgrenadier unit and its commander, Gerhard Franz, finally received his belated promotion to major general on December 1, 1944. He had made a fine professional comeback, and the "lost order" incident was at last behind him.

By the end of March 1945, the 256th Volksgrenadier was part of the 1st Army and was defending a sector on the middle Rhine. After six months of combat against the lavishly equipped Americans, without receiving replacements in sufficient quantity or of adequate quality, the division was down to kampfgruppe strength. General Franz nevertheless led it into action against an overwhelming American attack at Bitburg on April 8. When the battle was over, the 256th had ceased to exist as an organized combat force. Only small remnants of the division retreated to the east, where they were absorbed into other divisions, and the 256th Volksgrenadier Division passed into history. General Franz was not with it at the time. He was in a U.S. POW camp.

The former chief of staff of the Afrika Korps was discharged from the prison camps in 1947. He settled in Bad Wildungen, where he died on December 24, 1975.

Ulrich Kleemann was born in Langensalza on March 23, 1892, and entered the service as a Fahnenjunker in the 21st Dragoon Regiment in 1911. He was commissioned second lieutenant in 1913 and attended the Officers' Riding School at Paderborn from October 1913 to late June 1914. He spent virtually all of the war with the 21st Dragoons. He was twice severely wounded, was decorated with both grades of the Iron Cross, was promoted to first lieutenant in mid-1916, and became regimental adjutant on April 1, 1918.[4]

After the armistice, Kleemann commanded the 12th Volunteer Squadron in "the war after the war." In late September 1919, however, he was accepted into the 100,000-man army and was assigned to the Reichswehr's 113th Cavalry Regiment. He spent almost the entire 1919–35 period in cavalry assignments, much of it with the 18th Cavalry Regiment at Stuttgart-Cannstadt, where he commanded a squadron. He was promoted to Rittmeister (captain of cavalry) in 1923 and to major in 1933.

On October 15, 1935—the day it was activated—Ulrich Kleemann became commander of the 1st Motorcycle Battalion at Erfurt (1935–38) and was promoted to lieutenant colonel in 1936. This transfer eventually led to his permanent separation from the mounted arm, as German cavalry officers at this time resented the evolving motorized branch. Kleemann, however, had gone as far as he could with the cavalry and, on January 1, 1938, assumed command of the 3rd Rifle Regiment of the 3rd Panzer Division. His headquarters was at Eberswalde, Brandenburg, in Wehrkreis III. He was promoted to full colonel on October 1.

In September 1938, Kleemann and his regiment prepared for the invasion of Czechoslovakia, and took part in *Fall Grun*, the occupation of the Sudetenland. It is interesting to note that among his fellow regimental commanders in the 3rd Panzer Division were Colonel Walter Nehring (5th Panzer Regiment) and Colonel Ludwig Cruewell (6th Panzer Regiment), two future commanders of the Afrika Korps.

Meanwhile, Kleemann led the 3rd Regiment in the Polish campaign and did well in the attack from Pomerania across the Polish Corridor, where it linked up with the 3rd Army, attacking west from East Prussia. The 3rd Rifle Regiment then redeployed and, as part of Guderian's XIX Motorized Corps, pushed into eastern and central Poland. Kleemann's performance in Poland led to his promotion to command of the 3rd Rifle Brigade of the 3rd Panzer Division, which he commanded from December 4, 1939, to January 5, 1942. The 3rd Brigade's home station was also Eberswalde, but Kleemann was there only occasionally. He was on the Lower Rhine with his brigade in late 1939 and, as part of 6th Army, fought in the Netherlands and Belgium in May 1940. Then the 3rd Rifle redeployed and, as part of Panzer Group Guderian, took part in the final conquest of France in May and June 1940.

After Paris surrendered, Kleemann's brigade returned to Germany and did not see action again until Germany invaded the Soviet Union on June 22, 1941. As part of the 2nd Panzer Group, he fought in the huge battles of encirclement at Smolensk and Kiev, among others. He was decorated with the Knight's Cross on October 13, 1941, and was promoted to major general on November 1.

During Stalin's great winter offensive of 1941–42, Ulrich Kleemann fell ill or was wounded and gave up command of the depleted 3rd Rifle Brigade on January 5, 1942. (Because of its heavy casualties, the brigade would be dissolved later that year.) After he recovered, Kleemann was sent to North Africa as commander of the 90th Light Division. He assumed command on April 1, 1942. Here he was reunited with his old comrades from the 3rd Panzer Division: Nehring (now commanding the Afrika Korps) and Cruewell (now commander of Group Cruewell and deputy commander of Panzer Army Afrika). It is almost certain that they recommended Kleemann to Rommel, but this cannot be proven at this late date. In any case, he proved to be an excellent selection.

Figure 7.1
The Battle of Mersa Matruh

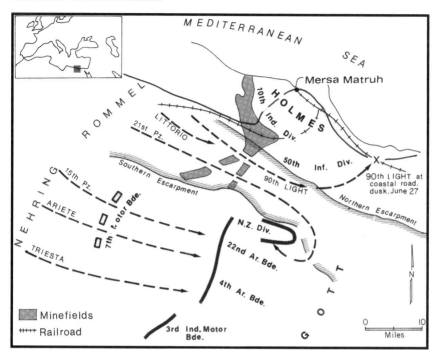

Ulrich Kleemann led the 90th Light through some of the worst fighting of the North African war, including the battles of the Gazala Line, the Cauldron, Bir Hacheim, the capture of Tobruk, and the invasion of Egypt. From an authorized strength of around 15,000 men, the 90th Light was gradually reduced to a strength of less than 1,500 troops. A very daring officer, Kleemann drove east with almost reckless abandon and cut off the British X Corps (10th Indian and 50th Infantry Divisions) east of Mersa Matrush on June 27, despite the fact that he had only 1,600 men at the time, was outnumbered more than 10 to 1, and was 15 miles from the nearest Axis unit (see Figure 7.1).[5] Fortunately for Kleemann, the British did not try to break out until the following evening and, by that time, the 90th Light had been reinforced by elements of the Italian X and XXI Infantry Corps. Only 60% of the British corps escaped in the confused breakout.[6] The next day, Kleemann and the Italians captured Mersa Matrush, along with a rearguard of 6,000 men and 40 destroyed tanks.

Rommel was finally checked near El Alamein on June 30. Kleemann was absent from July 13 to August 10, 1942, for reasons not disclosed by the records. He was temporarily replaced by Colonel Carl-Hans von Lungershausen. In any case, his division (now a kampfgruppe) figured prominently in almost every phase of the 1st Battle of El Alamein. At last, on September 8, 1942, General Kleemann was seriously wounded while leading an attack against the British 23rd Armoured Brigade west of Alam Halfa Ridge. He was in the hospital for months and did not return to active duty until May 28, 1943, when he assumed command of Assault Division Rhodes. Thirteen days later he was promoted to lieutenant general, to date from May 1. In September 1943, he was awarded the Oak Leaves for his service in Libya and Egypt.

Sturm-Division Rhodos was officially activated on May 31, 1943, and was created out of parts of the 22nd Air Landing Division and Fortress Division Crete. Stationed on the Greek island of Rhodes in the eastern Aegean, it included Grenadier Regiment Rhodes (formerly the 440th Grenadier Regiment); Fuesilier Battalion Rhodes (formerly the Fuesilier Battalion, 41st Infantry Division); Panzer Battalion Rhodes (consisting of two companies, equipped with captured tanks); and a light anti-aircraft company, a signals company, and an engineer company, plus a field replacement battalion.[7] The division was under the direct command of Luftwaffe Colonel General Alexander Loehr's Army Group E.

Kleemann remained in Rhodes until August 31, 1944, when he went on leave. While he was away, Italy defected from the Axis. Kleemann rushed back to the Balkans, where Loehr placed him in charge of the newly formed LXXXXI Corps z.b.V. ("for special purposes"), which controlled miscellaneous forces in the Salonika area of Greece and garrison units on the Aegean islands. Kleemann was relieved of this assignment on October 9 and two days later assumed command of the IV Panzer Corps. He was promoted to general of panzer troops on October 20, 1944.

The newly formed IV Panzer Corps was formed from the remnants of the IV Corps, which had been destroyed in Romania. (Its commander, General of Infantry Friedrich Mieth, had been killed.) The IV Panzer absorbed the Operations Staff Eastern Hungary, as well as part of the staff of Assault Division Rhodes and Staff, 17th Panzer Grenadier Brigade. Attached to Army Group South, it fought in Hungary and Austria. Most of Kleemann's combat units, however, were cut off in Budapest, where they were destroyed in February 1945.

Fourth Panzer Corps was redesignated Panzer Corps Feldherrnhalle (FHH) on November 27, 1944. Kleemann commanded it for the rest of the war, except for the period December 22 to 28, 1944, when he was acting commander of the 8th Army. (The former army commander, General of Infantry Otto Woehler, had been named commander-in-chief of Army Group South on December 22 and his permanent replacement, General of Mountain Troops Hans Kreysing, did not arrive until

December 28.) By 1940 standards, the FHH was a very weak panzer corps indeed. In February 1945, it included the badly understrength 13th Panzer and 2nd FHH Panzer Divisions, as well as the 503rd Heavy Panzer Battalion (equipped with Tiger tanks) and some strong combat engineer components. Kleemann led the FHH in battles in Slovakia and Upper Austria, and managed to surrender his command to the British at the end of the war.

Kleemann was one of many highly competent German generals who have been largely forgotten today, but he helped make the German Wehrmacht the terror of the world for six years, in spite of the "genius" of the Fuehrer. Not charged with any war crimes, he was released from the POW camps in 1947 and settled in West Germany. He was killed in an automobile accident near Oberursel in the Taunus Mountains on January 3, 1963. He was 70 years old.

Wilhelm von Thoma was born in Dachau, a town near Munich, on September 11, 1891. His father died when he was one year old, so he was raised by his mother, who saw to it that he got a good education. In 1912, he graduated from the Ludwig Humanist Gymnasium (high school) in Munich and joined the Royal Bavarian Army as a Fahnenjunker on September 9 of that same year. He was commissioned in the 3rd Bavarian (Prince Karl) Infantry Regiment of the Bavarian 11th Infantry Division on August 1, 1914.

Later that month, Germany invaded Belgium and France. Thoma was at the front from the beginning, fighting in the Vosges, in the Battle of Lorraine, and in the Battle of Nancy-Epinal. On September 25, during the Battle of the Somme, he received his first wound when a bullet grazed his head. Four days later, a piece of shrapnel struck him in the shin. He nevertheless remained with the troops and was named regimental adjutant on January 24, 1915.

Thoma and the 3rd Bavarian fought in the decisive Battle of Gorlice in Galicia in May 1915, when the Czar's armies were routed. He also took part in the capture of Brest-Litovsk and in the pursuit to and through the Pripet marshes. The 3rd was sent to Serbia that fall, and Thoma was hit in the chest in October. The following year, the regiment was sent to the Western Front, where it fought in the Battle of Verdun. In the summer of 1916, it was transferred back to the east to bolster the sagging Austrians, who were being hard pressed by the Russians. On July 5, 1916, the Czar's forces launched another offensive. Thoma and his regimental commander had just arrived at an Austrian command post when the Russians hit and quickly routed most of the Austrians. Thoma and his colonel held the command post, however, and, acting on his own, Lieutenant von Thoma decided to make a stand. Impressed with Thoma's coolness and absolute disregard for his own safety, enough Austrians rallied on him to form a small battalion. They beat back three major Russian attacks and gave the Bavarian 11th Infantry Division time to plug the hole in the Central Powers' line. For his courage, Wilhelm von Thoma was decorated with one of Germany's highest medals, the Bavarian Max Joseph Military Order for exceptional "Courage on Behalf of the Fatherland." With it came the non-hereditary title *Ritter* or Knight.

After this victory, Thoma fought in the Battle of Kovel, in the Vulcan Mountains (on the Romanian border), and in the conquest of Romania, which ended with the capture of Bucharest on December 6. After this, Leutnant von Thoma and his regiment were transferred back to the west, fighting in the trenches in the Upper Alsace in the spring of 1917, in the battles of the Aisne and Champagne, in Flanders, and in the trenches between the Maas and the Mosel. Thoma was promoted to first lieutenant in 1917 and continued to distinguish himself in the field. Back on the Western Front in 1918, he was hit in the wrist by a grenade fragment on April 25. He was named commander of the 3rd Machine Gun Company (Bavarian 3rd Infantry Regiment) a week later. On May 14, 1918, he was given a tremendous vote of confidence for a lieutenant when he was named commander of the I Battalion. His luck, however, ran out on July 18. The day before, the fifth and final "Ludendorff Offensive" had been defeated. The U.S. Army, backed by heavy French tank support, launched their Aisne-Marne counteroffensive. Fighting southwest of Soissons, Thoma's battalion put up a fierce defense but was unable to check the Americans. Thoma himself was among the prisoners. He remained a prisoner of war until October 1919.[8]

After his release from prison, Thoma joined Major General Ritter Franz von Epp's Freikorps and fought in "the war after the war." In January 1921 he became part of the Reichsheer's 19th Infantry Regiment (where he served as a company commander) and, in July 1922, joined the Bavarian 7th Motorized Battalion as battalion adjutant. Here, on November 8 and 9, 1923, he took part in suppressing Adolf Hitler's Beer Hall Putsch in Munich. He commanded the 2nd Company of the 7th Motorized (2/7th Motorized) from 1925 to 1929.

Thoma was already one of the most experienced motorized officers in the Reichswehr when he was transferred to the Prussian 3rd Motorized Battalion in 1929. He returned to the 7th Motorized in 1931, but served on detached duty to the Motorized Demonstration Command in Berlin and to the staff of the 7th Infantry Division in Munich, where he was the motor transport officer (1931–34). He was a major when the Nazis took power in 1933.

On August 1, 1934, Thoma transferred to Motorized Demonstration Command Ohrdruf, where Germany's first entirely tank unit was being formed. It was equipped with the small and inferior Panzer Mark I tanks, which were armed with two machine guns and had no main battle gun. It had a crew of two. (A second motorized demonstration command was later created at Zossen. Together with Ohrdruf, they formed the nucleus of the German panzer branch, the *Panzerwaffe*.)

On October 1, 1935, the day the first three panzer divisions were officially created, Ritter von Thoma was named commander of the II Battalion, 4th Panzer Regiment. The II/4th was part of Heinz Guderian's 2nd Panzer Division in Wuerzburg. He was promoted to lieutenant colonel in 1936 and in September of that year was sent to Spain, where he led the German experimental tank forces against the Reds as part of the famous Condor Legion. (The men of this unit, which was called Group *Imker* [Beekeeper], were volunteers from the 6th Panzer Regiment of the 3rd Panzer Division.) Thoma's unit consisted of two (later three) companies equipped with Panzer Mark Is. Although they spent some time training Franco's Nationalists, Group Imker was also frequently involved in combat, often against the T-26, a Soviet tank that was superior to the Panzer Mark I. German panzer tactics, however, were superior to those of the Reds and usually won the day. Thoma himself was personally involved in 192 armored combats during the Spanish Civil War and earned the highest Spanish decorations for his incredible courage, as well as a promotion to colonel in 1938. He also played a major role in the defeat of the Royalist and Communist forces and was partially responsible for the ultimate victory of Franco's Republicans.

When he returned home, Colonel General Walter von Brauchitsch, the commander-in-chief of the army, offered him command of a panzer brigade. Thoma asked for a regiment instead. This did not impress Brauchitsch and probably damaged Thoma's career. In any case, he assumed command of the 3rd Panzer Regiment of the 2nd Panzer Division at Dresden on June 1, 1939. He led his unit in the invasion of Poland with considerable success. The regiment then redeployed to the Western Front. Thoma, meanwhile, was named general of mobile troops (*Gen.d.schnellen Tr.*) at OKH on March 5, 1940. He was promoted to major general on August 1, 1940.

After the French campaign, Ritter von Thoma was given command of the 17th Rifle Brigade of the 17th Panzer Division, which he led in the massive frontier battles around Brest-Litovsk in June 1941. He also took part in the battles of encirclement around Minsk and Smolensk. Meanwhile, his divisional commander, Lieutenant General Hans-Juergen von Arnim, was seriously wounded on June 26, and Arnim's temporary replacement (and a follow holder of the Max Joseph Order), Major General Ritter Karl von Weber, was mortally wounded south of

Smolensk on July 18.[9] Thoma succeeded Weber. Of his new divisional commander, Colonel General Guderian recalled: "He had been famous for his icy calm and exceptional bravery ... and now he proved his ability once again."[10] Thoma commanded the 17th Panzer Division on the Eastern Front until September 15, 1941, when Arnim returned. The Bavarian knight resumed command of the 17th Rifle until October 14, when he was named commander of the 20th Panzer Division, also on the central sector of the Russian Front. He fought in the Battle of Moscow and in the subsequent Soviet Winter Offensive of 1941–42, winning the Knight's Cross in the process.

Thoma gave up command of the 20th Panzer Division in the summer of 1942 and, after two months' leave, was officially named commander of the Afrika Korps on September 1, 1942. (He did not arrive at corps headquarters, however, until September 17. Until then, the Afrika Korps was commanded by General von Vaerst.)

Montgomery's great offensive began on October 23, 1942 (Figure 7.2), and Georg Stumme, the acting commander of Panzer Army Afrika, was reported as missing in action the next day. As the ranking German general, Ritter von Thoma assumed command of the army and checked the British advance, at least for the moment. He was, however, immensely relieved when Erwin Rommel returned from Europe and resumed command of the army.

Thoma fought like a tiger in the 2nd Battle of El Alamein and inflicted terrible casualties on the British 8th Army (which lost more than 500 tanks in this battle), but could not prevent it from virtually destroying the Afrika Korps. It had 293 tanks on October 23. By November 4, it had only 24 "runners" left. Rommel had ordered a general retreat the previous day, but Adolf Hitler had reversed this order and commanded him to "stand fast, yield not a yard of ground, and throw every gun and every man into battle."[11]

At 8 A.M. on November 4, the British attacked the center of the Axis line with 200 tanks. Thoma counterattacked with everything he had left. Remarkably, with odds of 10 to 1 against him, Wilhelm von Thoma turned back the first attack. Later that morning, however, he made his last stand at Tel el Mampsra, a 16-foot-high sand dune west of Kidney Ridge. Thoma deployed the Afrika Korps on either side of the dune and personally assumed command of the Kampfstaffel in the center.

When Fritz Bayerlein, the chief of staff of the Afrika Korps, arrived, he found Thoma wearing all of his many decorations. "Bayerlein, the Fuehrer's order is madness," Thoma declared. "It's the death warrant of the Army. How can I explain it to my men?" He then ordered the colonel to establish an Afrika Korps headquarters at El Daba, some distance to the rear, in effect sending Bayerlein to a place of safety.

Figure 7.2
El Alamein

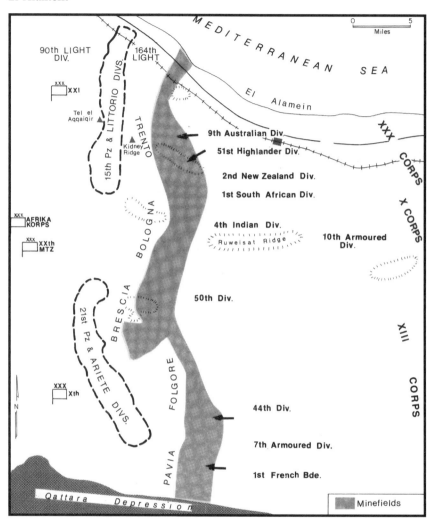

"I shall remain here and conduct the defense of Tel el Mampsra in person, as Rastenburg [i.e., Fuehrer Headquarters] orders." Does the general want to die? Bayerlein asked himself.[12]

Bayerlein left at once. At 11 A.M., Thoma's aide appeared at El Daba. He also had been sent away on a pretext. He reported to Bayerlein that Thoma's force had been almost destroyed—tanks, flak guns, antitank guns—everything. Alarmed, Bayerlein jumped into a "reece" (reconnaissance) vehicle and rushed back to the front. British tank fire forced him to abandon his vehicle, but he proceeded on foot to the crest of a sand dune, about 200 yards away from Tel el Mampsra. Here he could see that the aide had not exaggerated: the Afrika Korps had been practically wiped out. All Thoma had left was a handful of badly wounded men. His own command tank had been hit several times and now lay knocked out and burning nearby. Like some kind of weird ghost, the general stood beside a burning panzer, deliberately exposing himself to heavy machine gun fire. Miraculously, not a bullet touched him.

Suddenly, the firing stopped. Several Sherman tanks and a jeep approached the veteran panzer leader. Ritter von Thoma got into the jeep without saying a word. The Battle of Tel el Mampsra was over.

Bayerlein turned, ran to the west, and finally reached safety. When he reported to Erwin Rommel and Siegfried Westphal, the operations officer begged him to keep the story to himself. "Otherwise Thoma's entire family will suffer for it."[13]

Field Marshal Sir Bernard Law Montgomery appreciated a brave man, and there was none braver than Ritter Wilhelm von Thoma. He invited the former commander of the Afrika Korps to dinner that evening, and the two hit it off famously. Thoma later admitted that he was "staggered" by what Montgomery knew and that "he seemed to know as much about our position as I did myself."[14] Each invited the other to visit his home after the war. Certain members of the news media tried to get Monty into trouble by reporting the event and expressing their outrage that the commander of the 8th Army would entertain a "Nazi" general. British Prime Minister Churchill, however, would have none of it. "Poor von Thoma," Sir Winston moaned. "I, too, have dined with Montgomery."

A hero of three wars, Thoma remained in prison until 1947, where he met B. H. Liddell Hart. The famous British military historian wrote of Thoma:

A tough but likeable type ... loves fighting for the zest of it, but would fight without ill-feeling, respecting any opponent. In the Middle Ages he would have been perfectly happy as a knight-errant, challenging all comers at any crossroad for the honor of crossing spears with them. The advent of the tank in warfare was a godsend to such a man, giving him a chance to relive the part of the mail-clad knight.[15]

Thoma made perhaps the most serious mistake of his military career as a prisoner of war. On March 22, 1943, during a conversation with another former commander of the Afrika Korps, he told General Cruewell of a secret rocket-testing facility located at Peenemuende on the Baltic coast. Unknown to the Germans, the British Secret Intelligence Service (SIS) planted a microphone in the room. The SIS thus learned the location of one of the Third Reich's most important secret bases. Later, after reconnaissance flights confirmed this information, the Allies bombed the place and inflicted serious damage upon it.

Thoma was held in several POW camps, including Island Farm (Bridgend, Glamorgan), Trent Park (Barnet, Middlesex), and Wilton Park (Beaconsfield, Buckinghamshire). His health deteriorated in prison, and one of his legs had to be amputated. The British officials (with whom he had excellent relations) fitted him with an artificial limb. He was repatriated to Germany and released on November 25, 1947.

After World War II, there was not enough housing to go around in the former Third Reich. Montgomery, however, reportedly made sure that no one was billeted at the Thoma home, other than his relatives. (Thoma was a lifelong bachelor and had no children of his own.) The former commander of the Afrika Korps, however, had been wounded at least 14 times in his career, and the stress of his life had taken its toll. He died at Dachau, the town of his birth, on April 30, 1948, at the age of 56.

Another officer of whom Rommel thought very highly was Dr. Rudolf Boeckmann.

Boeckmann was born in Silschede, Westphalia, on April 16, 1895, and graduated with the *Abitur* from the Gevelsberg *Realgymnasium* in 1913. He spent three semesters studying philosophy and theology at the University of Halle/Saale before joining the army when World War I began. Initially he was a war volunteer with the 7th Field Artillery Regiment in Wesel, but he joined the 50th Reserve Field Artillery Regiment in January 1915. A "90-day wonder," he received his commission as a second lieutenant of reserves later that year. The 50th Reserve Artillery alternatively fought in Russia and France. In March 1918, young Boeckmann became a battery commander. He won both grades of the Iron Cross, as well as the Knight's Cross of the Hohenzollern House Order, and was voluntarily discharged in 1919, because he had no interest in a military career. After the war, he went back to school and received the *Dr. Phil. promoviert* in philosophy, theology, and Germanic studies from the University of Muenster in 1921. After that, he taught at the *Oberrealschulen* in Hagen and Hameln.

Boeckmann was recalled to military duty on August 17, 1939, as the Wehrmacht prepared to invade Poland. He was initially sent to the Artillery School at Jueterbog, where he caught up on developments in his field. In 1940, he served in France. The following year, he took part in Operation "Barbarossa," the invasion of Russia, and earned the Iron

Cross, 1st Class. In September, however, OKH placed him in "Fuehrer Reserve, Africa." He was named commander of the 480th Heavy Artillery Battalion, which was part of Arko 104, and he was soon regarded as an expert at blowing apart British positions. Colonel Fritz Krause, the senior artillery commander in Panzer Army Afrika, soon came to rely on his advice, and even General Rommel was impressed with his ability to slam the enemy. He would often call his artillery command and ask: "Krause, what does Boeckmann say?"[16] He was promoted to major of reserves on April 1, 1942.

On July 17, 1942, during the first battle of El Alamein, the British launched a surprise attack southwest of El Alamein. Boeckmann beat it back, employing direct fire over open sights. For this act of skill and courage, he was awarded the Knight's Cross.

On September 14, Boeckmann's luck ran out when a fragment from an exploding British shell struck him in the head. He was medically evacuated back to Europe and was in the Reserve Hospital at Garmisch until August 1943. While there, he was promoted to lieutenant colonel of reserves.

After he finally regained his health, Rudolf Boeckmann was selected to attend the Regimental Commanders' Course. He was promoted to colonel of reserves on August 1, 1944, and was given command of the 187th Artillery Regiment of the 87th Infantry Division, which was then fighting in the northern sector of the Eastern Front. On September 19, after less than seven weeks in the Soviet Union, the veteran Afrika Korps artilleryman was killed in action near Siimusti, Estonia.

Willibald Borowietz, the last commander of the 15th Panzer Division, was born in Ratibor, Silesia, on September 17, 1893. He entered the service as a Fahnenjunker on March 5, 1914, and went to war as a noncommissioned officer in August 1914, as a sergeant and deputy officer (*Offiziers-Stellvertreter*) in the 156th Infantry Regiment. He was promoted to Faehnrich in October and was commissioned Leutnant on January 1, 1915. Meanwhile, he served on the Western Front. He was slightly wounded at Cutry-Ugny on August 24, 1914, and seriously wounded at St. Andre on September 10. Sent back to Breslau to recover, he was given a wounded leave and did not return to duty until the end of the year. Even then he did not return to the front, but rather was assigned to the 2nd Machine Gun Replacement Company of Wehrkreis VI, where he underwent machine gun training. He was then assigned to the machine gun company of the 271st Reserve Infantry Regiment. He became the machine gun company commander in June 1915 and held his post until January 1916, when he became commander of the 123rd Machine Gun Troop (*MG-Scharfschuetzen-Abteilung 123*) in the 269th Reserve Infantry Regiment.[17]

After a staff assignment at Spandau, which lasted from June 1917 to June 1918, Borowietz rejoined the 156th Infantry Regiment. He served successively as regimental signals officer, deputy regimental adjutant, and adjutant of the II Battalion. Promoted to first lieutenant on October 18, 1918, he fell ill late that month and was sent to the Reserve Hospital in Wiesbaden. He had just returned to the 156th Infantry's replacement battalion when the armistice was signed.

Except for brief temporary duty assignments, Lieutenant Borowietz commanded a company in the 156th from December 1918 to June 1919, when he was seconded to the commander of armored vehicles in Army Frontier Guard Command South. He was not selected for the Reichsheer and was discharged in early 1920. He had already joined the Silesian State Police as a first lieutenant by then and was stationed in Breslau. Postings to the Higher Police School at Eiche and the Technical Police School in Berlin followed. He became a police captain in 1921 and a major of police in 1935.

Borowietz rejoined the army as a territorial major (E) in 1935. He did not become a member of the active (regular) army until 1941. He was initially assigned to the mobile combat school (*Kraftfahrschule*), but joined the staff of the Panzer Troops School in late 1937. When World War II began, he was on the staff of the general of mobile troops at OKH, where he had been since the previous February. On September 9, 1939, however, he was given command of the 50th Antitank (*Panzerabwehr*) Battalion of the 4th Light Division, which he led in the last four weeks of the Polish campaign. This Austrian formation then returned to St. Poelten, Austria (Wehrkreis XVII), where its parent unit was converted into the 9th Panzer Division. Borowietz (who was promoted to lieutenant colonel on April 1, 1940) led the battalion in the Netherlands and French campaigns of 1940. The 50th Panzerabwehr was redesignated the 50th *Panzerjaeger* (Tank Destroyer) Battalion in February 1941.

Borowietz remained with the 9th Panzer Division and was named commander of its 10th Rifle Regiment on June 1, 1941. He distinguished himself in the invasion of Yugoslavia and on the Russian Front, where he fought in the battles of encirclement at Uman, Kiev, and Bryansk, and in the subsequent drive on Moscow. That summer, his brigade destroyed 92 enemy tanks, 16 guns, and 12 anti-aircraft guns in a single battle. For this accomplishment, Borowietz was awarded the Knight's Cross on July 24, 1941. The following year he fought at Voronesk, Orel, and Orscha, and in the Rzhev salient, and was promoted to full colonel in February 1942. He was transferred to the 10th Panzer Division in November 1942 and was named commander of the 10th Panzer Grenadier Brigade on November 18. The division was then in Italy and embarking for Tunisia. Meanwhile,

Lieutenant General von Vaerst, the commander of the 15th Panzer Division, was earmarked for higher command. Borowietz was selected to replace him in command of the 15th Panzer. Borowietz led the 15th Panzer Division in the retreat through western Libya and in Tunisia, where it fought its final battles. He was promoted to major general on January 1, 1943, and, in May 1943, as Army Group Afrika was collapsing, he was awarded the Oak Leaves to his Knight's Cross and received a special promotion to lieutenant general. (There were many such promotions as resistance in North Africa collapsed, but Borowietz's promotion does confirm that Berlin thought he had done a good job as a divisional commander.)

Willibald Borowietz remained in POW camps for the rest of the war. Ironically, he was killed in an accident in the prison camp at Clinton, Mississippi, on July 1, 1945—almost two months after the end of the war.

CHAPTER VIII

THE OTHER COMMANDERS

COMMANDERS OF PANZER ARMY AFRIKA

Panzer Army Afrika was formed on August 15, 1941, as Panzer Group Africa. It was upgraded to Panzer Army Afrika on January 21, 1942, and was redesignated 1st Italian-German Panzer Army on October 1, 1942. It surrendered in Tunisia on May 12, 1943.

The commanders of the panzer army were as follows: General of Panzer Troops/Colonel General/Field Marshal Erwin Rommel (August 15, 1941–September 25, 1942); General of Panzer Troops Georg Stumme (September 25–October 24, 1942); General of Panzer Troops Ritter Wilhelm von Thoma (October 24–25, 1942); Rommel (October 25–November 26, 1942); General of Panzer Troops Gustav Fehn (November 26–December 2, 1942); Rommel (December 2, 1942–February 26, 1943); and Italian General Giovanni Messe (February 23–May 12, 1943).

The story of Erwin Rommel is well known. He was born in Heidenheim, Swabia (a district in Wuerttemberg, in southwestern Germany) on November 15, 1891, the son and grandson of schoolteachers. He joined the Imperial Army as a Fahnenjunker in the 124th Infantry Regiment in 1910. He served in World War I, mainly in infantry and mountain units, and earned the *Pour le Merite* in 1918. This medal was the equivalent of the Congressional Medal of Honor when awarded to someone of such junior rank. Rommel emerged from the war as a captain. Selected for the Reichsheer, he did not score high enough on his Wehrkreis examination to be selected for the General Staff, a fact that he resented.

Rommel spent the Weimar years (1919–33) and the peacetime years of the Nazi regime (1933–39) alternating mainly between command positions and staff (instructional) positions. He also wrote a book,

Infantry in the Attack, based upon his World War experiences, which became a bestseller in Nazi Germany. He became a colonel, commander of the Infantry School at Weiner Neustadt (south of Vienna, Austria), and served three temporary duty tours as commander of Adolf Hitler's bodyguard. He was promoted to major general on August 23, 1939, with a date of rank of August 1.

Hitler liked the dynamic Swabian so, when Rommel asked to be given command of a panzer division, Hitler gave him one. Rommel distinguished himself as commander of the 7th Panzer Division in Belgium and France, leading to his promotion to lieutenant general (effective January 1, 1941) and to command of the Afrika Korps (February 14, 1941). Later, the Desert Fox commanded Panzer Group Afrika (from September 1, 1941), Panzer Army Afrika (January 21, 1942), the 1st Italian-German Panzer Army (October 24, 1942), and Army Group Afrika (January 1–March 9, 1943). He was promoted to general of panzer troops (July 1, 1941), colonel general (January 30, 1942), and field marshal (June 22, 1942). In the meantime, he established the legend of the Desert Fox, captured Tobruk, and won many victories.

On July 10, 1943, Rommel became commander of Army Group B, which was then reforming in Munich. (It had been mauled on the Eastern Front in the winter of 1942–43.) Rommel commanded it in the occupation of northern Italy (1943) before being assigned the major role in the defense of Western Europe, under Field Marshal von Rundstedt's OB West. Here he was able to check—but not defeat—the Allied D-Day invasion on June 6, 1944. He waged a brilliant but ultimately unsuccessful campaign in Normandy from then until July 17, 1944, when he was critically wounded in an Allied fighter-bomber attack.

Rommel was peripherally involved in the July 20, 1944 attempt to overthrow Adolf Hitler. When his role in the plot was discovered, he was given the choice of committing suicide or standing trial before the People's Court. If he chose the former, he was told no action would be taken against his wife and son. He took a fatal dose of poison near his home at Herrlingen on October 14, 1944.

For biographies of Georg Stumme and Ritter Wilhelm von Thoma, see Chapter VII.

Gustav Fehn was born in Nuremberg, Franconia, on February 21, 1892, and joined the Imperial Army as a Fahnenjunker on July 24, 1911. He was commissioned in the 67th Infantry Regiment in January 1913 and soon transferred to the 98th Infantry Regiment. He spent virtually the entire 1914–17 period with this unit, serving on the Western Front as a battalion adjutant, company commander, battalion staff officer, and regimental adjutant. He fought in the Battle of the Marne

(1914), the Argonne (1914–16), Verdun (1916), in the Ardonne again (1916), on the Somme (1916), back to the Argonne (1917), and in the Champagne sector (1917). He was named adjutant of the 89th Reserve Infantry Brigade on December 21, 1917, and spent the rest of the war with this unit on the Western Front.[1]

Fehn spent almost the entire Reichsheer period in the 12th Infantry Regiment, serving as a company commander from 1927 to 1932. He was assigned to the 5th Cavalry Regiment from 1932 to 1935, and was commander of the I Battalion, 33rd Infantry Regiment at Darmstadt from 1935 to 1937.[2] He was on the staff of the 33rd Infantry from 1937 to 1939, and became commander of the regiment on April 1, 1939. He led it on the Saar Front (1939–40) and in the Western campaign of 1940, where he fought in Belgium and France. He was meanwhile promoted to first lieutenant (1916), captain (1923), major (1933), lieutenant colonel (1935), and colonel (1938).

Fehn distinguished himself in the French campaign and was promptly rewarded. On July 30, 1940, he was named commander of the 4th Rifle Brigade and a promotion to major general became effective two days later. He was decorated with the Knight's Cross on August 5.

The 4th Rifle was part of the 4th Panzer Division and consisted of the 12th and 33rd Rifle Regiments and the 34th Motorcycle Battalion. Fehn directed it in the preparation for the invasion of the United Kingdom. On November 11, 1940, however, he was named commander of the 5th Panzer Division, which was then stationed in Poland.

Fehn's new division was sent to Romania in January 1941. Three months later, it took part in the invasion of eastern Yugoslavia and then turned south into Greece. The 5th Panzer played a major role in driving the British forces and their allies from the mainland of Europe. In July 1941 it was sent to Russia and Army Group Center, where it took part in heavy fighting all the way to the gates of Moscow. It remained on the central sector during Stalin's winter offensive of 1941–42 and in the defensive battles of 1942 and 1943. Fehn, meanwhile, was promoted to lieutenant general on August 1, 1942, and was given command of the XXXX Panzer Corps on November 1, 1942. He was promoted to general of panzer troops the same day.

Gustav Fehn led the XXXX Panzer for only two weeks. He handed over command of the corps to Hermann Balck and left Russia on November 13. Three days later he arrived in Libya and assumed command of the Afrika Korps, which he led in the retreat across Libya. On November 26, after only 10 days in Africa, Rommel named him acting commander of Panzer Army Afrika, much to the surprise of General Fehn. The Desert Fox then flew to Germany to try to make Hitler see that Germany's strategic position in North Africa was hopeless. He was unsuccessful.

Rommel returned to Libya on December 2, and Fehn resumed command of the Afrika Korps. He led it in the retreat to Tripoli, which the Germans abandoned on January 20. Meanwhile, on January 15, 1943, Gustav Fehn was seriously wounded in a battle against the British. He would not be able to return to active duty for six months.

After he finally recovered from his wounds, Gustav Fehn was named acting commander of the LXXXVI Corps, headquartered in Dax, southwestern France. He only held this command for seven weeks; then, after six weeks in Fuehrer Reserve, he was named commander of the XXI Mountain Corps in Serbia and Croatia. Although he had been considered a good panzer corps and division commander, Fehn spent the rest of the war in the Balkans. On July 20, 1944, he exchanged commands with General of Infantry Ernst von Leyser. From then until the end of the war, he was commander of the XV Mountain Corps. He surrendered it to Tito's Yugoslavian guerillas on May 8, 1945. Most of Fehn's men were subsequently murdered, including General Fehn. On June 5, 1945, he was shot, without benefit of trial.

Perhaps the most distinguished Italian soldier to emerge from the World War II era, Giovanni Messe was born on December 10, 1883, near the city of Brindisi. He joined the Italian Army in 1901 and took part in the conquest of Libya. Later he fought in World War I, earned several decorations, and served as aide to King Victor Emmanuel III from 1923 to 1927. He then transferred to the *Bersaglieri*, a branch of elite motorized infantry units that can still be recognized from the peculiar hats they wear, which are decorated with capercaillie feathers. For eight years, he commanded the 9th Bersaglieri Regiment. In 1935, Messe was promoted to brigadier general and was given command of the 3rd (Motorized) Celebe Brigade in Verona. After successfully leading this unit in the 2nd Italo-Abyssinian War, he was promoted to major general and was named deputy commander of an armored division in Ethiopia (1935–36).

After spending three years as inspector of Celere Troops (1936–39), Messe briefly commanded the 3rd Celere Division (1939), and was then transferred to Albania (which had recently been annexed by Italy) as deputy GOC (General Officer Commanding) of Occupation Corps Albania. He led the Celere Corps in the Greco-Italian War in 1940–41 and—unlike most other Italian generals—actually experienced some success against the Greeks. That winter, however, the Greeks launched a major counteroffensive, hurled back the latter-day Romans, and conquered one fourth of Albania. The following spring the German Wehrmacht intervened and overran Greece and Yugoslavia.

Meanwhile, Hitler invaded the Soviet Union on June 22, 1941. Mussolini pledged assistance and, on July 10, 1941, the *Corpo di*

Spedizione Italiano in Russia (the CSIR or the Italian Expeditionary Force) was formed under the command of Generale di Corpo d'Armata Francesco Zingales. Before he could cross into Russia, however, General Zingales fell ill in Vienna and was replaced by Giovanni Messe on July 14. This command grew from 60,000 men in 1941 to 200,000 by 1942.

The CSIR fought as part of the German 11th Army and later as part of General Ewald von Kleist's 1st Panzer Group on the Eastern Front. It did well initially, and Messe was decorated with the Knight's Cross. In early 1942, however, the CSIR was redesignated XXXV Corps and became part of Generale d' Armada Italo Gariboldi's Italian 8th Army. This force generally fought well until the winter of 1942–43, but was plagued by a lack of transport, inferior equipment, and poorly trained officers. When Stalin launched Operation "Uranus," which led to the encirclement of the German 6th Army in Stalingrad, 8th Army was smashed and almost disintegrated. Fortunately for Messe, he had been recalled to Italy on November 1, 1942, and he was not involved in the Stalingrad debacle.

Giovanni Messe's next assignment was to command the 1st Italian-German Panzer Army (the former Panzer Army Afrika, it was also called the 1st Italian Panzer Army and the 1st German-Italian Panzer Army). He was genuinely flattered to succeed Erwin Rommel in this post and was proud to have the Afrika Korps under his command, and said so at every appropriate opportunity. He worked smoothly with his Teutonic allies except for his German chief of staff, Fritz Bayerlein, who was Messe's inferior both as a commander and as a leader. Bayerlein routinely interfered with his orders, and Messe was no doubt relieved when he was sent back to Europe.

General Messe led the 1st Army as well as anyone could have expected, but the material superiority of Montgomery's British 8th Army was simply too great. On May 13, 1943, with his army already destroyed, Messe gave himself up to the British. The day before, he had been promoted to the rank of field marshal.

Like most Italian officers, Messe was a royalist. After the Italian government capitulated and was forced to flee Rome one step ahead of the Germans, Messe was released from prison, and in September 1943 he was named chief of staff of the Royal Italian Army, which was being reorganized and reformed to fight for the Allies against the Germans and Mussolini's rump Fascist Republic. In 1947, two years after the Third Reich surrendered, Messe retired after a military career of 46 years.

Marshal Messe had always been popular with his troops (both German and Italian). After he left the service, he was elected president of the Italian Veterans Association, a post he held until his death. In

1953, he decided to see if his popularity extended to the general public as well and ran for public office. He was elected to the Italian senate that same year but only served one term. He then again retired from public service to write his memoirs, which included a book about the final campaign in Tunisia. (Apparently he did not care for politics.)

After an active retirement, Giovanni Messe died in Rome on December 19, 1968, at the age of 85.

COMMANDERS OF THE AFRIKA KORPS

The commanders of the German Afrika Korps (DAK) included Lieutenant General/General of Panzer Troops Erwin Rommel (February 14–August 15, 1941); Lieutenant General Ferdinand Schaal (August 15–September 1, 1941); Lieutenant General/General of Panzer Troops Ludwig Cruewell (September 1, 1941–May 29, 1942); Lieutenant General Walther Nehring (May 29–August 31, 1942); Lieutenant General Gustav von Vaerst (August 31–September 17, 1942); Lieutenant General Ritter Wilhelm von Thoma (September 17–November 4, 1942); Colonel Fritz Bayerlein (November 4–13, 1942); General of Panzer Troops Gustav Fehn (November 13, 1942–January 15, 1943); Lieutenant General Heinz Ziegler (January 15–February 28, 1943); and Lieutenant General/General of Panzer Troops Hans Cramer (February 28–May 12, 1943).

The stories of Rommel, Cruewell, and Nehring have already been told.

Ferdinand Schaal was born in Freiburg, Brunswick on February 2, 1889. He joined the army as a Fahnenjunker in 1908, was commissioned in the 22nd Dragoon Regiment in 1909, fought in World War I, and served in the Reichsheer. He became commander of the 16th Cavalry Regiment in 1934, the year he was promoted to colonel. Later he commanded the 1st Panzer Brigade (1935–39) and the 10th Panzer Division (1939–41), which he led in France and on the Russian Front. He was promoted to major general in 1938, to lieutenant general in 1939, and to general of panzer troops to date from October 1, 1941. He was picked to succeed Erwin Rommel as commander of the Afrika Korps but only held the command two weeks (August 15–September 1, 1941).[3] Apparently, for some reason, he was not acceptable to Erwin Rommel. In any case, he was named acting commander of the XXXIV Corps Command on the Eastern Front on September 2 and was appointed permanent commander of the LVI Panzer Corps on September 13, 1941.

General Schaal led the LVI Panzer on the Eastern Front until August 1, 1943, fighting in the drive to and retreat from Moscow, in the Soviet winter offensive of 1941–42, in the Rzhev salient, and in the Spass-Demjamsk zone in the central sector. After two years on the Russian

Front, he took a month's leave and, on September 1, 1943, assumed command of Wehrkreis Bohemia-Moravia. His headquarters was Prague, and his territory was the former Czech area of Czechoslovakia. Charged with providing trained replacements for the field army, Schaal recognized that the Nazis were leading Germany to a disastrous defeat. He welcomed the July 20, 1944 coup, even though he was not deeply involved in the plot and apparently did not know of the planned assassination attempt. This saved his life. He was nevertheless arrested on July 21, 1944, and spent the rest of the war in prison.

After his release, General Schaal retired to Allensbach/Konstanz, where he died on October 9, 1962.

Gustav Friedrich Julius von Vaerst was born in Meiningen on April 19, 1894. He entered the service as a Fahnenjunker in the Hessian 14th Hussar Regiment in 1912 and was commissioned in early 1914. When World War I broke out, Vaerst went to the field as an orderly officer with the 22nd Cavalry Brigade and initially fought on the Western Front, including the battles of Lille and Ypres. He returned to his regiment in December. It was transferred to the Eastern Front the following month and served there until December 1916. Vaerst, meanwhile, was detached to the brigade staff as an orderly officer from April 1, 1915 to May 26, 1916, when he again returned to the 14th Hussars, where he served as deputy regimental adjutant until September 21, 1917, when he became adjutant of the regiment. He served on the Dutch-Belgian border before the 14th was sent back to the Eastern Front, where it remained for the rest of the war. Vaerst assumed command of the 3rd Squadron on November 11, 1918—the day the armistice took effect. He commanded the squadron during the evacuation of the Ukraine (November 1918–January 1919).

Vaerst led the 2nd Squadron of the Hessen-Homburg Volunteer Hussar Regiment in early 1919 and helped protect the German border against the Poles. In November he was accepted into the Reichsheer and was assigned to the 11th Cavalry Regiment. After a tour with the 16th Cavalry Regiment (1920–21), he served on the staff of Wehrkreis VII in Munich (1921–22). He remained in the cavalry until 1938; in the meantime, he earned an army-wide reputation for his exceptional marksmanship with a carbine and even received a commendation from General of Infantry Baron Kurt von Hammerstein-Equord.

On January 20, 1938, he was named commander of the 2nd Rifle Regiment of the 2nd Panzer Division in Vienna. He became commander of the 2nd Panzer Brigade (also in Vienna) when World War II began and led it in the Polish campaign. Later, he commanded it in Luxembourg, Belgium, and France (1940); in Greece (1941), and on the Eastern Front (1941). His divisional commander, Lieutenant General

Richard Veiel, wrote in his officer evaluation that he was a "Splendid man of high personal standards. Practical, clear, calm and determined in his leadership and issuance of commands before the enemy!"[4]

Near the end of 1941, he was ordered to report to Panzer Group Afrika, and assumed command of the 15th Panzer Division on December 9. He led it until May 26, 1942, when he was severely wounded. He returned to duty on August 8, fought in the battles of El Alamein, and led it until November 11, 1942, when he reported himself sick and returned to Europe. (After Nehring was wounded on August 31, Vaerst was also acting commander of the Afrika Korps until September 17.)

Gustav von Vaerst remained on furlough until March 9, 1943, when Erwin Rommel left North Africa forever. Rommel was replaced as commander-in-chief of Army Group Afrika by Juergen von Arnim. Vaerst, who had been promoted to general of panzer troops as of March 1, 1943, succeeded Arnim as commander of the 5th Panzer Army.

Vaerst proved to be an excellent army commander and did what could be done to check the Allies in Tunisia. By the beginning of May, however, his supply lines had collapsed completely. He was unable to prevent the Americans from breaking his lines during the first week of May. Vaerst resisted to the maximum and, when he ran out of fuel, sent his last panzers into battle with their tanks full of Tunisian wine. It was all to no avail. The Allies broke into his rear, and he was captured by the Americans near Bizerta on May 9. By May 13, all Axis resistance in North Africa had ceased.

General von Vaerst remained in the POW camps until 1947. Upon release he settled in Stockheim, where he died on October 10, 1975.

Wilhelm von Thoma's life is described in Chapter VII. He was temporarily succeeded by Fritz Bayerlein.

Bayerlein was born in Wurzburg (Wuerzburg), Bavaria on January 14, 1899, the son of a senior police inspector. He entered the army as a Fahnenjunker in 1917 and took the field with the 9th Infantry Regiment in May 1918. Remaining in the Reichsheer, he was commissioned second lieutenant in 1922. He commanded the machine gun company of the 21st Infantry Regiment and then the regiment's motorcycle detachments. In May 1932, he took his Wehrkreis examinations and scored high enough to undergo General Staff training. On June 1, 1935, he joined the staff of the 15th Infantry Division at Kassel and by 1936 was division Ia. In 1937, he became commander of the divisional armored car company.

Promoted to major in 1938, Bayerlein was named Ia of XV Motorized Corps and became Ia of the 10th Panzer Division when the war began. In February 1940, he was appointed Ia of Guderian's XIX

Panzer Corps, which did so well in the French campaign. This led to Bayerlein's promotion to lieutenant colonel in October. He remained with Guderian when his headquarters was upgraded to 2nd Panzer Group and fought in the early stages of the Russian campaign; then he was sent to North Africa, where he served as chief of staff of the Afrika Korps (October 5, 1941–November 4, 1942), acting commander of the Afrika Korps (November 4–13, 1942), and chief of staff of the 1st Italian-German Panzer Army (December 7, 1942–March 1943). Promoted to major general on March 1, 1943, he was wounded in action and left North Africa on May 2, 1943—just in time to escape the surrender of Army Group Afrika. He was unemployed until October 1943, when he assumed command of the 3rd Panzer Division on the southern sector of the Eastern Front. On January 10, 1944, he was named commander of the Panzer Lehr Division, then forming in France. Bayerlein commanded the division in the Normandy campaign, the Falaise Pocket, the retreat to the Seine, and the retreat to the West Wall. He was promoted to lieutenant general on May 1, 1944.

Panzer Lehr was rebuilt in the fall of 1944 and committed to the Battle of the Bulge. It spearheaded the advance of the XXXXVII Panzer Corps on Bastogne. On the evening of December 18, General of Panzer Troops Baron Heinrich von Luettwitz received an intercepted radio message, informing him that two American airborne divisions were heading for Bastogne. The veteran panzer general was not worried. He estimated that they could not possibly arrive before noon on December 19. Surely Lieutenant General Fritz Bayerlein, the commander of the elite Panzer Lehr, could capture the town by then.

He should have.

Bayerlein's abilities as a commander are, in my view, highly overestimated by British and American historians. Immediately after the war, Bayerlein cooperated with Western historians and befriended B. H. Liddell Hart, arguably the most distinguished military historian of his day, and helped Hart edit *The Rommel Papers*. Not surprisingly, Hart was very sympathetic to Bayerlein, who was able to pass himself off as a highly capable commander and General Staff officer. Subsequent Western historians have generally followed the lead set by Hart. This view was certainly not universally held in the German Army at the time, however; indeed, it seems to be a minority opinion. Major General Gerhard Franz, the chief of staff of the Afrika Korps in late 1942 when Bayerlein briefly served as acting commander, had nothing good to say about him,[5] and General of Panzer Troops Baron Hasso von Manteuffel, who commanded the 5th Panzer Army in the Battle of the Bulge, also had serious reservations about him. Bayerlein and Erwin Rommel had a falling out in early 1943, and the Desert Fox threatened to sack him. When Rommel was given command of an army group later that year, he made no effort to have Bayerlein transferred to his staff, which was a common practice in the Wehrmacht at that time. On the other hand, Rommel had several other of his "Africans" assigned to his new headquarters. When Bayerlein was the German chief of staff of the 1st Italian Panzer Army in Tunisia in 1943, he practically commanded the German units in that campaign until he was wounded and evacuated. He failed to make any attempt to cooperate with the army's commander, Italian General Giovanni Messe, who clearly demonstrated in Tunisia that his tactical instincts were superior to Bayerlein's. Bayerlein is hardly ever mentioned in the divisional history of the *Panzer Lehr*,[6] which is very odd in a book of this nature, although other commanders are praised. The late Friedrich von Stauffenberg, an expert on the panzer branch, also felt that Bayerlein was vastly overrated by Anglo-American historians.[7] Another prolific historian, Brigadier General S. L. A. Marshall, also held a poor opinion of him, noting that he was highly critical of the mistakes of other commanders, but, when his own mistakes were pointed out, he only laughed. Certainly Bayerlein's performance during the Battle of the Bulge was very poor, and, on one critical day, he was more interested in seducing a captured American nurse than in the activities of his division.[8]

Bayerlein's initial mistake in the drive to Bastogne was to ask Belgian civilians if the roads to the small towns of Oberwampach and Niederwampach were good. They replied that they were. They were lying—and Bayerlein should have suspected that. He nevertheless started down the road (the general himself was in the lead tank) and got a few hundred meters before the dirt roads turned into mud. He nonetheless pressed on and reached Niederwampach, six miles from Bastogne, before 8 o'clock on the evening of December 18. An hour later he reached Mageret and was on the main road to Bastogne. Here, he paused and asked another Belgian civilian for information. The civilian, who was an Allied sympathizer (like most Belgian civilians), replied that an American armored force of 50 Shermans, 25 self-propelled guns, and dozens of other armored vehicles had passed through Mageret heading east. He also said it was being commanded by an American major general. Bayerlein swallowed this cock-and-bull story. Convinced that Mageret was defended by a divisional-sized force, Bayerlein confined himself to cutting the Longvilly-Bastogne road, deploying his panzers east of Mageret and laying mines. Actually, this sector was defended by very weak forces. Bastogne was his for the taking, but Bayerlein let the opportunity pass. It was a critical mistake in the history of the Third Reich.

Bayerlein continued in command of the Panzer Lehr Division until the end of the Battle of the Bulge, even though he was "in a complete daze," according to Friedrich von Stauffenberg.[9] (Certainly a little combat fatigue at this stage of the war is easy to understand.) He was relieved of his command on January 25, 1945, but was assigned to the hard-pressed 7th Army as a reserve panzer officer. Here he was engaged in organizing stragglers into ad hoc formations. On March 6, 1945, however, General of Cavalry Count Edwin von Rothkirch und Trach accidentally drove into American lines and was captured. As the senior available officer, General Felber gave Bayerlein command of the LIII Corps and ordered him to retake the Ludendorff Bridge at Remagen. He reacted slowly and failed. Field Marshal Walter Model, the commander of Army Group B, was so dissatisfied with Bayerlein's performance that he transferred all of the LIII Corps's armor to General of Infantry Carl Puechler's LXXIV Corps.

Bayerlein surrendered to the U.S. 7th Armored Division on April 16, 1945. He was released from prison in 1947 and retired to Wuerzburg. Here he contributed to Chester Wilmot's exhaustive *The Struggle for Europe* but refused to assist Milton Shulman in *Defeat in the West*. Stauffenberg suggests that this was because of Bayerlein's deep-seated anti-Semitism.[10]

Bayerlein also assisted B. H. Liddell Hart in the writing of *The Other Side of the Hill* and in editing *The Rommel Papers*. He also collaborated with Hans Karl Schmidt (a/k/a Paul Carell) in the production of *Hitler Moves East, Foxes of the Desert, Scorched Earth*, and *Sie Kommen*. In influencing these historians, the less than candid Bayerlein succeeded in partially rewriting history.

Fritz Bayerlein contracted a liver disease while serving in North Africa. It finally killed him. He died in Wuerzburg on January 30, 1970.

Gustav Fehn was covered under the commanders of Panzer Army Afrika.

Heinz Ziegler was born in Trakennen, East Prussia, on May 19, 1894. He joined the Kaiser's army as a Fahnenjunker in 1912 and was commissioned in the 15th Foot Artillery Regiment at Thorn in 1914. During World War I, he served as a battery commander and earned the Hohenzollern House Order with Swords, as well as the Iron Cross, 1st Class and 2nd Class. After the war he was selected for the Reichsheer, where he was named the Ib (chief supply officer) of the Bromberg Frontier Guards Zone, suggesting that he also took the abbreviated (three-month) General Staff course near the end of the war. Subsequently, he was assigned to the 2nd Artillery Regiment at Stettin and again commanded a battery. From 1925 until 1931 he was on the staff of the Army Command, which later became OKH (the High Command of the Army). Ziegler was promoted to colonel and named commander of the 98th Artillery Regiment in Steyr, Austria, in November 1938.

Ziegler was good at office politics and used this talent to maximum advantage to advance himself; he also made important friends easily. On September 1, 1939, the day World War II began, the Home Army was officially activated in Berlin. Its commander, Fritz Fromm, was officially chief of army equipment and commander-in-chief of the Replacement Army. That same day, Heinz Ziegler joined Fromm as his chief of staff for replacement forces. He became chief of staff of Wehrkreis IV in Breslau on September 13, and was appointed chief of staff of the XXXXII Corps on February 1, 1940. After playing a minor role in the French campaign, Ziegler's corps remained on occupation duty along the Channel coast until August 1941, when it was sent to the Eastern Front and took part in the Siege of Leningrad. That winter, it was transferred to the Crimean peninsula, where he temporarily commanded a motorized brigade. Ziegler, meanwhile, was promoted to major general effective January 1, 1942. That spring, he managed to be transferred back to Berlin and the Home Army.

On December 3, 1942, General of Panzer Troops Hans-Juergen von Arnim visited Fuehrer Headquarters in East Prussia, where he was promoted to colonel general and named commander of the 5th Panzer Army in Tunisia. That same day, Heinz Ziegler was promoted to lieutenant general and was named deputy army commander of the 5th Panzer Army, despite the fact that he had never commanded anything beyond a brigade.

The position of deputy army commander was not a normal one in the German Wehrmacht. Most armies did not have deputy commanders and, when they did, the post was created for an individual and was not a table of organization and equipment (TOE) position. Ziegler had managed to secure himself a promotion, but General von Arnim found him to be of no great help.[11]

After General Fehn was critically wounded on January 15, 1943, Ziegler was the senior general available to command the Afrika Korps. He held the post until February 28, 1943, when Fehn's permanent replacement, Hans Cramer, arrived from Russia and took command of the DAK.

Although not rated highly by von Arnim (or apparently by Rommel), Ziegler did a good job as commander of the DAK. During the six weeks he commanded the Afrika Korps, the 1st German-Italian Panzer Army evacuated Tripoli (which fell on January 20), got out of Libya, and turned on their new and inexperienced American opponents at Kasserine Pass. In the week before he was replaced, Ziegler had the outstanding moment of his military career when, acting on the orders of Field Marshal Rommel, he ambushed elements of the U.S. 1st Armored Division east of Sidi Bou Zid, where he destroyed 98 American tanks (Figure 8.1). This action earned him the Knight's Cross.

Figure 8.1
The Tunisian Bridgehead

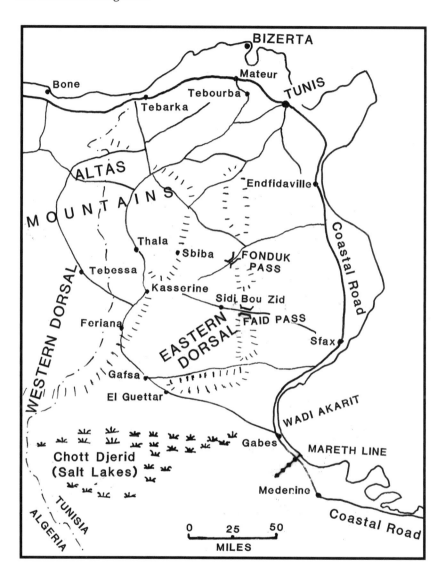

Ziegler then returned to the staff of Army Group Afrika, where Rommel (and later Arnim) employed him in tasks of much less responsibility.

As Army Group Afrika crumbled, Arnim sent Ziegler back to Europe on a pretext. Generally speaking (although certainly not true in every case), as the end came for the Axis forces in Africa, the best of the German commanders opted to stay and shared the fate of their men. The others escaped to Europe at the first convenient opportunity. Among the formations destroyed in Tunisia (called "Tunisgrad" by the German civilians) was the 334th Infantry Division. Hitler ordered it rebuilt in May 1943. On May 24, Heinz Ziegler arrived in France to supervise the formation of the new 334th. He held this post until October 21, 1943, when he became acting commander of the III Panzer Corps on the Eastern Front. He held this post for less than five weeks. On November 25, 1943, General of Infantry Friedrich Schulz replaced him and held the position until January 9, 1944, when the permanent commander, General of Panzer Troops Hermann Breith, returned and resumed command.

Ziegler, meanwhile, was promoted to general of artillery on January 1, 1944, and was placed in charge of a special economic staff under OKW the following month. He held this post until the fall of 1944, by which time most of the foreign areas that could be exploited economically had been lost. Finally, from October 24 to November 22, 1944, Heinz Ziegler was acting commander of the 14th Army in Italy. It was his last assignment.

Ziegler was placed in Fuehrer Reserve after his return from Italy and was never reemployed. He avoided Soviet captivity at the end of the war and settled in Goettingen. He died on August 21, 1972.

Hans Cramer was born in Minden, Westphalia, on July 13, 1896. Educated in cadet schools, he joined the Imperial Army as a Fahnenjunker in the 15th Infantry Regiment when World War I began. Cramer was in the field by late October and was commissioned second lieutenant on Christmas Day, 1914. He successively was a company commander (1915–16), battalion adjutant (1916–18), and commander of the 1st Machine Gun Company of the 15th Infantry. He fought in numerous battles, including the Battle of Picardy (where his division, the 13th Infantry, suffered 40% casualties), Avre, and the 3rd Battle of the Somme. He earned both grades of the Iron Cross and the Wounded Badge in Silver, indicating that he was wounded at least three different times. On August 8, 1918, he was captured by the British. Released in 1919, he applied for the Reichsheer, was accepted, and was promoted to first lieutenant in 1925. He transferred to the cavalry in 1923 and was assigned to the 13th Regiment. He passed his Wehrkreis exam and from 1927 to 1929 underwent General Staff training.

Rittmeister as of 1931, Cramer served on the staff of the 13th Cavalry Regiment (1930–33), on the staff of the 1st Cavalry Division (1933–34), as an instructor at the Cavalry School in Hanover (1934–38), and as commander of the Cavalry Demonstration and Experimentation

Battalion (1938–39). He was promoted to major in 1936 and lieutenant colonel in 1939.

When World War II began, Hans Cramer assumed command of the Panzer Reconnaissance Demonstration (*Lehr*) Battalion, which he directed until November 1940, when he was earmarked to command a panzer regiment. In preparation for this assignment, the Army Personnel Office assigned him to the staff of the 10th Panzer Division, where he underwent an informal period of instruction for this position. He was then sent to Darmstadt, where he assumed command of the 8th Panzer Regiment of the 15th Panzer Division on March 22, 1941.

Cramer did not remain in Germany long. His regiment was ordered to Italy, where it boarded ships and sailed for Tripoli. Lieutenant Colonel Cramer was soon in action in North Africa, were he commanded his regiment for four months. On May 16, 1941, he launched a surprise attack and captured the important British position of Sidi Azeiz. Without pausing, he headed for Capuzzo and overran it as well. He then played a major role in the capture of Halfaya Pass. Neumann-Silkow and Rommel recommended him for the Knight's Cross, which he received on June 27. Shortly thereafter, however, he was badly wounded while leading an attack on Sollum. He was promoted to colonel on October 1, 1941—in the hospital.

On April 1, 1942, after he recovered, Cramer was named chief of staff to the general of mobile troops (*Schnellen Truppen*, also translated as "fast troops") at the High Command of the Army in Zossen. He was named acting general of fast troops on September 1, 1942, and this appointment was made permanent on November 1, the day he was promoted to major general.

The Russians launched their Winter Offensive of 1942–43 on November 19, 1943, and encircled the German 6th Army at Stalingrad on November 23, wrecking the XXXXVIII Panzer Corps in the process. Hitler sacked its commander, Lieutenant General Heim, on November 20, and Hans Cramer was sent to Russia as acting commander, to salvage what he could. He directed the corps until November 26, when he was replaced by Heinrich Eberbach. Eberbach, however, was seriously wounded on December 1, so Cramer took command again until the permanent commander, General of Panzer Troops Otto von Knobelsdorf, arrived. Cramer, however, remained at XXXXVIII Panzer Corps Headquarters until December 10 as deputy corps commander.

I have not been able to establish Cramer's whereabouts with certainty from December 11, 1942 to February 21, 1943, but apparently he remained on special assignment with Field Marshal Erich von Manstein's Army Group Don. In any case, he was promoted to lieutenant general on January 22, 1943, after less than two months' time in grade as a major general—a very rapid promotion indeed. On January

22, 1943, he was named commander of *Generalkommandos z.b.V. Cramer*, a corps-level special purposes unit. Its purpose was to form a new corps headquarters. In March 1943, the unit became Headquarters, XI Corps, replacing the original XI, which had been destroyed in Stalingrad. Cramer, however, left Russia forever in February. After a brief leave he was sent to Tunisia, where he assumed command of the Afrika Korps on or about February 28, 1943 (sources differ slightly as to the exact date).

Hans Cramer led the Afrika Korps in its last, hopeless battles in Tunisia in the spring of 1941. Together with Colonel General Hans-Juergen von Arnim, he surrendered to Lieutenant General Charles W. Allfrey, the commander of the British V Corps, at Ste.-Marie-du-Zit on May 12, 1943, shortly after he had been promoted to general of panzer troops, effective May 1. After a year in a POW camp in Wales, his health deteriorated to the point that the British repatriated him to Germany through the Swedish Red Cross. (He was suffering from severe asthma.) First, he was taken through south and southwestern England and was allowed to see the huge Allied build-up for D-Day. He was told, however, that he was being driven through southeastern England, suggesting that the invasion would come through the Pas de Calais sector. He reported this misinformation to Berlin on or about May 23, 1944.

On June 9, 1944, after the invasion had begun, Cramer was named an advisor to Panzer Group West in Normandy. After the Allies broke out, he became a special OKW advisor on the Western fortifications. His previous association with Rommel, however, had not gone unnoticed by the Nazis. He was involuntarily retired on August 17, 1944, with a retroactive retirement date of July 20, 1944—the date of the Stauffenberg assassination attempt.

General Cramer was taken prisoner by the British in May 1945 but was released in February 1946. He lived in Minden for a time and died at Hausberge on October 28, 1968.

COMMANDERS OF THE 15TH PANZER DIVISION

The commanders of the 15th Panzer Division during the North African campaign were as follows: Major General Heinrich von Prittwitz und Gaffron (March 22–April 10, 1941); Colonel Baron Hans-Karl von Esebeck (April 13–May 13, 1941); Colonel Maximilian von Herff (May 13–26, 1941); Major General Walter Neumann-Silkow (May 26–December 6, 1941); Colonel Erwin Menny (December 6–9, 1941); Major General Gustav von Vaerst (December 9, 1941–May 26, 1942); Colonel Eduard Crasemann (May 26–July 15, 1942); Major General Heinz von Randow (July 15–August 25, 1942); Major General/Lieutenant General von Vaerst

(August 25–November 10, 1942); and Colonel/Major General/Lieutenant General Willibald Borowietz (November 11, 1942–May 12, 1943).

As we have seen, General von Prittwitz was killed in action while on a reconnaissance of the Tobruk perimeter, April 10, 1941. Colonel Baron von Esebeck was severely wounded on May 13, 1941.

Maximilian von Herff was born in Hanover on April 17, 1893. He joined the army as a Fahnenjunker and was commissioned in the 115th Infantry Regiment in 1913. He fought in World War I (on the Western Front, including the Battles of Verdun and the Somme) and earned both classes of the Iron Cross. He was accepted into the Reichswehr, serving mainly in the 18th Cavalry Regiment at Stuttgart (1926–30) and in the 15th Infantry Regiment (1930–34). Promoted to lieutenant colonel in 1937, he became adjutant of Wehrkreis XVII in Vienna in early 1939 and apparently served with the XVII Corps in Poland and France. Except for two weeks as acting division commander, Herff (now a colonel) served as commander of the 115th Rifle Regiment in North Africa and, on his own initiative, stormed the British bases at Capuzzo and Sollum. He was rewarded with the Knight's Cross.

In the summer of 1941, Herff was called to Berlin. He had been transferred to the SS (by his own request) and became chief of Heinrich Himmler's Main Personnel Office. Here he was promoted several times, the last time to SS-Obergruppenfuehrer and General of Waffen-SS on November 9, 1944. This rank was standard for corps commanders. On May 2, 1945, he was captured by the British. He was taken to Scotland, where he died of natural causes on September 6, 1945, at the age of 52.

Walter Neumann-Silkow was born in Gross Silkow, Pomerania, the son of a Prussian Junker father and a Scottish mother. He entered the service as a Fahnenjunker in the 10th Dragoons in 1912. He was commissioned the following year, fought in World War I, served in the Reichsheer, and was named commander of the 7th Reconnaissance Regiment in 1938. He led it until early 1940, when he became commander of the 8th Rifle Brigade of the 8th Panzer Division. After distinguishing himself in the Western Campaign, he redeployed to Poland, where he was promoted to major general (April 1, 1941) and served a month as commander of the 8th Panzer Division (April 15 to approximately May 18, 1941), while its permanent commander, Major General Erich Brandenberger, was on leave. When Brandenberger returned, Neumann-Silkow was named to the 15th Panzer Division in North Africa. He assumed command on May 26 and led it in the Winter Battles. On December 6, 1941, shortly after the Siege of Tobruk was broken, General Neumann-Silkow was mortally wounded by British artillery fire. He died on December 9. A leader who was both immensely capable and immensely popular with his men, he was posthumously promoted to lieutenant general.

Colonel Erwin Menny was born in Saarburg in 1893. He joined the army as a Fahnenjunker in June 1912 and was commissioned in the 22nd Dragoons in February 1914. He fought in World War I (where he earned both grades of the Iron Cross), served in the Reichsheer, and transferred to the panzer branch in the early 1930s. In late 1938, as a lieutenant colonel, he became commander of antitank forces in Wehrkreis XVIII (Austria). A colonel from April 1, 1939, he commanded the 81st Rifle Replacement Regiment (1939–40), the 69th Rifle Regiment (1940–41), which he led in France, and the 15th Rifle Brigade in North Africa (1941–42). He earned the Knight's Cross for his part in Rommel's 2nd Cyrenaican Campaign of January 1942.

Menny briefly commanded the 15th Panzer Division after General Neumann-Silkow was wounded. He soon returned to the 15th Rifle, however, and led it in the battles of the Gazala Line and the conquest of Tobruk. He left Africa in mid-July 1942 and went to Russia as commander of the 18th Panzer Division (September 1942–May 1943). He then led the 387th Infantry Division (1943), the 333rd Infantry Division (1943), the 123rd Infantry Division, the 72nd Infantry Division (1943–44), and the 84th Infantry Division on the Western Front (1944). His division was overrun by the Americans in August 1944, and Menny (a lieutenant general since October 1, 1943) was captured. He was released from the POW camps in 1947 or 1948 and moved to Freiburg, Brunswick, where he died on December 6, 1949.

Eduard Crasemann was born in Hamburg on March 3, 1891. He entered the service as a Fahnenjunker in 1910, was commissioned in the artillery in 1911, fought in World War I, and was discharged in 1919. He returned to active duty as a captain in 1936. During World War II, he commanded the 5th Battery of the 73rd Artillery Regiment (1939–40), II/78th Artillery Regiment (1940–41), 33rd Panzer Artillery Regiment, 15th Panzer Division (acting commander, May 26–July 15, 1942), 33rd Panzer Artillery Regiment (July 15, 1942–January 17, 1943), 116th Panzer Artillery Regiment on the Eastern Front (1943), Arko 143 (1943–44), 26th Panzer Division in Italy (1944–45), and XII SS Corps on the Western Front (1945). He was captured in the Ruhr Pocket on April 16, 1945. He was reportedly promoted to general of artillery on April 20, 1945. In 1947, General Crasemann was convicted of executing 162 Italians in the Fucecchio Marshes in 1944 and was sentenced to 10 years imprisonment. He died in Werl Prison on April 28, 1950. For a full biography of Eduard Crasemann, see *Rommel's Lieutenants*.

Heinz von Randow is discussed in the next section.

Gustav von Vaerst is discussed under "Commanders of the Afrika Korps," above.

The story of General Willibald Borowietz, the last commander of the 15th Panzer Division, is told in Chapter VII.

COMMANDERS OF THE 5TH LIGHT/21ST PANZER DIVISION

The commanders of the original 5th Light/21st Panzer Division were as follows: Major General Baron Hans von Funck (January 1–February 7, 1941); Major General Johannes Streich (February 7–May 16, 1941); Major General Heinrich Kirchheim (May 16–31, 1941); Major General Johann von Ravenstein (May 31–November 29, 1941); Lieutenant Colonel Gustav-Georg Knabe (November 29–December 1, 1941); Major General Karl Boettcher (December 1, 1941–February 11, 1942); Colonel/ Major General Georg von Bismarck (February 11–July 21, 1942); Colonel Albert Bruer (July 21–early August 1942); Bismarck (early August 1942–August 31, 1942); Colonel Carl-Hans Lungershausen (September 1–18, 1942); Major General Heinz von Randow (September 18–December 21, 1942); Major General Baron Kurt von Liebenstein (December 12, 1942–January 1, 1943); Colonel/Major General Hans-Georg Hildebrandt (January 1–March 1943); and Colonel/Major General Heinrich-Hermann von Huelsen (March 15–May 12, 1943).

A second 21st Panzer Division was formed in 1943 and fought on the Western Front (1944–early 1945). It was transferred to the Eastern Front in early 1945 and was surrounded and destroyed in the Halbe Pocket in late April 1945.

Baron von Funck (1891–1979) commanded the division before it was sent to Africa. He later commanded the 7th Panzer Division (1940–43) and XXIII Corps (1943–44) on the Eastern Front and the XXXXVII Panzer Corps in Normandy (1944). An excellent commander, he was sacked by Hitler in September 1944—in part because Hitler remembered that he had been involved in a messy divorce/sex scandal in the early 1930s. Funck joined the army as a Fahnenjunker in the 2nd Dragoons in 1914 and was a colonel and German military attaché to Lisbon when World War II began. He later commanded the 5th Panzer Regiment (1939–40), the 3rd Panzer Brigade (1940), and the 5th Light Division (1940–41) before assuming command of the 7th Panzer. He was promoted to general of panzer troops on March 1, 1944.

Generals Streich, Kirchheim, von Ravenstein, and Boettcher were discussed earlier in this book.

Gustav Georg Knabe was born in Wichmannsdorf on July 8, 1897, the son of a schoolteacher. In August 1914, at the age of 17, he became a war volunteer in the 64th Prussian (8th Brandenburg) Infantry Regiment. He fought on the Western Front where he was promoted to second lieutenant, was wounded five times, and was awarded both grades of the Iron Cross.

In 1919 and 1920, Knabe led a tank platoon in the Baltic States as part of the East Prussian Freikorps. He was subsequently inducted into the Reichswehr and served mainly in the infantry until 1930. Then he transferred to the 1st Signals Battalion in Koenigsberg. From here, he attended the War Academy and became a General Staff officer, serving with the 1st Panzer Division and 2nd Light (later 7th Panzer) Division.

Knabe fought in the Western Campaign as commander of the II Battalion, 93rd Motorized Infantry Regiment. Later, in Africa, he commanded the 15th Motorcycle Battalion, and, in 1941, helped capture Sollum and Capuzzo. He was promoted to lieutenant colonel and was decorated with the Knight's Cross on June 1, 1941. He was then given command of the 104th Panzer Grenadier Regiment, which he led in the Sidi Rezegh battles. He briefly commanded the 21st Panzer Division during the Winter Campaign.

Gustav Knabe developed severe circulatory problems in late 1941 and was forced to leave North Africa. After his recovery, he was promoted to colonel and became a department head in the Panzer Inspectorate. He was attached to the training and organizational staff of the Romanian Armored Forces. While on an inspection trip, he was seriously injured in an automobile accident. He still had not recovered when the war ended.

Colonel Knabe returned to civilian life and died in Celle on December 13, 1972.

Georg von Bismarck was born in Neumuehl in 1891 and joined the 6th Jaeger (Light Infantry) Battalion as a second lieutenant at Oels, Silesia, on November 18, 1911. During World War I, he fought at Verdun, in the Carpathians, and in Italy. He won both grades of the Iron Cross and was awarded the Royal House Order of the Hohenzollerns with Swords for storming a mountain pass.[12] His battalion was also used as a shock unit on the Western Front. After the armistice, he served with Frontier Guard Silesia in "the war after the war," and was accepted into the Reichsheer in 1920. In 1924, he became a company commander in the 2nd Motorized Battalion at Stettin. He quickly saw the potential of motorized units and spent the rest of his career in armored or motorized commands. As a lieutenant colonel, he assumed command of the 7th Cavalry Rifle Regiment (later 7th Rifle Regiment) in 1938 and led it in Poland, Belgium, Luxembourg, and France. The 7th Rifle was part of the 7th Panzer Division, which was commanded by Erwin Rommel, who was impressed by Bismarck's performance.

After France, Bismarck was named commander of the 20th Rifle Brigade of the 20th Panzer Division on December 10, 1940. He led it on the Eastern Front, fighting in the fierce battles of Minsk, Vitebsk, Ulla, Smolensk, Vyazma, and others. Because of the strain of the Russian Front, his divisional commander's health collapsed, and Bismarck assumed command of the 20th Panzer on September 10, 1941. He led it until December 18, when he was succeeded by Ritter Wilhelm von Thoma and, at Rommel's request, was sent to Libya. He assumed command of the 21st Panzer Division on February 11, 1942, and led it in every major battle until he was killed in action at El Alamein on August 31, 1942. (He was inside a panzer that exploded. Sources differ as to whether it ran over an antitank mine or was hit by a British fighter-bomber or an antitank gun.)

Bismarck was an outstanding tactical leader and was the best division commander in Panzer Army Afrika at the time of his death. He was promoted to major general on March 1, 1942, and received a posthumous promotion to lieutenant general, effective August 1, 1942. A full description of Bismarck's career can be found in *Rommel's Lieutenants* by Samuel W. Mitcham, Jr.

Colonel Albert Bruer was born in 1897 and joined the Imperial Army as a 17-year-old war volunteer in 1914. He fought on the Western Front with the 165th (5th Hanoverian) Infantry Regiment and earned a commission. Not retained in the Reichsheer, Bruer joined the state police in Berlin in 1920. His unit was absorbed into the Wehrmacht in 1936. Bruer went with it as a captain.

Bruer initially commanded the 6th Battery of the 41st Motorized Artillery Regiment at Ulm. Later, his battery was transferred to Neckarsulm and became part of the newly formed 71st Motorized Artillery Regiment. Bruer (now a major) served on the staff of the II Battalion during the French campaign of 1940.

Alfred Bruer briefly commanded the 612th Artillery Regiment in 1941. In June of that year, after his promotion to lieutenant colonel, he was named commander of the 155th Panzer Artillery Regiment of the 21st Panzer Division. Promoted to full colonel in 1942, he assumed command of the division after General von Bismarck was wounded on July 21, 1942. During the 1st Battle of El Alamein, Bruer faced a British tank attack. He skillfully deployed his artillery, let the British tanks advance, and then smashed the attack with flanking fire. For this action, he was awarded the Knight's Cross.[13]

When Georg von Bismarck returned to headquarters in early August 1942, Alfred Bruer resumed command of his regiment, which he led in Egypt, Libya, and Tunisia. He surrendered it on May 12, 1943.

Released from prison in 1947, Colonel Bruer settled in Schwaebisch-Gmund, where he died on February 12, 1976.

Major General Heinz von Randow was born in Grammow on November 15, 1890. He joined the 18th Dragoon Regiment as a Fahnenjunker in 1910. Commissioned in 1911, he fought in World War I, served in the Reichsheer, and became commander of the 13th Cavalry Regiment as a lieutenant colonel in late 1937. On September 1, 1939, the day World War II began, Randow assumed command of the 1st Cavalry Brigade on the Western Front. After Poland fell, he was named commander of the 26th Infantry Regiment of the 30th Infantry Division (October 26, 1939–end of February 1941), leading it in the Netherlands and Belgium in 1940. It redeployed to Poland in July 1940 and to Romania and Bulgaria in 1941, in preparation for the invasion of Yugoslavia and Greece. Randow, however, was transferred back to the 1st Cavalry Division in Poland. Here he assumed command of the 2nd Cavalry Brigade (1941–42), which he led on the Russian Front. He took command of the 17th Rifle Brigade of the 17th Panzer Division on April 1, 1942 and led it in the Orel sector until early July 1942, when he was sent to North Africa.

Heinz von Randow commanded the 15th Panzer Division from July 15 to August 25. On September 1, he assumed command of the 21st Panzer Division, which he led in the 2nd Battle of El Alamein and the retreat to Libya. On December 21, 1942, during the retreat to Tripoli, he was killed in action.

Randow was promoted to colonel on February 1, 1939, and to major general on April 1, 1942. He was posthumously promoted to lieutenant general.

Major General Baron Kurt von Liebenstein served as acting commander of the division from December 12, 1942 to January 1, 1943. Apparently, he also simultaneously commanded the 164th Light Afrika Division at the same time. (For a German general to command two divisions [or even two armies] simultaneously was a rare occurrence but was certainly not unheard of.) When his replacement arrived, Liebenstein returned to the 164th Light.

Colonel/Major General Hans-Georg Hildebrandt commanded the division from January 1 to March 1943. Born in Fraustadt in 1896, he attended cadet schools and entered the Imperial Army as a Faehnrich on August 2, 1914. Ten weeks later, he was commissioned second lieutenant in the 36th Fusilier Regiment, which fought on the Western Front throughout World War I. Hildebrandt later joined the General Staff, served in the Reichsheer, and became Ia of the XIV Motorized (later Panzer) Corps on October 1, 1938, the day he was promoted to lieutenant colonel. From 1938 until October 1940, Hildebrandt served General of Infantry Gustav von Wietersheim, a steady, professional and talented motorized infantry commander. He fought in Poland and France and was promoted to colonel on October 1, 1940. That same day, he was sent to southwestern France and named chief of staff of the XXXIX Panzer Corps, which was commanded in 1941–42 by General of Panzer Troops Hans-Juergen "Dieter" von Arnim. (The XIV Panzer Corps was later destroyed in Stalingrad.)

The XXXIX Panzer was transferred to Poland in the spring of 1941. It invaded Russia as part of General Hoth's 3rd Panzer Army and fought at Vilna, Minsk, and Smolensk, among other places. In September 1941, the corps was transferred to the northern sector of the Eastern Front, where it saw action at Cholm and the Rzhev salient. Hildebrandt either fell sick or was wounded on September 30, 1942, and returned home to Germany. Arnim, meanwhile, became a colonel general and assumed command of 5th Panzer Army on December 3, 1942. He immediately "pulled some strings" and had his former chief of staff sent to North Africa. Hildebrandt assumed command of the 21st Panzer Division on January 1, 1943.

Hildebrandt was a better chief of staff than he was a panzer division commander. He was also not up to par physically. He was sent back to Europe on March 15, 1943, and remained unemployed until early 1944. Arnim's recommendation that he be promoted, however, was acted upon, and he became a major general on April 1, 1943.

General Hildebrandt was named commander of the 715th Infantry Division in Italy on January 5, 1944. A reasonably good static infantry commander, he led the 715th until July 1944, when he again took an extended leave. (He was promoted to lieutenant general on June 1, 1944.) When he returned, he was named German liaison officer (and virtual commander) of the Italian 3rd Infantry Division of Mussolini's rump Fascist republic. He was engaged in antipartisan operations until the end of the war. He managed to surrender to the Anglo-Americans on May 3, 1945, and remained in prison until the beginning of November 1947. He retired to Frankfurt/Main and died there in 1967.

Colonel/Major General Heinrich-Hermann von Huelsen was the last commander of the 21st Panzer Division. Born in Weimar in 1895, he was a product of the German cadet schools. Huelsen entered the service in early 1914 as a lieutenant in the 4th Guards Regiment of Foot. He fought in World War I, but managed to get a transfer to the cavalry, where he spent most of his career. He became commander of the 11th Cavalry Regiment in 1938. On August 26, 1939, this unit, like most of the rest of the cavalry, was broken up to provide reconnaissance battalions for infantry divisions that needed them. Still a lieutenant colonel, von Huelsen was given command of the 44th Reconnaissance Battalion, which he led until the spring of 1941, when he assumed command of the 2nd Cavalry Regiment—part of the 1st Cavalry Division on the Russian Front. When this unit was converted into the 24th Panzer Division, Huelsen (now a full colonel) was sent to the Panzer School for five weeks and was given command of the 9th Rifle Brigade of the 9th Panzer Division on the Eastern Front in May 1942. He even served as acting divisional commander for a week at the end of July and early August 1942.

Because of its heavy casualties, the 9th Rifle Brigade was disbanded on December 15, 1942, and its men were sent to other units. As an excess officer, Heinrich-Hermann von Huelsen was sent back to Germany. In March 1943, however, another panzer divisional command came open: the 21st Panzer in Tunisia. Huelsen assumed command on March 15, 1943, and led it until its surrender on May 12, 1943. As Army Group Afrika was in the process of capitulating, Berlin signaled its headquarters that Huelsen was promoted to major general effective May 1.

From May 12, 1943 to February 17, 1947, Huelsen was a British prisoner of war. After his release, he settled in Kassel. He died in Celle in 1982.

COMMANDERS OF THE 90TH LIGHT DIVISION

The 90th Light Division was created on November 11, 1941 from the Staff, Special Purposes Division Command Afrika ("Stab, Div. Kdo. Afrika z. b. V."), which had been formed on June 26, 1941, in order to control miscellaneous formations and security units. It included the 155th Rifle Regiment (three battalions), which had been formed on June 7, 1941; the 361st Infantry Regiment (formerly the Afrika Regiment), which consisted of two battalions of former French Foreign Legions troops; the 580th Reconnaissance Company (later a battalion); the 361st Artillery Battalion; the 900th Engineer Battalion; and the 190th Signal Company. Its home station was Frankfurt/Oder. Gradually it was enlarged and, by June 1942, it included the 155th, 200th, and 361st Panzer Grenadier Regiments (two battalions each), the 190th Panzer Battalion, the 190th Antitank Battalion, the 90th Panzer Reconnaissance Battalion, the 190th Artillery Regiment (two battalions instead of the normal four), and the 190th Divisional Supply Unit.[14] Units thrown together in such an ad hoc manner seldom become elite divisions. For some reason, this one did.

Commanders of the 90th Light Division included Major General Max Suemmermann, Colonel Johann Micki, Major General Richard Veith, Major General Ulrich Kleemann, Colonel Carl-Hans von Lungershausen, Luftwaffe Major General Bernhard Ramcke, and Major General/Lieutenant General Count Theodor von Sponeck.

Max Suemmermann, the first commander of the 90th Light, was born in Muenster, Westphalia, on June 9, 1890. He entered the service as a Fahnenjunker in the fall of 1910 and was commissioned second lieutenant in the 117th Infantry Regiment. He fought on the Western Front in World War I, served in the Reichswehr, and was promoted to lieutenant colonel effective New Year's Day, 1935, and to colonel on August 1, 1937.[15] On October 12 of that same year he assumed command of the 105th Infantry Regiment at Trier, a unit that had been officially activated only six days before. Initially it was part of Guard Division Trier but became part of the 72nd Infantry Division on September 9, 1939. It remained in Wehrkreis XII during the "Phoney War" of 1939–40 and took part in the conquest of France in 1940.[16] After that, it was on occupation duty in Brittany and then Paris.

On February 19, 1941, Max Suemmermann was named commander of the 213th Infantry Regiment. He led this unit (part of the 73rd Infantry Division) in the Balkans campaign and in the initial advance into southern Russia. He was then sent to Africa, where he assumed command of what became the 90th Light Division on September 1, 1941. He was promoted to major general that same day.

Suemmermann fought in the Siege of Tobruk and in the Winter Battles of 1941, during which he did a good job. He also commanded the rear guard of the panzer group as it retreated in December 1941. On December 10, near Mamali, Libya, as he was conducting a delaying action against the British, he was killed by a fighter-bomber.

Johann Mickl, the senior regimental commander, reportedly succeeded Max Suemmermann but as an acting commander only. A native of the Austro-Hungarian Empire, Mickl was born in 1893 and considered himself an Austrian.[17] A World War I hero, he served in the Austrian Bundesheer from 1918 to 1938, when Hitler annexed the country. Mickl (then a lieutenant colonel) was transferred to the German Reichswehr and became commander of the 42nd Antitank Battalion. This unit was assigned to the 2nd Light Division, which later became the 7th Panzer Division that Erwin Rommel commanded from February 1940 to February 1941.

The Desert Fox was highly pleased with Mickl's performance in Belgium and France in 1940. He recommended that Mickl be promoted to colonel (which he was, effective June 1, 1940) and named him commander of the 7th Rifle Regiment (December 10, 1940). He also arranged for Mickl to be transferred to North Africa, where he became commander of the 155th Infantry Regiment on June 1, 1941.

Colonel Mickl was captured by the British in November 1941 and it appeared that his military career was over. He was thrown into an ad hoc POW cage to await transport to the rear. Mickl, however, quickly organized his fellow prisoners (several hundred of them), rushed and overwhelmed the surprised guards, and escaped on foot across the desert. They were fortunate enough to reach German lines, and a delighted Rommel saw to it that Mickl received the Knight's Cross.

Mickl apparently served as acting commander of the 90th Light from December 10 to 30, 1941, when he was succeeded by General Veith. Shortly thereafter he fell ill and was transferred back to Europe. Later he commanded the 12th Rifle Brigade (1942–43) and 11th Panzer Division (1943) on the Eastern Front before he was sent to the Balkans to command the 392nd (Croatian) Infantry Division (1943–45), which he led against Tito's partisans. He was promoted to major general on March 1, 1943, and to lieutenant general on April 1, 1944.

On April 9, 1945, as he was conducting a retreat on what had become part of the Eastern Front, he received the sixth wound of his career when he was struck in the head by a guerrilla's bullet. He died in the hospital at Rijeka the following day.

Richard Veith was born in Amberg, Bavaria, was educated in various cadet schools, and entered the service as a Faehnrich in 1909. He was commissioned Leutnant in the Bavarian 2nd Infantry Regiment in 1911. He fought on the Western Front in World War I, where he earned a promotion to captain (1918), both grades of the Iron Cross, and was wounded at least once. He served in the Reichsheer (1920–35), and was a major when Hitler took power in 1933. He was promoted to lieutenant colonel in 1934, to colonel in 1936, and was a member of the *Reichskriegsgericht* (Supreme Court of Military Justice) from April 1937 to November 1939. Veith became commander of the Austrian 135th Infantry Regiment of the 45th Infantry Division on November 10, 1939. He led this formation in France and was named commander of the 191st Replacement Division (*Division Nr. 191*) at Brunswick, Wehrkreis XI, on November 15, 1940. (Later this unit became the 191st Reserve Division.) Veith was promoted to major general on August 1, 1940, and became commander of the 90th Light Division in Libya on December 30, 1941.

Veith led the 90th Light until April 10, 1942, when he handed over his command to Ulrich Kleemann for reasons not made clear by the records. He either ran afoul of Erwin Rommel or fell ill—probably the former. In any case, he returned to active duty on the Eastern Front in June 1942, as a special purposes officer with Headquarters, Army Group North (1942–44). Later he performed the same function with Army Group Center (1944).

Veith was captured by the British in Hamburg on May 27, 1945, and was mainly held in the Island Farm Camp (Special Camp 11). He was released on May 17, 1948, and disappeared from the stage of history.[18]

Ulrich Kleemann, who commanded the 90th Light Division from April 10 to July 13, 1942, and from August 10 to September 8, 1942, was covered in Chapter VII, and Carl-Hans von Lungershausen, who served as acting commander from July 13 to August 10, 1942, is covered later.

After General Kleemann was wounded on September 8, 1942, Luftwaffe Major General Bernhard Ramcke, the commander of the newly arrived 2nd ("Ramcke") Parachute Brigade, served as acting commander of the division from September 8 to 17, 1942.[19] Then Major General Count Theodor von Sponeck, the division's last commander, arrived.

Count Theodor von Sponeck was born in Offenburg on January 24, 1896. He was educated in cadet schools and entered the service as a second lieutenant in the elite 1st Guards Grenadier Regiment on August 12, 1914. He fought on the Western Front in World War I, earned both grades of the Iron Cross, and served in the Reichsheer. While serving as commander of one of the first motorcycle companies, he developed the German motorcycle coat, which was later used throughout Europe. He was a lieutenant colonel and Ia of General of Panzer Troops Hermann Hoth's XV Motorized Corps when the Second World War began. He served in Poland and later led the 11th Rifle Regiment of the 9th Panzer Division in the Netherlands, Belgium, and France in 1940. The 9th Panzer was then sent east, where it helped overrun Serbia in the Balkans campaign of 1941. It crossed into Russia in July and played a major role in the battles of encirclement at Uman, Kiev, and Bryansk.

On January 26, 1942, Sponeck was badly wounded on the Eastern Front and did not return to active duty until he assumed command of the 90th Light Division. He received his promotion to major general on June 1, 1942, while he was still recovering from his experiences in Russia.

Count Theodor von Sponeck proved to be an excellent divisional commander. As Panzer Army Afrika retreated from El Alamein, the 90th Light Division became its rear guard. Sponeck brought up the rear all the way from Egypt to Tunisia and did a masterful job of delaying the enemy. Almost daily he had to hold and disengage when necessary—but never too early—while the rest of the army made good its escape. He had earned the Knight's Cross in Russia but was not awarded the Oak Leaves, probably because the Nazis hated his family. His older brother Hans had also been a brilliant divisional commander and had been seriously wounded while commanding the 22nd Air Landing Division in the Battle of Rotterdam. He had not done as well commanding the XXXXII Corps in the Crimea in late 1941, and had been arrested and held without trial since December 31, 1941, despite the efforts of a number of generals to have him freed.

In April and May 1943, as the Tunisian bridgehead teetered, crumbled, and finally collapsed, many senior German officers found or were given a reason or a pretext to escape. With his brother rotting in prison, the anti-Nazi Theodor made no effort to get out but rather stayed with his men until the end. He surrendered the 90th Light on May 12, 1943. A few days before, he had been promoted to lieutenant general, effective May 1.

Theodor von Sponeck did well to surrender. On July 20, 1944, Colonel Count von Stauffenberg launched his unsuccessful attempt to assassinate Adolf Hitler and overthrow the Nazi regime. Three days later, the SS dragged Hans von Sponeck out of his cell and shot him without benefit of trial. Theodor, meanwhile, was safe in an American prison in Dermott, Arkansas.

Sponeck was released from prison in 1947 or 1948. He lived in Baechingen/Dillingen after the war and died on July 13, 1982, at the age of 86.

COMMANDERS OF THE 164TH LIGHT AFRIKA DIVISION

The 164th Light Afrika Division was formed as the 164th Infantry Division on November 27, 1939, in the beautiful Saxon capital of Dresden, Wehrkreis IV. Later, its home station was transferred to Landau, Wehrkreis XII. It was an undersized German division by 1939 standards, having only two infantry regiments instead of the usual three and only one artillery battalion, instead of the standard four-battalion artillery regiment. It served as a training division in the Koenigsbrueck Maneuver Area until May 1940, when it was transferred to the OKH reserve at Bitburg. By now, it had received its third infantry regiment and its full compliment of artillery. The 164th did not see action in the French campaign but did spend several months on occupation duty in Reims. It was sent to Romania in early 1941 and first saw combat in Greece, during the successful drive on Salonika. It remained there until September 1941, when it was sent to Yugoslavia and then to Crete in November. On January 10, 1942, it was redesignated Fortress Division Crete.

After Rommel bogged down at El Alamein, the High Command sent the divisional staff to Africa and on August 15, 1942, the division became the 164th Light Afrika. It did not get to take all of its components to North Africa, however. The 164th consisted of two infantry regiments: the 125th Grenadier (made up from troops already in Libya and Egypt) and the 382nd Grenadier (consisting of troops from the fortress division). A third regiment from the original division (the 433rd

Grenadier) was sent in September. It also controlled the 164th Panzer Reconnaissance Battalion, the 220th Artillery Regiment (with only two battalions), and the 220th Divisional Support Unit, but it had no engineer troops. Eventually, in February 1943, it was given the 200th Engineer Battalion, which formally belonged to the 21st Panzer Division. By then, all three of its grenadier regiments had been reduced from three to two battalions because of casualties.[20] The 164th Light Afrika never distinguished itself to the degree the 15th Panzer, 21st Panzer, or 90th Light Divisions did, but it was nevertheless a very good division. It surrendered to the British on May 13, 1943, and has the distinction of being the last major German formation in North Africa to lay down its arms.

Commanders of the 164th include Colonel/Major General Konrad Haase (December 1, 1939–January 10, 1940) and Major General/ Lieutenant General Josef Folttmann (January 10–August 10, 1942).[21] The commanders in Africa were Colonel/Major General Carl-Hans Lungershausen (August 10, 1942–December 1, 1942), Colonel Siegfried Westphal (acting commander, December 1–29, 1942), Lungershausen again (December 29, 1942–January 15, 1943), Colonel/Major General Baron Kurt von Liebenstein (January 15–February 17, 1943), Major General Fritz Krause (February 17–March 13, 1943), and Liebenstein again (March 13–May 12, 1943).

Carl-Hans Lungershausen was born in Darmstadt on July 20, 1896. He joined the Imperial Army as a Fahnenjunker when World War I began in August 1914 and was commissioned second lieutenant in the 24th Dragoon Regiment the following year. During World War I, he served on the Eastern Front. Lungershausen served with the cavalry for most of his pre-World War II career, including a stint as commander of the I/8th Cavalry Regiment (1936–39). When the Second World War began, this unit was redesignated the 18th Reconnaissance Battalion and fought in Poland as part of the 18th Infantry Division. It was part of the spearhead of the German Army and fought in the major Battle of Kutno and at Warsaw.

Lungershausen, a lieutenant colonel since early 1939, was named adjutant of Fedor von Bock's Army Group B in October 1939. He served in the Netherlands, Belgium, and France, and in the preparation phase of Operation "Sea Lion"—the invasion of Great Britain, which was never launched. He was promoted to colonel on November 1, 1940. As the Wehrmacht prepared to invade Russia, Carl-Hans Lungershausen assumed command of the 7th Rifle Regiment of the 7th Panzer Division on June 1, 1941. He led this unit on the northern sector of the Russian Front and assumed command of its parent unit, the 7th Rifle Brigade, on April 1, 1942.

Colonel Lungershausen's tenure with the 7th Brigade did not last long. He was soon transferred to Africa, where he was earmarked to command the 164th Light Afrika Division. First, however, he served as acting commander of the 90th Light Division from July 13 to August 10, 1942. He assumed command of his own division (the 164th) on August 10, 1942. Shortly thereafter, he was called upon to temporarily replace Georg von Bismarck as commander of the 21st Panzer Division (September 1–18, 1942), while simultaneously retaining command of the 164th. (Bismarck had been killed in action on August 31.) Lungershausen then returned to his own command. He was promoted to major general on October 1, 1942.

General Lungershausen played a brilliant role in the 2nd Battle of El Alamein. On October 23, 1942, the first day of the offensive, Montgomery launched a massive artillery bombardment on the 164th Division. The general from Darmstadt ordered his gunners not to respond. Had they done so, the divisional artillery would no doubt have been destroyed. When the British 8th Army launched its ground attack, the attackers assumed the German guns must have been knocked out. Most of them, however, were still intact, and did not fire on the British tanks and infantry until they were easy targets. Lungershausen thus played a major role in checking the 8th Army on the first day of the offensive. Despite heavy casualties, the 164th Light Afrika held its positions until Rommel ordered a general retreat on November 4.

Lungershausen was probably wounded on December 1, 1942. In any case, he was temporarily succeeded by Siegfried Westphal, whose career is discussed in Chapter VI. Until the day he died, Westphal was very proud that he got to command the 164th, even if his tenure was relatively short.

Lungershausen resumed command on December 29, 1942. He still had not recovered his health, however, because he left Africa for the last time on January 15, 1943. He did not return to active duty until May 23, 1943, when he assumed command of the ad hoc Division Sardinia.

After Mussolini was deposed, Lungershausen did a masterful job in evacuating the island of Sardinia and assisted General Frido von Senger und Etterlin in evacuating Corsica, despite Allied aerial and sea supremacy. Back on the mainland, Division Sardinia was redesignated 90th Panzer Grenadier Division on August 1, and Lungershausen remained its commander. He was promoted to lieutenant general on September 1. Meanwhile, the division was sent to upper Italy to help disarm the Italian Army after Rome defected from the Axis.

In early 1944, the 90th Panzer Grenadier fought in the Cassino battles, but Carl-Hans Lungershausen was not with them. On December 20, 1943, he was placed in Fuehrer Reserve for six months. On July 1,

1944, he was assigned to Kesselring's OB Southwest and was named inspector of Italian units. He held this post until March 1, 1945, when it was apparently abolished and Lungershausen was sent home. He held no further appointments. After the war, he lived in Hamburg for a time, but eventually retired to the city of his birth. He died there on December 27, 1975.

Baron Kurt von Liebenstein was born in Jebenhausen on February 28, 1899, and joined the 26th Dragoon Regiment as a Fahnenjunker in 1916. He fought in World War I (where he won the Iron Cross, 1st and 2nd Classes), served in the Reichswehr, and was a major on the staff of the German military attaché to Paris in 1937. Before the beginning of the war, Liebenstein was transferred to the staff of OKH and was promoted to lieutenant colonel on April 1, 1939. In early 1940, he became Ia of the 10th Panzer Division, and in early 1941 he was promoted to colonel and named chief of staff of Guderian's 2nd Panzer Group on the Eastern Front (1941–42). He assumed command of the 6th Panzer Regiment of the 3rd Panzer Division on June 20, 1942, and led it in the battles around Kharkov, and in the drive across the Don, and into the Caucasus. He was named commander of the 3rd Panzer Grenadier Brigade of the 3rd Panzer Division in October 1942 but held the post only two weeks, as the brigade was dissolved on November 8. Now an excess officer, Baron von Liebenstein went on leave for about five weeks and was then given command of the 164th Light Afrika. He took charge on December 12, 1942, and led the division in the final retreats from Libya and in the Tunisian battles, mostly against the British 8th Army. He was injured in an automobile accident on February 17, 1943, and was incapacitated. He was forced to temporarily step down as divisional commander. Fritz Krause was selected as his temporary replacement.

Fritz Krause was the son of an artillery officer. He was born at Jueterbog, the home of the principle German artillery school, on January 29, 1895. He entered the service as a Fahnenjunker in 1913 and was commissioned second lieutenant in the 41st Field Artillery Regiment just before World War I began. He fought in the Great War, served in the Reichswehr, and became commander of the 36th Artillery Regiment of the 36th Infantry Division in late 1938. He was promoted to colonel in 1939. His home base was Kaiserslautern in northern Germany.

Krause directed the 36th Artillery in the Saar and in the Western campaign of 1940 (where he fought in Luxemburg, Verdun, and the conquest of France). He then took his regiment back to Germany and oversaw its conversion to a motorized unit. On January 20, 1941, he was named commander of the 104th Artillery Command (Arko 104) in France. Its home station was Potsdam, Wehrkreis III, an ancient garrison town near Berlin. Krause and his new command, however, were headed in the opposite direction. Arko 104 became the GHQ artillery unit for Panzer Group Afrika and began to arrive in Libya in April 1941.

Arko 104 distinguished itself in North Africa. The hard and often flat ground made for an excellent fragmentation effect, and artillery accounted for more personnel casualties than any other type of weapon in the Desert War. Krause, of course, had spent a lifetime in the artillery and naturally excelled here. He was, however, not a dynamic officer, and his contributions tended to be overlooked.

In late 1941, Fritz Krause was sent to Greece, where he assumed command of Arko 142. Rommel, however, remembered him. In the spring of 1942 he returned to Africa, fought in the capture of Tobruk and the drive to El Alamein, and was promoted to major general on July 1, 1942. He became Higher Artillery Commander Afrika (and commander of Harko Afrika) on September 1, 1942. He did a particularly good job at El Alamein, where he ran out of German shells, so he re-equipped his battalions with British guns because he had plenty of captured British shells.

Fritz Krause directed his GHQ units in the retreat across Egypt, Libya, and Tunisia. He was now seeking further advancement, however, so Rommel named him acting commander of the 164th Light Afrika Division on February 17, 1943. (He had been promoted to major general on July 1, 1942.) He served as commander of the division until March 13. A month later, on April 15, 1943, Dieter von Arnim made him acting commander of the 334th Infantry Division. It was too late by now to win many laurels in North Africa, however, as the Axis supply lines were collapsing. On May 9, 1943, Fritz Krause put on his finest dress uniform and surrendered his command to the Americans. Some of his comrades poked fun at him for his dress, but Krause considered it appropriate.

After more than four years as a prisoner of war, Fritz Krause was discharged. He retired to Ingelheim and lived quietly until his death on February 14, 1975.

Baron Kurt von Liebenstein was able to resume command of the 164th Light Afrika Divison on March 13, 1943. He had been promoted to major general on March 1, 1943, while he was still in the hospital. He led the division in its final battles, was awarded the Knight's Cross on May 10, 1943, and surrendered two days later.

General von Liebenstein was released from the POW camps in 1947 or 1948 and returned to Germany. When the West German Army (the

Bundesheer) was created in 1956, he was appointed major general (equivalent to lieutenant general on the old World War II scale) and was named commander of Wehrkreis V, which was headquartered in Stuttgart. He retired on September 30, 1960, but remained in Stuttgart until his death on August 3, 1975. The Lord Mayor of Stuttgart was Manfred Rommel, the son of the Desert Fox.

NOTES

CHAPTER I: THE SOURCES OF ROMMEL'S OFFICERS

1. T. N. Dupuy, *A Genius for War* (Fairfax, VA: 1984), pp. 47–48.

2. Charles de Gaulle, *The Army of the Future* (London: 1940), p. 47.

3. This figure excludes 300 medical and 200 veterinary officers, who were allowed by the Allies.

4. For the best English-language books on the Reichswehr during the Seeckt era, see James S. Corum, *The Roots of the Blitzkrieg: Hans von Seeckt and German Military Reform* (Lawrence, KS: 1992); and Harold J. Gordon, Jr., *The Reichswehr and the German Republic, 1919–1926* (Princeton, NJ: 1957).

5. Joachim Kramarz, *Stauffenberg: The Life and Death of an Officer, 15 November 1907–20 July 1940* (London: 1967), p. 38.

6. W. E. Hart (pseudo.), *Hitler's Generals* (New York: 1944), pp. 164–65.

7. One of the major flaws in the Treaty of Versailles from the Allied point of view was that the number of German NCOs was not restricted. By 1922, the Reichswehr had 48,680 NCOs (including corporals). This figure had increased in 1926, to the point that there were only 36,500 privates in the army—only about 35 percent of its total strength. See Corum, p. 47.

8. Ibid., p. 82.

9. Ibid., pp. 82–84.

10. Ibid., pp. 85–86.

11. Wiener-Neustadt is located south of Vienna in present-day Austria.

12. Siegfried Knappe, "Soldaten" (unpublished manuscript in the possession of the author). It was later published by Crown Publishers in New York. Knappe rose to the rank of major and was chief of operations of the LVI Panzer Corps during the Battle of Berlin. After he was released from Soviet captivity and escaped to West Germany, he moved to Ohio, where he died in 1997.

Notes

CHAPTER II: THE FIRST CYRENAICAN CAMPAIGN

1. Friedrich von Stauffenberg, "Panzer Commanders of the Western Front" (unpublished manuscript in the possession of the author).

2. Ibid.

3. Paul Goerbig (1895–1974) became commander of the 67th Panzer Battalion of the 3rd Light Division. Sieckenius was given command of the 66th Panzer Battalion, 2nd Light Division. See Samuel W. Mitcham, Jr., *Rommel's Lieutenants* (Westport, CT: 2006).

4. U.S. Army Military Intelligence Service, "Order of Battle of the German Army" (Washington, DC: April 1943).

5. Hartlieb (1883–1959) had replaced von Vietinghoff as commander of the 5th Panzer Division on October 18, 1939. He was sacked on May 29, 1940. He later commanded a replacement division and an army rear-area, but he never received another promotion or another field command.

6. Erwin Rommel, *The Rommel Papers*, ed. B. H. Liddell Hart (New York: 1953), p. 110.

7. David Irving, *The Trail of the Fox* (New York: 1978), p. 78.

8. Heinz W. Schmidt, *With Rommel in the Desert* (London: 1951), p. 45.

9. Ibid.

10. Fritz Stephans assumed command of the 5th Panzer Regiment on July 1, 1941. He was mortally wounded on November 25, 1941, and died in a New Zealand hospital that the Afrika Korps had captured.

11. Walter Brauchitsch (1881–1948), the son of a Prussian general of cavalry, was named commander-in-chief of the army on February 4, 1938. Hitler sacked him on December 19, 1941, for his failure to take Moscow. He died in Allied captivity. Franz Halder (1884–1972) was a Bavarian. He was promoted to chief of the General Staff in the shake-up of February 2–4, 1938, and was fired by Hitler on September 24, 1942. He dabbled in the anti-Hitler conspiracy before the war. Arrested in 1944, he ended the war in a concentration camp. Both he and Brauchitsch were artillery officers.

12. Wolf Keilig, *Die Generale des Heeres* (Friedburg: 1983), p. 149.

13. Hans-Henning Holtzendorff, "Reasons for Rommel's Successes in Africa, 1941–1942," Foreign Military Studies MS D-004, Office of the Chief of Military History, U.S. Army (Washington, DC: n.d.).

14. Keilig, p. 130.

15. Frank Kurowski, *Knight's Cross Holders of the Afrikakorps*, trans. David Johnston (Atglen, PA: 1996), p. 61; Keilig, p. 44.

16. Georg Tessin, *Verbaende und Truppen der deutschen Wehrmacht und Waffen-SS, 1939–1945* (Osnabrueck: 1979–86), vol. 2, pp. 173, 294–95. The 3rd Panzer Brigade Staff was also transferred to the 5th Light and was used to form the divisional headquarters. The 3rd Panzer Reconnaissance Battalion, 39th Anti-tank Battalion, and I/75th Artillery Regiment were also transferred from the 3rd Panzer Division to the 5th Light. The new division also received the 200th Special Purposes Infantry Regiment Staff (from Wehrkreis III), the 2nd and 6th

Machine Gun Battalions, and the 605th Antitank and 606th Fla Battalion, a light anti-aircraft unit (all former GHQ units). The Staff, 200th Infantry Regiment, and the 2nd Machine Gun Battalion were transferred to the 15th Panzer Division that fall.

17. Kurowski, p. 61; Keilig, p. 44.

18. Ernst Bolbrinker, "5th Panzer Regiment (13–14 April 1941)," Foreign Military Studies MS D-088, Historical Section, U.S. Army–Europe (n.p.: n.d.).

19. http://home.wxs.nl/~j.n.houterman/bio/german/HeerB2.htm#Bo (accessed November 8, 2006).

20. Dermot Bradley, Karl-Friedrich Hildebrand, and Markus Brockmann, *Die Generale des Heeres* (Osnabrueck: 1993–2004), vol. 6, pp. 469–70.

21. Ibid.

22. Tessin, vol. 8, p. 322.

23. Other members of the "Court of Honor" included Field Marshal von Rundstedt, Colonel General Guderian, General of Infantry Walter Schroth, General of Infantry Karl Kriebel, and Lieutenant General Karl-Wilhelm Specht. Major General Ernst Maisel, the chief of the Officers' Education and Welfare Office Group, was the protocol officer on the court.

CHAPTER III: THE SIEGE OF TOBRUK

1. The 2nd Panzer Regiment was formed from the 7th Cavalry Regiment "Breslau" and part of the II Battalion, Demonstration Command (*Lehrcommando*) Ohrdruf. It was later transferred to the 16th Panzer Division and was decimated in the Stalingrad campaign, where its parent division was destroyed. A rebuilt 2nd Panzer Regiment fought in Italy and on the Eastern Front.

2. Keilig, p. 263.

3. Kuehn led the 14th Panzer Division in Yugoslavia and in the invasion of Russia, where it fought mainly in the Ukraine. It suffered heavy losses at Rostov in late 1941 and was destroyed at Stalingrad in early 1943. Kuehn, meanwhile, was promoted to general of panzer troops and was named chief of army motorization in February 1943. He was killed in an Allied bombing raid on Berlin on February 15, 1944. He had previously commanded the 4th Panzer Regiment (1935–38), the Panzer Troops School (1938–39), the 14th Panzer Brigade (1939–40), the 3rd Panzer Brigade (1940), and was acting commander of the 3rd Panzer Division (1940).

4. Keilig, p. 84.

CHAPTER IV: CRUSADER

1. Wahlstaff, which was near Strehlen, was the home of the Bluecher family, and Field Marshal Bluecher, who smashed Napoleon's Imperial Army at Waterloo, was buried there. Rowland Ryder, *Ravenstein* (London: 1978), pp. 8–9.

2. Ryder, p. 9. Manfred von Richthofen, the famous "Red Baron" and the leading fighter ace of World War I, also attended Wadstatt. Like Ravenstein, he disliked it intensely but, again like Ravenstein, highly praised the senior cadet academy at Gross-Lichterfelde.

Lieutenant General Friedrich von Loeper (1888–1983) commanded the 1st Light Division (1938–39), the 81st Infantry Division (1939–40), the 10th Infantry Division (1940–42), the 178th Reserve Panzer Division (1942–44), the Tatra Panzer Division (1944–45), and Division Ludwig (1945) during World War II.

3. Ryder, p. 21.

4. Kurowski, p. 216.

5. Unlike the American tradition, Imperial Germany's highest decoration was sometimes awarded to field marshals and senior generals for directing major campaigns, or to high-ranking royalty (including allies) for no apparent reason. The same would apply to the Knight's Cross during World War II.

6. Kurowski, p. 261.

7. Karl Jarres was born in Remschied on September 21, 1874. He served as Oberbuergermeister of Remschied (1910–14) and Duisburg (1914–33), was national minister of the interior from 1923 to 1925, and was vice chancellor under Dr. Gustav Stresemann and Wilhelm Marx (1923–24).

8. Ryder, p. 32. See also Samuel W. Mitcham, Jr., *Why Hitler?* (Westport, CT: 1997). Dr. Jarres died in Duisburg on October 20, 1951.

9. Giraud was captured on the morning of May 19, 1940.

10. Schmidt, p. 95.

11. Ibid.

12. Ryder, p. 172.

13. Rommel was born on November 15, 1891.

14. Sources for the section on Cruewell include Tessin, vol. 3, pp. 202–3; Bradley, Hildebrand, and Brockmann, vol. 2, pp. 480–82; and Keilig, p. 63.

15. Tessin, vol. 3, pp. 202–3.

16. Guenther Angern was the commander of the 11th Rifle Brigade and was an acting commander only. Cruewell's permanent replacement, Major General Baron von Esebeck, arrived on August 26. Angern, a native of Kolberg, East Prussia, then returned home on leave. He assumed command of the 16th Panzer Division on September 15, 1942, and led it in the Stalingrad campaign. Rather than surrender to the Russians, he killed himself on February 2, 1943. He was promoted to major general effective September 1, 1942.

17. Cruewell replaced Lieutenant General Ferdinand Schaal, who only commanded the corps for 15 days (September 1–15, 1941). Lieutenant General Philipp Mueller-Gebhard was initially slated to replace Schaal, but Rommel apparently blocked his appointment. Mueller-Gebhard (1889–1970) commanded the 13th Infantry Regiment (1936–39), the 169th Replacement Division (1939–41), and the 72nd Infantry Division (1941–43). He had no tank or motorized infantry experience at all.

18. Desmond Young, *Rommel: The Desert Fox* (New York: 1965), p. 81.

19. Irving, p. 131.

20. Young, p. 91; Rommel, p. 181; and Paul Carell, *Hitler Moves East* (Kansas City, MO: 1966), p. 133.

21. Irving, p. 171.

22. Bradley, Hildebrand, and Brockmann, vol. 2, pp. 99–100.

23. I. S. O. Playfair, *The Mediterranean and Middle East*, vol. 3, *British Fortunes Reach Their Lowest Ebb* (London: 1960), p. 78.

24. Kurowski, p. 59.

25. As soon as it was learned that Ravenstein was captured, Lieutenant Colonel Gustav-Georg Knabe assumed command of the 21st Panzer Division.

26. Tessin, vol. 9, p. 237.

27. Hans von Luck, *Panzer Commanders* (New York: 1989), p. 89.

28. Wolf Heckmann, *Rommel's War in Africa*, trans. Stephen Seago (Garden City, NY: 1981), p. 126.

29. After Operation "Battleaxe," the Western Desert Force was redesignated XIII Corps. Sir Noel Beresford-Peirse was given command of the Sudan and was replaced by Lieutenant General A. R. Godwin-Austen. Meanwhile, Headquarters, 8th Army was formed in Egypt and took charge of all British forces in Libya and Egypt, including XIII Corps. It was initially commanded by General Sir Alan Cunningham. Another major headquarters, XXX Corps, was formed at the same time to control the British armor. It was initially commanded by Lieutenant General V. V. Pope, a noted tank expert who was killed in an airplane crash on October 5, 1941. He was succeeded by Major General C. Willoughby M. Norrie, the former commander of the 1st Armoured Division.

30. General von Ravenstein later met di Giorgis in captivity and recorded that he was "intelligent, is urbane, charming, certainly likeable"; Ryder, p. 124.

31. The 555th Infantry Division was formed in Wehrkreis VI on February 10, 1940, and included the 624th, 625th, 626th, and 627th Infantry Regiments (three battalions each), the 555th Artillery Regiment, the 555th Observation Battalion, and the 555th Divisional Supply Unit. It was officially dissolved on August 31, but the actual process took a few weeks longer to complete. See Tessin, vol. 11, pp. 154, 336.

CHAPTER V: THE GAZALA LINE AND TOBRUK

1. Carell, *Hitler Moves East*, p. 179.

2. Ibid.

3. Marie Pierre Koenig (1898–1970) was born in Caen, France. He fought in World War I, served in Morocco, fought in Norway and Belgium in 1940, and escaped via Dunkirk when Hitler overran France and the Low Countries. He joined Charles de Gaulle's Free French Forces as a colonel and fought in Syria and Lebanon (1941). After Bir Hacheim, he served as the Free French delegate to SHAEF (General Eisenhower). In June 1944 he was named commander of the Free French Forces of the Interior (FFI) and, on August 21, 1944, was

named military governor of Paris. After the war he was commander of the French Occupation Zone in Germany (1945–49) and briefly served as defense minister in the 1950s. He was posthumously promoted to marshal of France.

4. Irving, p. 177.

5. Carell, *Hitler Moves East*, pp. 179–82.

6. For reasons not made clear by the records, General Hecker was absent June 1–25, 1944. During this time, the 3rd Panzer Grenadier was commanded by Lieutenant General Hans-Guenther von Rost.

7. http://www.axishistory.com (accessed November 8, 2006).

8. Others were created late in the war. The army formed the 3rd and 4th Cavalry Divisions, and the SS formed the 8th, 22nd, and 37th SS Cavalry Divisions, as well as the I Cossack Cavalry Corps (1st and 2nd Cossack Cavalry Divisions).

9. The regiments were named after their commanders, Lieutenant Colonel Karl Ens, Colonel Theodor Koerner, and Lieutenant Colonel Fritz Fullriede. Ens had commanded a regiment in the Afrika Korps before he was seriously wounded. Fullriede had commanded the 961st (Penal) Grenadier Regiment in Tunisia from December 1942 to early April 1943, when he was also wounded. Koerner was a veteran engineer officer.

10. The move was partially political. Goering had nominated Stahel to command all forces in Sicily, instead of the extremely competent Hube, and Kesselring—who wanted to minimize Goering's influence on the conduct of operations—may have wanted to get him out of the way, which he certainly did. Stahel later distinguished himself on the northern sector of the Eastern Front.

11. Samuel Eliot Morison, *History of United States Naval Operations in World War II*, vol. 9, *Sicily, Salerno, Anzio* (Edison, NJ: 1962), p. 209.

12. Martin Blumenson, *Sicily: Whose Victory?* (New York: 1968), p. 96.

13. C. J. C. Molony et al., *The Mediterranean and Middle East*, vol. 5, *The Campaign in Sicily, 1943, and the Campaign in Italy, 3 September 1943–31 March 1944* (London: 1973), p. 168.

14. Stauffenberg, "Panzer Commanders of the Western Front."

15. James Lucas, *Hitler's Enforcers* (London: 1966), p. 104.

16. Oswald Lutz, who was born in Oehringen on November 6, 1876, entered the service in 1894 as a Fahnenjunker in a Bavarian railroad battalion in 1894 and was commissioned in the 1st Bavarian Engineer Battalion in 1896. He fought in World War I, served in the Reichsheer, and was promoted to major general in 1931. He became a lieutenant general on February 1, 1933 (the day after Hitler assumed power) and became the first general of panzer troops on November 1, 1935. Hitler sacked him during his bloodless purge of the Reichswehr on February 2, 1938. Lutz learned of his involuntary retirement in a particularly tasteless manner: he heard about it on the radio. He was succeeded by his chief of staff, Heinz Guderian, who never lifted a finger to help him. Lutz's only World War II service began in September 1941, when he was

named chief of a special transition staff in Frankfurt/Oder. He was placed in retirement again at the end of May 1942 and was never reemployed. He died in Munich on February 26, 1944. See Keilig, p. 213.

17. Lucas, p. 108.

18. Tessin, vol. 4, pp. 93–94, 97. The 18th Panzer Division would be reorganized as the 18th Artillery Division in October 1943. It would suffer heavy losses on the southern sector of the Eastern Front and would be dissolved on July 27, 1944.

19. Lucas, p. 110.

20. Carell, *Hitler Moves East*, p. 163.

21. Ibid., pp. 163–65.

22. Otto Heidkaemper (1901–69) had been Rommel's Ia when he commanded the 7th Panzer Division in France. He later served as Ia of the 4th Panzer Division and chief of staff of the XXIV Panzer Corps, 3rd Panzer Army, and Army Group Center—all on the Eastern Front. Sacked by the pro-Nazi Field Marshal Schoerner in January 1945, he ended the war as a lieutenant general, commanding the 464th Infantry Division, which he managed to surrender to the Americans. For a full description of Heidkaemper's career, see Mitcham, *Rommel's Lieutenants*.

23. Heinz Guderian, *Panzer Leader* (New York: 1967), p. 326.

24. Lucas, pp. 116–17.

25. Kurowski, p. 32.

CHAPTER VI: THE STAFF

1. Kurowski, p. 127.

2. Bradley, Hildebrand, and Brockmann, vol. 5, p. 191.

3. Ibid., pp. 191–92.

4. Ibid.

5. Panzer Group Afrika was officially upgraded to Panzer Army Afrika on January 30, 1942.

6. The 58th Infantry Division later fought in Luxembourg and France (1940) and on the northern sector of the Eastern Front (1941–45). It surrendered in East Prussia at the end of the war. See Carell, *Hitler Moves East*; and Kurt von Zydowitz, *Die Geschichte der 58 in Infanterie-Division, 1939–1945* (Kiel: 1952).

7. The XXVII Corps was sent to central Russia in October 1941 and was destroyed on July 28, 1944. See Tessin, vol. 4, p. 250.

8. Keilig, p. 369.

9. Young, p. 111.

10. Rommel, p. 167; and Paul Carell, *The Foxes of the Desert* (n.p.: 1972), p. 84.

11. Heckmann, p. 251.

12. Young, p. 111.

13. Hans-Otto Behrendt, *Rommel's Intelligence in the Desert Campaign, 1941–1943* (London: 1985), p. 64.

14. Christian Zweng, ed., *Die Dienstlaufbahnen der Offiziere des Generalstabes des deutschen Heeres, 1935–1945* (Osnabrueck: 1995, 1998), vol. 2.

15. Eric Hansen was born in Hamburg in 1889, entered the service as a Fahnenjunker in the 9th Dragoons in 1907, fought in World War I, and served in the Reichsheer. He was a lieutenant general commanding the 4th Infantry Division when World War II began. He served with the German mission to Romania (October 1940–41) before assuming command of the LIV Corps on June 1, 1941. He led the LIV on the Eastern Front until January 1943, when he returned to Romania as chief of the military mission and German military commander in Romania. He was definitely a better corps commander than a mission chief. He had few diplomatic skills and was taken in by the Romanians. He was captured by the Russians on August 26, 1944, but unlike most of the men of the 6th Army, he survived his 11 years in prison. Released in October 1955, he returned to Hamburg, where he died in 1967.

16. Verner R. Carlson, "Portrait of a German General Staff Officer," *Military Review* 70 (April 1990):69–81.

17. F. W. von Mellenthin, *Panzer Battles*, trans. H. Betzler (New York: 1971), p. xi.

18. Horst von Mellenthin, who was six years older than F. W., was born in Hanover on July 31, 1898. He attended the cadet schools, entered the service as a Faehnrich in early 1915, and was commissioned in the 6th Field Artillery Regiment in June of that same year. He fought in World War I, served in the Reichsheer, and by 1937 was a major and chief of the attaché group in OKH. He was assigned to the 677th Artillery Regiment in late 1939. Later he commanded the 67th Infantry Regiment (1943), was acting commander of the 23rd Infantry Division (August 1943), and was named acting commander of the 93rd Infantry Division in September 1943. He received his own division—the 205th Infantry—in December 1943 and led it until January 1945, when he became acting commander of the XXXVIII Panzer Corps. He commanded the XI Corps for three days in March 1945 and was named commander of the VIII Corps on March 19. He served the entire 1941–45 period on the northern sector of the Eastern Front and was promoted to lieutenant colonel (1939), colonel (1941), major general (1943), lieutenant general (1944), and general of artillery (March 16, 1945). A holder of the Knight's Cross with Oak Leaves, Horst von Mellenthin died at Wiesbaden on January 8, 1977. F. W. wrote an excellent chapter about Horst in his "other" book, *German Generals of World War II* (Norman, OK: 1977).

19. Carlson, p. 71.

20. Mellenthin, *Panzer Battles*, p. 32.

21. Ibid., p. 38.

22. Ibid., p. 54.

23. Ibid., p. 51.

24. Carlson, p. 74.

25. Ibid., pp. 74–75.

26. Rommel, p. 253.

27. Ferdinand Heim (1895–1977) entered the service as a Fahnenjunker in the 13th Field Artillery Regiment in June 1914. He fought in World War I, served in the Reichsheer, and was a full colonel and chief of staff of the XVI Motorized (later Panzer) Corps when World War II began. He fought in Poland and became a branch chief in OKH in early 1940. He became chief of staff of 6th Army on September 3, 1940, assumed command of the 14th Panzer Division on July 1, 1942, and became commander of the XXXXVIII Panzer Corps on November 1, 1942. He was released from prison in August 1944 and was given command of the fortress of Boulogne on the English Channel. He surrendered to the British on September 23, 1944.

28. Werner Friebe (1897–1962) was a Silesian. He entered the service as a war volunteer in September 1914 and received a commission in the infantry in 1916. Selected for the Reichsheer in 1920, he was a lieutenant colonel and Ia of the 20th Motorized Infantry Division when World War II began. He became chief of staff of the XXXXVIII Panzer Corps on January 1, 1941, and was promoted to colonel later that year.

After being sacked as chief of staff of the XXXXVIII Panzer, he served as chief of an instructional staff from January 1943 to January 1944. He assumed command of the 8th Panzer Division on April 1, 1944.

29. Heim was temporarily replaced by Major General Hans Cramer (November 20–26), Major General Hans Eberbach (November 26–December 1), and Cramer again (December 1–4). Knobelsdorff arrived on December 4, 1942, and assumed permanent command of the corps.

30. Hermann Balck (1893–1982) was of Swedish-Finnish ancestry and was nicknamed "the cool Nordic" by von Mellenthin because he was "absolutely unshakable" under fire. An infantry lieutenant in World War I, he remained in the army and rose from lieutenant colonel to general of panzer troops during World War II. He commanded the 1st Rifle Regiment (October 1939–late 1940), 3rd Panzer Regiment (1940–41), and 1st Panzer Brigade (1941–42) before spending six months as the general of mobile troops at OKH (1942–43). He returned to the Eastern Front and commanded the 11th Panzer Division (1942–43) and Panzer Grenadier Division "Grossdeutschland" (1943). He briefly commanded the XIV Panzer Corps in Italy (September–October 1943) until he was seriously injured when the reconnaissance airplane in which he was flying crashed. When he recovered in late 1943, he returned to the Eastern Front as commander of the XXXX Panzer Corps (1943), XXXXVIII Panzer Corps (1943–44), and 4th Panzer Army (1944). Later he commanded Army Group G on the Western Front (1944) and 6th Army in Hungary and Austria (late 1944–45). He surrendered to the Americans in 1945 and was released from a POW camp in 1947. A very brave man, he held the Knight's Cross with Oak Leaves, Swords, and Diamonds. See Carlson, p. 76; and Keilig, p. 19.

31. Carlson, p. 78.

32. Ibid., p. 71.

Notes

33. Ibid., p. 78.

34. Behrendt, p. 65.

35. Ibid., p. 57.

36. The 4th Infantry Division became the 14th Panzer Division on August 15, 1940. It later took part in the conquest of Yugoslavia and was destroyed at Stalingrad in early February 1942.

37. From April 1, 1934, until the end of World War II, German senior medical officer ranks were as follows: *Oberfeldarzt* (lieutenant colonel), *Oberstarzt* (colonel), *Generalarzt* (major general), *Generalstabsarzt* (lieutenant general), and *Generaloberstabsarzt* (general of medical services).

38. The 228th Infantry Division was transferred to the Muenster sector of Germany in May 1940 and remained there until the fall of France. It was dissolved in August 1940. See Tessin, vol. 8, p. 228.

39. Before Barnewitz arrived, Wehrkreis XII also included the Lorraine district of France (including the city of Nancy), but this region had been lost in the fall of 1944.

40. Keilig, p. 70.

41. Sources for the section on Hoesslin essay include Kurowski, pp. 152–54; www.das-ritterkreuz.de (accessed November 8, 2006); and http://ritterkreuz.heim.at (accessed November 8, 2006).

42. Hubert von Hoesslin was born in Augsburg in 1882. He was a cadet page at the court of the Bavarian king at the turn of the century. After being educated in the cadet schools, he joined the Bavarian Army as a Faehnrich in 1900 and was commissioned into the Bavarian cavalry in 1902. In 1914, the Bavarian Army was incorporated into the Imperial German Army, and most of it was sent to the Western Front in World War I. Hubert was discharged after 20 years' service as a Rittmeister (captain of cavalry). From 1922 to 1934, he was an archivist at the Bavarian Military Archives. Recalled to active duty as a major of reserves in 1935, he served in Wehrkreise XII and XIII, mainly as an Ib (logistical General Staff officer). He was officially made a regular army officer in 1941 and was promoted to major general in 1943. He served as chief of staff of Wehrkreis XII from 1940 to late 1943, when he retired. He was discharged from the service on the last day of 1944, apparently because it was suspected that he knew about the plot to assassinate Hitler. He was, however, never brought to trial. He died in 1968. See Keilig, p. 146.

43. Peter Sauerbruck was a captain in the General Staff and Ib of the 14th Panzer Division during the Stalingrad campaign (1942). He was given command of a battle group during the siege. He was awarded the Knight's Cross on January 4, 1943. He later rose to the rank of lieutenant colonel.

44. Fromm, who had commanded the Replacement Army since the beginning of the war, was in a sense successful, because there were not enough witnesses left to convict him of conspiracy or treason. When it came to killing people, however, Adolf Hitler was nothing if not resourceful. He had Fromm executed for cowardice on March 19, 1945.

45. Stauffenberg, "Panzer Commanders of the Western Front."

46. Wolfgang von Kluge, who was nine and a half years younger than Field Marshal Guenther von Kluge, was born in Stettin in 1892. He was also educated in cadet schools and entered the army as a lieutenant in the 11th Field Artillery Regiment in 1912. He fought in World War I, where he served as a battalion adjutant and a battery commander. Remaining in the Reichsheer and the Wehrmacht, he was a colonel on the staff of a field inspectorate when World War II began. In late 1940, he assumed command of the 31st Artillery Regiment. In October 1941 he became commander of Arko 107 on the Eastern Front and assumed command of the 292nd Infantry Division on October 1, 1942—the day he was promoted to major general. A promotion to lieutenant general followed on April 1, 1943. He was seriously wounded on July 20, 1943. After months in the hospitals, he took command of the 357th Infantry Division in the West in late 1943. On July 6, 1944, he became commander of the 226th Infantry Division. He was subsequently named commander of the isolated German garrison at Dunkirk but was relieved of his command in September 1944. Hitler had him expelled from the army at the end of 1944. He retired to Kiel, where he died in 1976.

CHAPTER VII: EL ALAMEIN

1. Carell, *Hitler Moves East*, p. 519.

2. Stumme was succeeded as commander of the XXXX Panzer Corps by General of Panzer Troops Baron Leo Geyr von Schweppenburg. Boineburg managed to regain command of his division in late August, after his successor was killed in action, but was run over by a tank in December and was never again able to exercise field command. He was, however, able to command the 325th Security Division in Paris.

3. Ian Kershaw and Andrew Close, *The Desert War* (n.p.: 1975), p. 42; I. S. O. Playfair and C. J. C. Molony, *The Mediterranean and Middle East*, vol. 4, *The Destruction of the Axis Forces in Africa* (London: 1966), pp. 2–30.

4. Bradley, Hildebrand, and Brockmann, vol. 6, pp. 49–97.

5. Mellenthin, *Panzer Battles*, p. 127.

6. B. H. Liddell Hart, *History of the Second World War* (New York: 1972), vol. 1, p. 279.

7. Tessin, vol. 14, p. 207.

8. For an even more detailed description of Thoma's career, see http://www.specialcamp11.fsnet.co.uk (accessed November 8, 2006).

9. Karl von Weber died in the military hospital at Krassnyi on July 20, 1941. Born in 1892, he joined the Bavarian Army in 1911 and served in the infantry. He was commander of the 93rd Infantry Regiment from October 1, 1937, before assuming command of the 17th Panzer Division. He was promoted to major general on December 1, 1940.

10. Guderian, p. 98.

11. Michael Carver, *El Alamein* (New York: 1962), p. 177; and Playfair and Molony, pp. 475–76.

12. Carell, *Foxes of the Desert*, p. 296.

13. Irving, p. 235.

14. B. H. Liddell Hart, *The Other Side of the Hill* (London: 1951).

15. Ibid.

16. Kurowski, p. 55.

17. Sources for the section on Borowietz are Keilig, pp. 46–47; Tessin, vol. 5, p. 164; and Bradley, Hildebrand, and Brockmann, vol. 2, pp. 157–59.

CHAPTER VIII: THE OTHER COMMANDERS

1. Bradley, Hildebrand, and Brockmann, vol. 3, pp. 427–28.

2. The 33rd Infantry Regiment was part of the 13th Motorized Infantry Division and later became the 4th Panzer Division.

3. http://www.lexikon-der-wehrmacht.de/Gliederungen/KorpsSonstige/ AfrikaKorps.htm (accessed November 8, 2006).

4. http://www.powcamp.fsnet.co.uk (accessed November 8, 2006).

5. British interrogation of Major General Gerhard Franz, on file at the Air University Archives, Maxwell Air Force Base, Alabama.

6. Helmut Ritgen, *Die Geschichte der Panzer-Lehr-Division im Westen, 1944– 1945*. (Stuttgart: 1979).

7. Stauffenberg, "Panzer Commanders of the Western Front."

8. Ibid.

9. Friedrich von Stauffenberg, "Papers" (unpublished manuscript in the possession of the author).

10. Ibid.

11. Ibid.

12. Kurowski, p. 53.

13. Ibid.

14. Tessin, vol. 6, p. 111.

15. Kielig, p. 340.

16. Later, the 105th Infantry Regiment was transferred to Romania and fought in northern Greece. It then spent four years on the Eastern Front, ending the war in Silesia. See Tessin, vol. 6, p. 199.

17. For a complete biography of General Mickl, see Mitcham, *Rommel's Lieutenants*.

18. Veith (prisoner number A451669) was six feet tall and weighed 189 pounds. He had brown hair and blue eyes. For a photograph, see http:// www.specialcamp11.fsnet.co.uk (accessed November 8, 2006).

19. Ramcke's brigade was later expanded into the 2nd Parachute Division. He later distinguished himself in the Battle of Brest, where he was finally forced to surrender in September 1944.

20. Tessin, vol. 7, pp. 140–41.

21. Konrad Haase, the first commander of the 164th Infantry Division, was born in Dresden in 1888. He entered the service as a Fahnenjunker in the 12th

Artillery Regiment in 1908, was commissioned in 1909, fought in World War I, and was discharged as a captain in 1919. He joined the police as a captain that same year and rose to lieutenant colonel of police. He rejoined the army in 1935 and was promoted to colonel in 1936, to major general effective January 1, 1940, and to lieutenant general exactly two years later. During World War II, he served as commander of the 11th Infantry Regiment, commander of the 164th Infantry Division, commander of the 365th Infantry Division (1940), Field Command 365 (1940), the 302nd Infantry Division (1940–late 1942), and as a special-purposes general with Army Group South, B and C (OB South) (1943–45). In Italy (1943–45), he commanded military police. A prisoner of war until 1947, he settled in Hahnstaetten and died in 1963.

Joseph Folttmann (1887–1958) was a Silesian. He entered the service as an officer-cadet in 1907, was commissioned in the infantry in 1908, fought in World War I, and served in the Reichsheer. He commanded the 52nd Infantry Regiment (1935–38), the 103rd Infantry Regiment (1938–39), the 256th Infantry Division (1939–40), the 164th (1940–42), Fortress Division Crete (1942), and the 338th Infantry Division (1942–44). He headed Special Staff II at OKH from early 1944 until April 7, 1945, when he was placed in Fuehrer Reserve. He surrendered to the Americans the day Hitler committed suicide and was a prisoner of war until 1947. He lived in Aachen after the war.

BIBLIOGRAPHY

Behrendt, Hans-Otto. *Rommel's Intelligence in the Desert Campaign, 1941–1943.* London: 1985.

Blumenson, Martin. *Sicily: Whose Victory?* New York: 1968.

Bolbrinker, Ernst. "5th Panzer Regiment (13–14 April 1941)." Foreign Military Studies MS D-088, Historical Section, U.S. Army–Europe. N.p.: n.d.

Bradley, Dermot, Karl-Friedrich Hildebrand, and Markus Brockmann. *Die Generale des Heeres.* 7 vols. Osnabrueck: 1993–2004.

Carell, Paul. *The Foxes of the Desert.* N.p.: 1972.

———. *Hitler Moves East.* Kansas City, MO: 1966.

Carlson, Verner R. "Portrait of a German General Staff Officer." *Military Review* 70 (April 1990):69–81.

Carver, Michael. *El Alamein.* New York: 1962.

Corum, James S. *The Roots of the Blitzkrieg: Hans von Seeckt and German Military Reform.* Lawrence, KS: 1992.

Dupuy, T. N. *A Genius for War.* Fairfax, VA: 1984.

Gaulle, Charles de. *The Army of the Future.* London: 1940.

Gordon, Harold J., Jr. *The Reichswehr and the German Republic, 1919–1926.* Princeton, NJ: 1957.

Guderian, Heinz. *Panzer Leader.* New York: 1967.

Hart, B. H. Liddell. *History of the Second World War.* 2 vols. New York: 1972.

———. *The Other Side of the Hill.* London: 1951.

Hart, W. E. (pseudo.). *Hitler's Generals.* New York: 1944.

Heckmann, Wolf. *Rommel's War in Africa.* Translated by Stephen Seago. Garden City, NY: 1981.

Hildebrand, Karl Friedrich. *Die Generale der deutschen Luftwaffe, 1935–1945.* 3 vols. Osnabrueck: 1990–92.

Holtzendorff, Hans-Henning. "Reasons for Rommel's Successes in Africa, 1941–1942." Foreign Military Studies MS D-004, Office of the Chief of Military History, U.S. Army. Washington, DC: n.d.

Irving, David. *The Trail of the Fox.* New York: 1978.

Bibliography

Keilig, Wolf. *Die Generale des Heeres*. Friedburg: 1983.

Kershaw, Ian, and Andrew Close. *The Desert War*. N.p.: 1975.

Knappe, Siegfried. "Soldaten." Unpublished manuscript in the possession of the author.

Kraetschmer, E. G. *Die Ritterkreuztraeger der Waffen-SS*. 3rd ed. Preussisch Oldendorf: 1982.

Kramarz, Joachim. *Kriegstagebuch des Oberkommando des Wehrmacht (Fuehrungsstab)*. 4 vols. Frankfurt-am-Main: 1961.

———. *Stauffenberg: The Life and Death of an Officer, 15 November 1907–20 July 1940*. London: 1967.

Kurowski, Franz. *Knight's Cross Holders of the Afrikakorps*. Translated by David Johnston. Atglen, PA: 1996.

Lucas, James. *Hitler's Enforcers*. London: 1966.

Luck, Hans von. *Panzer Commanders*. New York: 1989.

Mehner, Kurt, ed. *Die Geheimen Tagesberichte der deutschen Wehrmachtfuehrung im Zweiten Weltkrieg, 1939–1945*. 12 vols. Osnabrueck: 1984–99.

Mellenthin, F. W. von. *German Generals of World War II*. Norman, OK: 1977.

———. *Panzer Battles*. Translated by H. Betzler. New York: 1971.

Mitcham, Samuel W., Jr. *Rommel's Lieutenants*. Westport, CT: 2006.

———. *Why Hitler?* Westport, CT: 1997.

Molony, C. J. C., et al. *The Mediterranean and Middle East*. Vol. 5, *The Campaign in Sicily, 1943, and the Campaign in Italy, 3 September 1943–31 March 1944*. London: 1973.

Morison, Samuel Eliot. *History of United States Naval Operations in World War II*. Vol. 9, *Sicily, Salerno, Anzio*. Edison, NJ: 1962.

Playfair, I. S. O. *The Mediterranean and Middle East*. Vol. 3, *British Fortunes Reach Their Lowest Ebb*. London: 1960.

Playfair, I. S. O., and C. J. C. Molony. *The Mediterranean and Middle East*. Vol. 4, *The Destruction of the Axis Forces in Africa*. London: 1966.

Ritgen, Helmut. *Die Geschichte der Panzer-Lehr-Division im Westen, 1944–1945*. Stuttgart: 1979.

Rommel, Erwin. *The Rommel Papers*. Edited by B. H. Liddell Hart. New York: 1953.

Ryder, Rowland. *Ravenstein*. London: 1978.

Schmidt, Heinz W. *With Rommel in the Desert*. London: 1951.

Stauffenberg, Friedrich von. "Panzer Commanders of the Western Front." Unpublished manuscript in the possession of the author.

———. "Papers." Unpublished manuscript in the possession of the author.

Tessin, Georg. *Verbaende und Truppen der deutschen Wehrmacht und Waffen-SS, 1939–1945*. 17 vols. Osnabrueck: 1979–86.

Thomas, Franz, and Guenter Wegmann. *Die Ritterkreuztraeger der deutschen Wehrmacht, 1939–1945*. Vol. 1, *Sturmartillerie*. Osnabrueck: 1985.

U.S. Army Military Intelligence Service. "Order of Battle of the German Army." Washington, DC: April 1943.

U.S. War Department. "Histories of 251 Divisions of the German Army Which Participated in the War (1914–1918)." Compiled from the Records of the Intelligence Section, General Staff, American Expeditionary Forces. Washington, DC: 1920.

Young, Desmond. *Rommel: The Desert Fox*. New York: 1965.

Zweng, Christian, ed. *Die Dienstlaufbahnen der Offiziere des Generalstabes des deutschen Heeres, 1935–1945*. 2 vols. Osnabrueck: 1995, 1998.

Zydowitz, Kurt von. *Die Geschichte der 58 Infanterie-Division, 1939–1945*. Kiel: 1952.

INTERNET SOURCES

http://home.wxs.nl/~j.n.houterman/bio/german/HeerB2.htm#Bo

http://www.axishistory.com

http://www.ritterkreuz.at

INDEX

Rank listed is the highest attained by that individual.

Index

Index

Index

About the Author

SAMUEL W. MITCHAM, JR., is an internationally recognized authority on Nazi Germany and the Second World War. He is the author of twenty-one books, including *Rommel's Lieutenants* (Praeger Security International, 2007), *Panzers in Winter* (Praeger Security International, 2006), and *Crumbling Empire* (Praeger, 2001). A former Army helicopter pilot and company commander, he is a graduate of the U.S. Army's Command and General Staff College.